Public Works, Government Spending, and Job Creation

PUBLIC WORKS, GOVERNMENT SPENDING, AND JOB CREATION

The Job Opportunities Program

Robert Jerrett, III
Thomas A. Barocci

PRAEGER

PRAEGER SPECIAL STUDIES • PRAEGER SCIENTIFIC

Library of Congress Cataloging in Publication Data

Jerrett, Robert.
    Public works, government spending, and job creation.

    Bibliography: p.
    Includes index.
    1. Public service employment--United States--
History. 2. United States--Public works--History.
I. Barocci, Thomas A., joint author. II. Title.
HD5724.J47   331.1'1'0973   79-15972
ISBN 0-03-051336-7

The main body of this material was gathered
under Contract #6-36375, between Abt Associates
Inc. and the Economic Development Administration,
Department of Commerce. The opinions expressed
herein are those of the authors, not those of
EDA/DOC. This study (except the historical
analysis in chapter 1) is part of public domain.

Published in 1979 by Praeger Publishers
A Division of Holt, Rinehart and Winston/CBS, Inc.
383 Madison Avenue, New York, New York 10017 U.S.A.

9 038 987654321

Printed in the United States of America

PREFACE

The national rate of unemployment in the 1970s has been disturbingly high in all stages of the business cycle. The rate in the 1974-75 recession was higher than in any downturn since the great depression. Currently, after four years of expansion and dramatic growth in employment, the rate of unemployment is above 5.5 percent. There is virtual unanimity of opinion that the "full" rate of unemployment cannot be less than 5.5 percent.

It is not surprising, therefore, that most observers are skeptical of the value of government programs aimed at putting unemployed workers into jobs. At best, they find program costs to exceed program benefits. At worst, they find no benefits at all. Adding to the general frustration is the failure on the part of many researchers who evaluate such programs to produce unequivocal conclusions as to which programs work well and which do poorly.

Against this background, the current volume must be seen as a silver lining on a cloud hanging over government efforts to cope with cyclical and structural unemployment and as a major contribution to the art and the prestige of program evaluation. The authors report on a painstaking and scientifically sophisticated evaluation of a modest countercyclical program known as "Title X" which served in 1975-76 as a precursor to the ten times larger and well heralded Ford-Carter initiatives known as the "Local Public Works Program." They do offer many unequivocal conclusions, and many of these are encouraging to those who still harbor hope and dream that government programs can be effective.

Benjamin Chinitz

ACKNOWLEDGEMENTS

Chapters 2 through 8 of this book are derived from a study directed by Dr. Jerrett at Abt Associates Inc., for the Economic Development Administration (EDA). Chapter 1 was written by Dr. Barocci, who was also consulting economist on, and regular contributor to, the study. Because an effort of this scale and importance can be successful only when a team of professionals provides dedicated and effective contributions, the authors express special thanks to the following key contributors. Dr. Bennett Harrison, professor of urban studies at MIT, provided guidance and insight throughout the study, particularly in the development of the statistical-control model and in the approach to indirect and induced effects. Louise Strayhorn, deputy project director on Abt's evaluation, was responsible for survey management and led the research into long-term impacts. Dr. Charles Fairchild provided much of the early input into study designs and assistance in analyses and data processing. Dr. Jonathan Silberman took responsibility for much of the analysis in the net labor cost study. Timely advice and review were received from Dr. Benjamin Chinitz, Dean Ericson, Steven Fosburg, Vincent A. Scardino, and Dr. David Stevens. Data processing was handled by Thomas Cerva, Sanford Friedman, Michael Hagerty, and Jo Jasztrab. Finally, continuing coordination and production would not have been possible without the efficient and selfless assistance of Judith Sobel and Julie Gabaldon.

Special recognition should also be given to Norman L. Thompson, of the Program Analysis Division of the Economic Development Administration. As EDA's technical representative, he devoted a level of interest, energy, and expertise to this study that is rare on government contracts. His contributions and those of Dr. Anthony Sulvetta are greatly appreciated. Finally, the services of the EDA's Information System and Services Division, including, particularly, Christos Kyriazi, Aaron Cohen, Henry Woodward, and Carl Payne, should be noted.

CONTENTS

LIST OF TABLES

LIST OF FIGURES

INTRODUCTION

In response to alarmingly high unemployment and a faltering economic recovery from the 1970-71 recession, Congress created the Job Opportunities Program in December 1974. This program constituted one of three major sections of the Emergency Jobs and Unemployment Assistance Act (PL 93-567), each of which was intended to ameliorate recessionary unemployment problems. The first section extended unemployment insurance benefits to a maximum of 65 weeks, providing 26 weeks of federally financed special unemployment assistance (SUA), on top of state benefits and federal supplemental benefits. The second section established Title VI of the Comprehensive Employment and Training Act of 1973 (CETA). Under Title VI, the U.S. Department of Labor (DOL) allocated funds to its network of prime sponsors to hire unemployed persons for public-service employment (PSE) program positions on state- and local-government payrolls. Title VI contained a "maintenance-of-effort" clause intended to prevent the use of PSE money to pay the wages of regular public employees.* The regulations also called for an expenditure of 90 percent of the money on wages and the remaining 10 percent on administrative expenses.† Since its initial authorization, CETA Title VI has superseded CETA Title II as the principal support for PSE among DOL prime sponsors.

The third section (par. 301) of the act, authorized the Job Opportunities Program by adding Title X to the Public Works and Economic Development Act of 1965. The stated purpose of the new title was to "provide emergency financial assistance to stimulate, maintain or expand job creating activities in areas, both urban and rural, which are suffering from unusually high levels of unemployment." Under the auspices of the Economic Development Administration (EDA), the Job Opportunities Program (Title X) awarded almost $500 million in fiscal-year (FY) 1975 EDA funds to support projects involving "such activities as rehabilitation of buildings, street paving and repairs, painting, park developments,

---

*This provision was later relaxed as the dire fiscal position of some of the states and cities came to the attention of DOL officials and Congress. In fact, in subsequent funding of Title VI this provision was officially deleted altogether.

†This provision precluded purchase or rental of materials and equipment for PSE employees. In some instances the locality contributed the needed money, and in others, existing materials were used or the jobs represented almost pure service. However, the CETA regulations allowed for the transfer of money allocated under one title to another. If this were done, the regulations of the title under which the person was hired would be applied. For example, if the CETA-VI money were transferred to Title I, and persons hired were put into work-experience positions, the prime sponsor could spend 20 percent of the total for materials and equipment. Some prime sponsors did, in fact, take this route.

environmental improvements and other community improvement projects."[1] The Title X funds were distributed in two rounds, $125 million being allocated in June 1975, and an additional $375 million being distributed in November and December 1975. Supplemental funds from 43 sponsoring federal agencies, and state, local, and private sources brought the total investment to about $758 million. (Although there has not been additional funding since the 1975 appropriations, a number of projects were still in operation as of April 1977.)

The response to the program by governmental units across the country was remarkable. Over 50 federal agencies and offices, and regional commissions received applications. Some merely forwarded them to EDA, while others selected what they regarded as the best ones before sending them.* Eventually, EDA received more than 18,000 project proposals,[2] of which 2,255 were approved for funding. Using the employment estimate made from applications, the agency predicted that 100,000 persons would be employed at "prevailing wages" (as determined under provisions of the Davis-Bacon Act).

As a countercyclical program, the Title X funds were not intended to be distributed equally among states or regions, the legislation recognizing that employment problems caused by the recession were not spread evenly.[3] Instead, priority in selection was given to projects in areas of substantial unemployment.†

Once an area was designated as eligible for assistance, funding was to be given, according to Title X, only to those programs or projects—

1. that would contribute significantly to the reduction of unemployment in the eligible area;
2. that could be initiated or strengthened promptly;
3. that could have a substantial portion completed within 12 months after such allocation is made;
4. that are not inconsistent with locally approved comprehensive plans for the jurisdiction affected, where such plans exist; and
5. that would be approved on the basis of giving first priority to programs and projects that are most labor intensive.

These priorities then became regulations that emphasized the area unemployment rate, labor match, and labor intensity.[4] In addition, the regulations added three

---

*For example, the regional offices of the EDA received over 15,000 applications, only 491 of which were sent on to Washington for possible final approval. A similar ratio applied to the Community Services Administration.

†Eligible areas included those with an unemployment rate of over 6.5 percent for three consecutive months, areas designated under CETA as having substantial unemployment, and areas already receiving other EDA funds.

nonstatutory project-selection factors: contributory funds and labor leverage, indirect benefits, and cost effectiveness.

As one of relatively few counterrecessionary job-creation programs funded in the United States since World War II, the Job Opportunities Program shared with other efforts the objective of supporting temporary subsidized jobs for the unemployed, thereby providing a short-term countercyclical stimulus to areas with high unemployment and sluggish economies. However, a brief review of countercyclical jobs programs reveals the uniqueness of Title X. Such programs have basically been of two types: accelerated public works and public-service employment. Public-works programs have been administered by the Economic Development Administration (formerly called the Area Redevelopment Administration). Public-service employment programs have been conducted under the auspices of the Department of Labor.

The first major postwar public-works employment program was the Accelerated Public Works (APW) program, which funded projects on a local/federal cost-sharing basis in areas with high unemployment or depressed local economies. Authorized in 1962, the program had provided $852 million in federal funds to projects by July 1964, or about one-half of the total project costs.[5] In response to the 1970–71 recession, the Public Works Impact Program (PWIP) was created to support projects which provided "immediate useful work to unemployed and underemployed persons."[6] PWIP, like APW, focused on highly impacted areas, but, unlike APW, put a priority upon funding small projects involving quick startup and short duration. EDA spent approximately $92 million on PWIP in 1972 and 1973, out of total project costs of $134 million. When Title X authorized $500 million for 1975, it represented the largest single postwar fiscal-year investment by the federal government in public-works jobs. However, in October 1976, a far larger appropriations bill for the new Local Public Works Employment Act was signed, authorizing $2 billion for antirecessionary public-works projects (Title I) and $1.25 billion in countercyclical fiscal assistance (Title II) to state and local governments. Subsequently, supplemental appropriations added another $4 billion to the program.

Public-service employment programs were not utilized after World War II for countercyclical objectives until the 1970s. Most categorical programs under the Manpower Development and Training Act (MDTA) of 1962 and the Economic Opportunity Act (EOA) of 1964 addressed structural problems of the disadvantaged, with principal stress placed upon training and employability development. Then, in 1971, Congress passed the Emergency Employment Act (EEA) to fund public-service jobs as an antirecessionary tool. Between FY 1972 and FY 1974 about $2.5 billion in EEA funds was provided under the Public Employment Programs (PEP) to local agents on the basis of unemployment rates and the number of unemployed. When the Comprehensive Employment and Training Act of 1973 introduced a more decentralized, decategorized approach to program funding and planning, Title II of CETA picked up the public-service employment initiative from the PEPs. The continuing rise in unemployment then spurred Congress to add a new Title VI to CETA, under which subsidized public-service employment was expanded. Both Titles II and VI allocate monies according to formulas based upon unemployment, with Title II subject to greater restrictions; under the two programs, public-service employment reached the level of about 310,000 jobs, about twice the level attained under the PEP.

In general, public-works and public-service employment programs have differed from one another in several important respects. Public-works programs, for example, usually utilize a project-funding approach, under which applications to implement particular construction, rehabilitation, or related projects are screened individually and funded on a competitive basis. In contrast, most of the public-service employment funds are allocated as noncompetitive entitlement grants to support a wide variety of jobs in qualified state or local governments. Similarly, public-works programs have often reached the private sector (particularly, the construction trades) directly via subcontracting, whereas public-service employment has not. The capital needs of public-works programs have naturally tended to be greater than those for public-service jobs, with a lower proportion of funds going to wages and fringes. As a result, the cost per job tends to be higher for public-works jobs. A further operational program distinction is that EDA's public-works programs have channeled a higher proportion of funds into nonmetropolitan areas than has DOL. Related to this is the fact that DOL programs tend to target employment opportunities on the disadvantaged, while public-works programs do not. Finally, public-works programs have many other objectives, such as the creation or improvement of a physical asset that will have long-term impacts. Public-service employment programs also have had other, usually service, objectives, but the focus has been more upon providing temporary employment than is the case with public works.

The Title X program is unique for EDA and does not fit easily into either of the two general patterns described above. Like traditional public-works programs, it is project based, involves the private sector through subcontracts, has invested heavily in nonmetropolitan areas, and has produced or improved physical assets that may have long-term value. Unlike most public-works programs, its principal objective is employment and, unique to EDA, it has put a premium upon funding explicitly labor-intensive projects. Moreover, it is intended to focus on the long-term unemployed. In these respects, Title X is more similar to public-service employment programs of DOL. However, unlike either program type, the Job Opportunities Program has provided support to a wider variety of projects, from public- and civil-works construction to service projects, from renovation to training projects.

Thus, in many respects, Title X is a hybrid countercyclical employment program, combining the administrative arrangements and emphasis on construction and rehabilitation familiar to EDA with the employment focus of DOL programs. The resulting variety of locally initiated but centrally approved projects comprise a program which is distinctly different from others and a particularly fruitful subject for employment research.

STUDY OBJECTIVES

The study presented here was originally designed to be part of a broader evaluation of the Job Opportunities Program. The evaluation was structured by the Economic Development Administration, into three components: an administrative evaluation, an assessment of direct employment impacts, and a study of additional benefits. The first two studies were performed by the Program Analysis Division of the Economic Development Administration. The administrative evaluation examined the background and history of the program, documented and analyzed the policy decisions made by EDA in implementing the program, and assessed how the program's administration has affected its impact.[7] The direct-impact evaluation examined the amount of employment generated by the program, the cost of employment, the characteristics of employees, the labor intensity of projects, the duration of employment opportunities, and the relative effectiveness of different types of projects funded under the program.[8]

The third study, findings of which are reported in this volume, was conducted for EDA by Abt Associates Inc. This study had three principal objectives: to estimate the net cost of the Job Opportunities Program to federal, state, and local governments; to assess the jobs provided under Title X, in comparison with the employees' last jobs and usual occupations; and to examine, on a case-study basis, the potential long-term impacts of Title X projects upon local areas.

The net-cost analysis is the central feature of this study. Estimates of net program cost are important because policy makers generally make investment decisions based upon the estimated gross outlays for alternative programs.* Yet, gross costs overstate the true cost of a program to government, by ignoring the various financial returns and savings that accrue to different levels of government as a result of the program's expenditures. For example, providing employment to an unemployed person may save government money by terminating that person's unemployment-compensation claim or reducing dependence upon transfer payments such as Aid to Families with Dependent Children, or Medicaid. Moreover, the employee pays income taxes on earned wages, increasing the tax return to government. Since the returns to government will vary greatly with

---

*The concept of net cost addressed in this study should not be confused with related issues of budget substitution, issues which are not the focal point of the study.

different kinds of investments,[9] consideration of gross costs in making alternative funding choices may result in allocation decisions that are less than optimal.

The concept of net cost is rarely important in policy decisions, partly because the dynamics of returns are complicated to understand and partly because a careful net-cost methodology has not been developed or applied to major federal programs. The Job Opportunities Program study has provided the opportunity to create such a methodology and to use it to estimate the net cost of an important employment-creation program. Based upon empirical data, estimates are made for each source of financial return to government that results from Title X expenditures on wages, fringe benefits, goods, and services. Then the gross program costs are adjusted to account for the increased taxes (income, sales, excise, FICA, unemployment insurance [UI], and other taxes) and the savings in transfer payments (unemployment compensation, AFDC, food stamps, Medicaid, General Assistance, Supplemental Security Income, Social Security, publicly supported housing) that are attributable to Title X expenditures, and the indirect and induced effects of those expenditures. The result is a series of net-cost estimates that represent a more accurate measure of the actual cost of the Job Opportunities Program to taxpayers.

Since the principal objective of Title X has been to create temporary, subsidized employment opportunities, assessment of the jobs provided under Title X is also an important dimension of this study. The kinds of occupations demanded by different types of Title X projects will indicate to policy makers the particular labor market consequences of investments in varying types of projects. Moreover, comparison of Title X jobs with the employees' usual occupations and previous jobs can provide insight into whether Title X has provided meaningful employment or has merely offered a make-work wage alternative to other transfer subsidies. To address these issues, data on occupation, hourly wage, weekly earnings, and total earnings are supplemented by employee perceptions of their jobs.*

The third study objective was to examine the potential long-term impacts of Title X projects upon their local areas. Although primarily an employment program, Title X can also be viewed within the EDA mandate of stimulating local economic development. Thus, it is relevant to examine whether Title X projects have, in addition to providing short-term employment, had any longer-range effects upon local economies. Given the wide variety of projects funded under Title X, a broad range of infrastructural or human-capital improvements

---

*Available resources and time constrained the evaluation to one round of interviews conducted with employees, most of whom were in the program. A postprogram followup was not possible. Thus, the study focuses upon in-program effects on employees and does not pretend to address fully the potential long-term program impacts upon participants' subsequent experience.

were attempted. If they have added, directly or indirectly, to the economic potential of local areas, this fact would distinguish Title X from most employment programs. For example, in order to develop net-cost estimates, it was necessary to project the total person-months of employment and the number of persons employed by the Job Opportunities Program, in addition to estimating the program's total gross cost and cost components. Our independent projections parallel those made by EDA, but may differ from them somewhat, as a function of both projection methods used and the completeness of data available at the time of projection.*

The characteristics of Title X employees are a second area of complementarity and overlap between this study and the EDA direct-impact evaluation. Employee characteristics are of particular interest because Title X regulations did not specify any selected population segments as targets, or employee eligibility requirements, other than encouraging that employers hire persons who have exhausted unemployment benefits or been unemployed at least 15 weeks. Thus, analysis of Title X employee characteristics provides insight into the local constituencies of an employment program that is relatively free from federally imposed eligibility criteria. Moreover, it addresses the relevant policy question of whether or not a counterrecessionary employment program provides jobs to persons who are unemployed for cyclical reasons. These questions receive attention in the study, where data on Title X employees are contrasted with similar data on the CETA program and on the civilian labor force.

Although part of a more comprehensive effort, the study presented here stands alone as an assessment of many of the most significant dimensions of the Job Opportunities Program. It is important to policy makers because it provides a clear picture of the cost, employment, and long-term infrastructural impacts of a program option unique in its combination of the objectives of traditional public-employment and public-works programs. In many respects, Title X foreshadows the likely effects of "soft" public-works program options that have been under consideration for the past year. For researchers and students of labor market policies, the evaluation provides a full historical context for the program and detailed information about its relative effects. Moreover, it illustrates the importance of applying net-cost considerations to funding decisions and presents, for the first time, a precise methodology for determining net program costs to governments.

---

*The study was conducted during fiscal year 1977, while many Title X projects were still in operation. Thus, complete data on the spending and employment at all Title X projects were not available. For the Abt study, projections were made based upon data available from EDA as of April 15, 1977. These data encompassed reports from 543 completed projects, approximately 24 percent of all Title X projects.

ORGANIZATION OF THE BOOK

Chapter 1 places the Title X program in historical context by discussing in detail the series of programs and policies related to federal funding of public-works projects since the New Deal. The chapter discusses the programs in terms of level of effort, impacts, long-term value, and administrative issues, and gives a summary of program lessons learned. In addition, the chapter provides the interested reader with a comprehensive bibliography of information available on counterrecessionary public-works programs.

The second chapter offers a picture of the structure of the Title X program, analyzing funding levels and planned employment, by project type, and geographic distribution. Planned performance is then compared with projected actual experiences, utilizing data developed during the evaluation and derived from EDA reports. This comparison provides a setting for the discussion of Title X employees and jobs in the next chapter.

Chapter 3 details the individual characteristics of those employed under Title X. In addition to their basic sociodemographic characteristics, the chapter analyzes their labor-force status prior to program employment, individual and family income in the year prior to participation, duration of preprogram unemployment, and number and amount of transfer payments received by those participating. Title X employees are also compared with participants in adult programs funded under the Comprehensive Employment and Training Act. The chapter ends with a detailed description of the occupations funded under the program, including an analysis of the duration of employment and total earnings received from different types of jobs and by different types of employees.

The key analysis of net direct program costs forms Chapter 4. Gross program costs are adjusted to reflect returns to government from three types of sources: increased taxes generated by program labor expenditures, savings in transfer payments, and increased taxes from project expenditures on materials and other nonlabor items. Estimates of net government cost for the program and for different types of projects are made, based upon empirical data on 17 different tax and transfer sources. In addition, returns and savings to governments are discounted by estimates derived from projections of what the labor market experience of program participants would have been in the absence of the Title X program. Given the limited set of methodologies available to the study, an econometric model of monthly labor-force transitions for different age-race-sex cohorts was adapted to project employment (and, thus, returns to government) in the absence of the program.

Chapter 5 builds upon Chapter 4 by considering the likely indirect and induced (multiplier) effects of the program upon employment, income, and government cost. The implications of multipliers' effects are explored, and quantitative estimates of cost, income, and employment impacts are made for several possible scenarios of institutional and labor market behavior.

The in-program impacts of the Job Opportunities Program upon participants are analyzed in Chapter 6. The analysis is based upon comparisons of Title X jobs, wages, hours, and employees' perceptions of job quality with parallel measures of employees' prior and usual occupations. The analysis generates thoughts about occupational continuity and skill enhancement provided by the program. The same measures are used to form a tentative assessment of short-term, postprogram impacts in Chapter 7. This analysis is meant only to be suggestive, since it is based upon postprogram data available from only about 10 percent of the complete employee sample of 2,000. It does, however, suggest that Title X may have had some effect upon postprogram earnings, job quality, and career paths.

Finally, in Chapter 8, the potential long-term benefits of Title X projects are assessed. The analysis summarizes the findings from 52 project case studies to provide a first-order understanding of the longer-range impacts of projects upon the infrastructures and economic capabilities of local areas.

NOTES

1. "Requirements for Title X Assistance to EDA Programs," Subpart B, §313.24, *Federal Register* 40, no. 118 (June 18, 1975), p. 25672.

2. Economic Development Administration, U.S. Department of Commerce, "Summary of Title X Proposals," unpublished paper (Washington, D.C., March 7, 1976).

3. For empirical evidence of this, see Edward Gramlich, "The Distributional Effects of Higher Unemployment," *Brookings Papers on Economic Activity*, vol. 2 (Washington, D.C.: Brookings Institution, 1974); and Andrew Sun and Thomas P. Rush, "The Geographic Structures of Unemployment Rates," *Monthly Labor Review*, March 1975.

4. Under Title X, a project was considered labor intensive if "at least 60 percent of the project funds are to be expended for direct labor costs." Moreover, at least 50 percent of Title X funds were to be used to fund projects "in which no more than 25 percent of the funds will be used for nonlabor costs." See "Job Opportunities Program Interim Regulations" (parts 313.8 and 313.24), *Federal Register* 40, no. 101, p. 22537, and no. 118 (June 18, 1975), p. 25672.

5. See Economic Development Administration, U.S. Department of Commerce, *Public Works and Unemployment: A History of Federally Funded Programs (1975)* (Washington, D.C.: Government Printing Office, 1975), and Johannes U. Hoeber, "Some Characteristics of Accelerated Public Works Projects," *Redevelopment*, September 1964, pp. 3–4.

6. See Anthony J. Sulvetta and Norman Thompson, *An Evaluation of the Public Works Impact Program* (Washington, D.C.: Economic Development Administration, Department of Commerce, April 1975).

7. Program Analysis Division, Economic Development Administration, *Evaluation of the Administration of the Title X Program* (Washington, D.C.: Economic Development Administration, forthcoming).

8. Program Analysis Division, Economic Development Administration, *Evaluation of the Direct Employment Impacts on the Job Opportunities Program (Title X)* (Washington, D.C.: Department of Commerce, forthcoming).

9. See Congressional Budget Office (CBO), *Temporary Measures to Stimulate Employment: An Evaluation of Some Alternatives* (Washington, D.C.: Government Printing Office, September 2, 1972). The CBO, applying very rough procedures, estimated that gross expenditures of $1 billion result in an initial net cost ranging from $980 million to $615 million, depending upon which one of five counterrecessionary program options is selected.

Public Works, Government Spending, and Job Creation

PUBLIC WORKS PROGRAMS IN THE UNITED STATES, FROM FDR TO THE PRESENT

INTRODUCTION

Since 1960, between one-fourth and one-third of every construction dollar spent in the United States has gone for public works. These expenditures have occurred at all levels of government, including projects ranging from the rehabilitation of a commode in the Bronx Zoo to the building of Interstate 95. Public works were initially defined as durable and/or immobile, and have now come to include rehabilitation and maintenance activities under the same rubric.[1] Of the $39 billion spent on public works construction in 1975, we can attribute only about $1 billion-$2 billion to programs specifically funded for countercyclical job-creation purposes or special aid to lagging areas of the country.[2]

Government expenditures on all types of public works do not vary with business cycles to the degree that expenditures do in the private sector. However, there have been repeated charges that federal expenditures are not distributed equally across regions of the United States.[3] As private expenditures decline with a recession, there is always an attempt in Washington to persuade the federal program makers to compensate with debt-financed public-works expenditures by accelerating the construction of projects already underway, or by financing new ones proposed by the states and localities.*

---

*It is much more difficult financially and politically for a state or locality to assume countercyclical funding of public works, as the federal debt position is the business of Congress and the White House, while the debt posture of the states and localities is becoming more the business of regional and local financial institutions.

Even the deficit-conscious Ford administration passed a series of counter-cyclical spending programs, not the least of which was an increased investment in public works programs. The initiative for countercyclical and even structural public works construction comes from circles as diverse as the research departments of the AFL-CIO and the Brookings Institution to local representatives of the building trades and contractors' association. This country has had two periods of dependence on the financing of public works beyond what was deemed normal by the Congress: one period during the Great Depression, and the other, a sporadic but continuous flirtation since 1961. We will not address the issue of whether countercyclical employment policy is necessary,[4] although it is still the subject of hot debate in some quarters of the economics and political professions. In some sense, we are all Keynesians, and the issue now centers on how much countercyclical stimulus, and not whether it is needed.

The use of federal aid programs for the areas of the country experiencing economic stagnation or decline does not have a large consensus. Discussion often finds the proponents citing Marxian and Myrdalian theories of uneven development, with the opposing side riddled with phrases from a free-market handbook. The historical policy offshoot of these debates has always been a compromise, with the advocates gaining a program and the foes achieving lilliputian funding levels.[5]

Although the debate is interesting, it will not be addressed here. Instead, this chapter will concentrate on what we have learned and how we might apply this knowledge presently and in the future.

The chapter is divided into two major parts. The first presents a discussion of the public-works programs and policies utilized in the United States prior to the 1960s, with emphasis on the New Deal era. The second portion concentrates on programs implemented during the 1961-74 period, beginning with the Area Redevelopment Act of 1961 and ending with the Public Works Impact Program (PWIP) of 1972.

Under each major section of the chapter, the issues will center on the level of effort, program impacts, long-term value, and administrative issues. When appropriate, the public-works programs will be compared and contrasted with available evidence of the efficacy of alternative means of accomplishing the same end. For example, the utilization of public-service employment (PSE) programs will be a point of comparison in the contemporary context. Also, when possible, we will differentiate between programs aimed at structural problems and those aimed at cyclical employment problems. As the reader will soon see, it is often very difficult to distinguish the two, beyond the targets and areas identified in the legislative mandate.[6]

THE NEW DEALERS: FDR AND HARRY HOPKINS

When the New Dealers met, they did not have a series of cost-benefit analyses to look to, nor computer simulations of the likely impact of huge spending increases on the unemployment rate and the change in the consumer price index (CPI). Indeed, they didn't even have a copy of Paul Samuelson's *Economics*, where they could find out that debt-financed projects were effective as countercyclical devices. The programs of the New Deal were a series of perpetually adjusting experimental and demonstration programs approached with a level of funding never before attempted in a capitalist economy. The question of whether or not they were effective will never be completely resolved. Clearly, mistakes were made; some leaned on shovels and others built monuments to the ability of a great nation to survive a time of crisis.

The use of debt-financed public-works programs never pulled the country completely out of the Depression (it took World War II to do that), but it did provide work for millions of people, and it enhanced the climate for the long-run economic development of the nation.

Initial Responses and Experimentation: 1929-35

Nonintervention is the key word in describing the initial response of the federal government to growing unemployment in the first three years of the Great Depression. The stance of the Hoover administration was to ask Congress to speed up the appropriations for the previously planned ten-year public-construction agenda and to appropriate an additional $330 million for construction of federal projects.[7] Congress did, however, pass a bill authorizing $2.3 billion for direct grants to states and localities for public-works construction, only to have Hoover veto it with objections characterizing it as a "pork-barrel" proposal.[8] In 1932, the Emergency Relief Construction Act was passed as numbers emerged showing 24 percent unemployment and a drop in private-construction activities, from $8.7 billion in 1929 to $1.4 billion in 1932. This program provided federal money to states and localities and relied heavily on self-liquidating loans. The program reached its zenith in 1933, when it was directly responsible for the employment of approximately 3 million of the 13 million unemployed.[9]

When FDR took office he saw a desperate need to do something quickly while full-blown proposals could still be worked out in Congress and the White House. The Federal Emergency Relief Administration (FERA) was set up (under the Federal Emergency Relief Act of 1933) to disperse money to the states for direct and work relief. Unemployment was over 25 percent. This is analogous to the congressional extension of unemployment benefits in 1974 and the mandating of additional money by prelegislated formulas for the dispersion of welfare and unemployment insurance (UI) payments that were increasing across the country.[10] The regulations of the FERA stated that "all needy unemployed persons and/or their dependents shall receive sufficient relief to prevent physical suffering and maintain minimum living standards." This provision was the first legislatively mandated workfare program of the era. Those persons in need were employed for the number of hours required to compensate the difference between their income and the minimum living standard at federal wage rates.[11] In addition, grants were made for unemployable people as well; services under this program peaked in 1935 when over 16 percent of the civilian labor force (21 million persons) were receiving some sort of benefits. The federal government was still not directly involved in the administration of the program.

The year 1933 marked the first time the federal government became directly involved in operating a work-relief program. The Civil Works Administration (CWA) was established under executive order. The federal government directly operated the program, which provided jobs both for persons receiving relief and for those who were unemployed and not getting relief payments. Unemployment was the only criterion for eligibility for half the clients. Since there was a spreading prejudice against persons on relief, many who should have applied and, indeed, were eligible for relief, did not sign up. Unfortunately, the CWA got the stigma of a relief and make-work program, as the local relief offices filled as many jobs as possible from their rolls, and each placement led to a decrease in their own expenditures. As jobs became available, many new relief applicants appeared, as the wages paid on CWA projects were considered high.

Several major factors led to the termination of CWA after only seven months of operation (November 1933–July 1934). First, the program was initiated in midwinter, with most jobs being in short-term construction. Thus, in order to fill the number of open positions financed (over 2 million in the first two months), many of the localities created what could be called make-work efforts. Secondly, as noted above, the program was the first federal effort that directly provided jobs both for relief recipients and for unemployed persons, and was viewed as temporary. It should be mentioned that the hiring rate and the speed of implementation was very rapid: by mid-January 1934 (a month and a half after the executive order was issued), there were over 4.3 million persons working on CWA projects.[12] Even the highly praised speedy implementation of the Emergency Employment Act of 1971 could not hold a candle to the hiring rate under CWA.*

---

*Another interesting parallel of the CWA to present problems is the failure of the program to distinguish between the types of persons it was aiming to help—the cohort on relief or those who were in less severe straits, those who were simply unemployed. This could be taken in a present context as the failure to differentiate our programs aimed at the structurally unemployed and the cyclically unemployed. This is discussed later in the chapter.

As CWA expired, a new work-relief effort was begun under the FERA: the Emergency Work Relief Program (EWRP). Once again, relief status determined eligibility, and the program was to be a dual venture, with equal votes in the program for states and the federal government. As it turned out, the states had the major responsibility for operating the program, with many unfinished CWA projects getting most of the initial attention. Urban areas were the target, and virtually all of the participants were on relief, as opposed to only half under CWA. As in the first FERA program, employment hours per week were determined by the amount of money needed to make up the difference between what a person had and the minimum deemed necessary to get along. Almost 90 percent of the allocated $1.3 billion went to labor costs.[13]

The basic principle operating at this time was that states and localities were responsible for the physically unfit and otherwise unemployable persons, while the federal government had responsibility for able-bodied but unemployed persons. This distinction was the basis for the Works Progress Administration (WPA), which replaced the FERA late in 1935.

While CWA and EWRP were being planned and operated, the Congress was implementing parallel legislation. An agency that became important as a result of such legislation was the Public Works Administration (PWA), established in June of 1933. Under the National Industrial Recovery Act of 1933, over $3.3 billion was appropriated for the PWA, while the intention was later interpreted as follows: preparing a public-works program to be undertaken in the event of future necessity; providing employment for workers in building trades and in industries supplying construction materials; priming the pump of industry by placing large sums of money in circulation and by creating a demand for construction materials.[14] These goals are not unlike the goals listed in the legislation authorizing the latest round of countercyclical public work programs: the Local Public Works Act of 1976.

Several problems with the PWA prevented timely implementation, not the least of which was the failure of states to provide technical plans for the public construction they wanted. Another problem (familiar to those involved in the present public-works system) was the detailed and time-consuming review-and-appeal procedure for project selection, a problem which worsened as demand by state and local governments far outstripped the funding available. In fact, the delays in implementing the PWA program were precisely the reason that CWA was established in November 1933. One unique feature of the PWA was that the federal government, through ten different agencies, administered, planned, and ran projects directly. Federal agencies spent $1.8 billion of the total $5.9 billion allocated over the life of the program.

By the close of 1935, previous hopes that the end of the Depression was near began to wane, and the patchwork of programs underwent review by the White House and Congress. Although many were being employed and funds were stimulating the economy, there was still a long way to go—unemployment hovered around 20 percent. The federal government regrouped its efforts, primarily under the auspices of the Works Progress (later Projects) Administration. It is to this widely recognized program that we now turn.

Consolidation of Work-Relief Efforts: 1935-41

By 1935 there were 20 million people depending on relief of some kind, almost 17 percent of the total population. Hopes that the PWA would do the job were dwindling. The Committee on Economic Security reported the following to FDR:

> It is a sound principle that public employment should be expanded when private employment slackens, and it is likewise sound that work in preference to relief in cash or in kind should be provided for those of the unemployed who are willing and able to work.... The experience of the past year has demonstrated that making useful work available is the most effective means of meeting the needs of the unemployed.[15]

FDR responded immediately to this memorandum with an announcement to Congress that he wanted two new and expanded programs. He called for the passage of the Social Security Act to provide categorical help to the unemployable, and he asked for a federally administered public-works program for the unemployed. Within four months the Emergency Relief Appropriations Act of 1935 was passed in response to the latter request. This program authorized the appropriation of $4.88 billion to "provide relief, work relief and to increase employment by providing useful projects." The allocations were divided among federal agencies to sponsor temporary projects, and a new agency, the WPA, was established with an appropriation of $1.4 billion to finance "small useful projects."

Due to the dynamic leadership of Happy Hopkins, the WPA soon had administrative control over virtually all federal work-relief efforts. During 1936-43 the WPA averaged over 2 million persons a year on its employment rolls, with total allocations of almost $13 billion. This was by far the largest and most famous of all the New Deal programs and had become synonymous with public work-relief efforts in this era. The hallmark of the program was its adaptability. Hopkins was not averse to changing the goals, operations, and targets as he perceived the need for adjustments. In addition, there were annual congressional authorizations for the program, and Congress participated in annual alterations.

Although the objectives of the WPA are established in legal terms, it is more appropriate to quote Hopkins on the objectives, from a statement made to his staff in 1935:

> Never forget that the objective of this whole program as laid down
> by the President ... is the objective of taking 3,500,000 people off
> relief and putting them to work and the secondary objective is to
> put them to work on the best possible projects we can; but don't
> ever forget that first objective, and don't let me hear any of you
> apologizing for it because it is nothing to be ashamed of.[16]

Unfortunately, the objectives regarding who was to be employed on WPA projects were never really translated into explicit criteria, although in 1935 Hopkins asked Congress for enough money to employ one member of every needy family in the country.[17] It is interesting to note that at times there were implicit goals for the WPA to provide training, but these were never realized, as the unemployment at the time was viewed exclusively as a cyclical problem. What we would now term structural unemployment was generally ignored. However, an examination of the list of projects completed during the eight years of the WPA reveals a large number of projects that were, in the strict sense of the word, economic-development projects, not simply temporary measures to stimulate employment. The long-run effects of the WPA, and its enhancement of the climate for later economic development, are the most underestimated of all its accomplishments.[18]

There were several major changes in the administrative activities of the WPA vis-a-vis prior public works projects. These changes centered on the sponsors, hiring arrangements, and local contributions both during a project and after its completion. Instead of the previous arrangements with contractors, virtually all WPA projects were run directly through local or state governmental units rather than through a private contractor. This decision was made because the contractors were either unable or unwilling to hire those most in need, limiting their personnel to semiskilled and skilled workers. Of course, this method may have filled the efficiency needs of the program, but equity needs were left unmet.* Further, the WPA set up state and district offices to administer the program; 30,000 administrative personnel were hired, "without regard to the provisions of the civil service laws."[19] Again, we see that almost naive sensibility of the era in that it seemed intuitively obvious that creating a permanent civil-service structure for a temporary program would serve only to institutionalize the agencies and their employees.†

---

*This issue remains unresolved under the strategies designed for funding Title X of the Public Works and Economic Development (PWED) Act of 1965 and the Local Public Works Act of 1976; this is discussed later.

†The problem of civil-service laws and temporary employment programs is still unresolved either for the clients of programs like CETA-VI or the administrative personnel.

The projects themselves had to be sponsored by a state or local government unit or a federal agency, and that sponsor had to be legally empowered to carry out the work as well as be responsible for its maintenance.[20]

Approximately 96 percent of the projects under the WPA were initiated locally, with yearly local and state contributions averaging between 19 and 25 percent. Once the project was approved on the state level, the WPA district offices were charged with hiring workers and buying the necessary equipment and supplies. This setup was based on the conviction that local government units knew best what needed to be done, but were unable to administer it effectively; the historical consensus was that the WPA administrative network was quite efficient and successful. The lesson learned here could well have circumvented problems encountered by our national program planners who insisted that both the planning and administration of CETA had to be the responsibility of localities. Even in 1973 localities had little experience in running social programs.

Employment under a WPA project was based on need and employability, with specific provisions included against discrimination on the basis of race, age, and sex. Unfortunately, there was little enforcement of these provisions, as only 10-to-20 percent of project employees were female and/or nonwhite. The aged, however, were highly represented among the work force, although the young (under 18) were barred, as there were two separate programs for youths (the Civilian Conservation Corps and the National Youth Administration Work Program).[21]

Congress made explicit rules concerning WPA workers' acceptance of available private employment in a project area by stipulating that workers must leave the project if private-sector pay were at least the same as the WPA wage. Indeed, transition from WPA rolls to private employment remained a specific goal. Another problem with a contemporary ring emerged after Congress passed this provision. Those working on WPA projects, while paid less than similar private-sector workers, were virtually guaranteed full-time, full-year work, whereas regular private-sector jobs, particularly in construction, were only rarely full-year positions. Thus, even with the lower wages of WPA projects, many were reluctant to leave. Alden Briscoe, however, points out that "career WPA" workers were not a particularly large problem. In 1939, only about 16 percent of the workers had been on projects for three years or more.[22] In a reaction to charges by the media of "careers on WPA," Congress enacted legislation that automatically dismissed any WPA worker who had been working for 18 months or more. Those dismissed (almost 1 million over the last six months of 1939) had to remain off the project for at least 30 days. This process was called rotation. Many, of course, could not find permanent work and came immediately back after 30 days; as the mayor of Detroit reportedly commented, "It's pretty hard to rotate your appetite."

Wages paid on the WPA projects followed FDR's guidelines: "security payments which should be larger than the amounts now received on the relief roll, but . . . not so large as to encourage the rejection of opportunities for private employment." (This policy is similar to wage regulations under CETA-VI.) However, organized labor managed to use its influence to gain prevailing wages on WPA projects, not unlike the situation in current public-works programs. Thus, after Congress passed a prevailing-wage resolution, there was a catch-22: the "security" monthly wage policy was still in effect. Therefore, the workers who would surpass this security wage, if paid the prevailing wage, simply worked fewer hours per month.[23] Overall, wages paid on WPA projects in 1939 ranged from a low level in Mississippi of $19 per month to a high of $95 per month in Washington, D.C. The average hourly earnings on all projects financed under the Emergency Relief Employment Act were 48 cents per hour in 1939, with an overall average in the private-sector building trades of about $1.07 per hour.[24] Clearly, there were compromises reached at the local level between the security- and prevailing-wage differences.

The WPA projects were labor intensive, with nearly 90 percent of the federal contributions going directly to wages. The rules allowed for $7 worth of materials for each man-month of employment, although the local and state contributions (19-to-24 percent of the total) were often spent on materials. Thus the dual goal of labor intensiveness and usefulness of projects was accomplished. La Guardia Airport, for example, could not have been constructed with the federal materials allotment.

The overall economic impact of the WPA has never been the subject of serious economic analysis. However, as over $1.4 billion per year was spent on wages going to over 2 million families, we can be sure that virtually all of it was spent on necessities. The rate of spending, of course, has a positive impact on the countercyclical effect. The multiplier works more quickly if the money goes to wages than if it is spent on materials and equipment.[25] In current dollars this expenditure is equal to approximately $6 billion to $6.4 billion per year, far above the total PSE and public-works expenditures appropriated to smooth out the current recession. An equivalent level of effort in 1976 would result in employment stimulation in the range of 600,000 to 900,000 jobs for PSE and 350,000 to 450,000 for an accelerated public-works program.[26] Further comparison shows that the WPA, at its highest impact, employed 31 percent of the total unemployed in the country.[27] To equal this we would presently have to have almost 2.5 million persons on a public works or PSE program.

The WPA reached its highest level of activity in 1939 when $2.2 billion was spent on job creation; total federal receipts that year were only $5.1 billion. Further, the total government debt in 1939 was $3.6 billion, fully 70 percent as much as total receipts. Countercyclical policy was indeed taken very seriously in Washington.[28]

Before summarizing the accomplishments and lessons of the era, I cannot resist the temptation to list a few of the WPA accomplishments. The overall figures are truly impressive: 617,000 miles of roads built, 124,000 bridges and viaducts, and 120,000 public buildings. Perhaps specific examples will be more illustrative. La Guardia Airport in New York was a WPA project, as was Boston's Huntington Avenue subway. New York's Central Park zoo and Chicago's waterfront park were made possible by WPA dollars and men. Faneuil Hall in Boston and Independence Hall in Philadelphia, cornerstones of the nation's bicentennial celebration, were reconstructed by the WPA. Enough public buildings were constructed to put one in each of the 35,000 counties in the country. We are proud of our National Endowment for the Arts, but we would have to go much further to match the splendid achievements of the WPA's writers', musicians', and painters' projects under which people like Jack Levine, Willem deKooning, and Jackson Pollock were aided.[29] The list could go on and on, but even these few examples illustrate the products of the imagination and drive present in the crisis times of the 1930s.

On balance, I believe that the accomplishments of public-works projects in this era outweighed the tangles, given the inexperience of all of those involved in the planning and implementation of previously unattempted projects. However, many who criticized the works programs of the 1930s did so armed with evidence. For example, unemployment was still in the 16–18 percent range as the decade of the 1930s came to a close. Several blue-ribbon panels were set up to evaluate the efforts during the 1930s. For example, the National Appraisal Commission's criticism centered on the programs' inability to fully meet the needs of employable people.[30] However, after criticizing the programs' scope, they praised the performance, citing the utility of the work undertaken.[31] The National Resources Planning Board discredited the WPA on two counts: that it did not meet the needs of all unemployed persons, and that the objectives of the program were unclear. The same board also criticized the WPA for mixing the maintenance of work habits, skills, and morale with relief efforts.[32] Thus, almost all formal evaluations indicate that, if anything, the program level was too modest in size.

Summary

What lessons did we learn from the era of the Great Depression? The first conclusion that one researching this issue must draw is that, with the commitment and support of the public, the White House and Congress can, in consort, launch massive and unprecedented programmatic remedies for the unemployment problems of the nation.

More specifically, we can examine some of the levels of effort summarized in Tables 1.1 and 1.2. For example, the simple fact that the WPA managed to employ an average of 2 million persons a year is impressive; this was between one-quarter and one-third of the total unemployed. To equal this effort in the 1977 employment situation, we would have had to combine our countercyclical

TABLE 1.1

Some Parameters of Major Public Works Programs in the New Deal

Parameter	Community Works Administration (November 1933–July 1934)	Emergency Work Relief Program (March 1934–December 1935)	Public Works Administration (1933–39)	Works Projects Administration (1935–43)
Target groups	½ unemployed, ½ on relief	relief (urban areas)	unemployed	unemployed
Wages	high prevailing wage, with $.30-per-hour minimum	very low	medium, to maintain standard of decency	medium security wages and prevailing
Allocations (federal)	$860 million	$1.3 billion	$5.9 billion	$7.8 billion
Wages/total dollars (federal share, in percent)	79	89	N.A.*	88
State matching funds (percent of total)	10	N.A.	55–70 (for nonfederal portion of program)	19–25
Number of persons employed (various durations)	4 million, total	2.5 million, total	100,000–650,000 per month	2 million per year
Major activities	86% construction	majority were construction	medium-to-heavy construction	79% light, medium, and heavy construction

*N.A. Data not available.

Source: Bureau of the Census, U.S. Department of Commerce, *Statistical Abstract of the United States, 1941* (Washington, D.C.: Government Printing Office, 1942). Also based on author's calculations.

TABLE 1.2

Statistics for 1936, 1939, 1975, Compared with WPA Information for 1936 and 1939

Statistical Item	1936	1939	1975
Civilian Labor force (000s)	53,440	55,600	93,129
Number employed (000s)	44,410	45,750	84,783
Number unemployed (000s)	9,030	9,480	7,830
Unemployment rate (percent)	20.3	17.1	8.5
GNP (billions of dollars)	82.48	90.49	1,449.0
Federal government receipts (billions of dollars)	4.12	5.16	285.3
Federal deficit (billions of dollars)	4.95	3.60	71.3
Number employed (000s, WPA only)	3,062	2,436	N.A.*
Wage expenditures on WPA (billions of dollars)	1.834	1.578	N.A.
Wages as percent of GNP	2.25	1.75	N.A.
Number employed on WPA as percent of total unemployment	33.9	25.7	N.A.
Average wages paid, WPA	$0.46 per hour	$0.48 per hour	N.A.

*N.A. Data not applicable.

Sources: Bureau of the Census, U.S. Department of Commerce, *Statistical Abstract of the United States* (Washington, D.C.: Government Printing Office, various years); *Economic Report of the President, 1976* (Washington, D.C.: Government Printing Office, 1977); and various WPA documents.

programs to employ between 2 and 2.5 million persons—at least five times the actual effort. Further, Table 1.2 shows that the percentage of GNP devoted exclusively to the WPA during 1936 and 1939 was 2.25 percent and 1.75 percent, respectively. In a present context this would mean appropriations in the neighborhood of $25 billion–$33 billion per year. Admittedly, the comparisons can be questioned for relevance, but they are nevertheless illustrative of the magnitude of the WPA program.

John K. Galbraith points out that over the 1934–38 period the various programs were only able to employ 14 percent of the total unemployed.[33] Even with this conservative estimate, we would have to put over 1 million persons to work in order to equal the achievement of the 1930s.

Assessment of the overall economic impact of the programs is difficult as there are no analytically sound studies available; the major economic-assessment tools were yet to be invented. Predictions about what the situation would have been without the New Deal programs are equally imprecise, but enlightening. We would either have reverted to reliance on continuation of the poor-law concept or launched a massive program of federal relief. Neither would have left us with the series of physical accomplishments that resulted. The stimulation of private industry resulting from materials-and-equipment purchases would have been delayed or missed altogether.

On the administrative side we can bring a great deal of knowledge to bear in the present context. The issue which first comes to mind is the fact that projects were almost always initiated by local and state levels of government and administered through federal branch offices. Some attribute the lessening of abuses to this arrangement. Further, when the WPA made local contributions mandatory, the local governmental units responded with between 19 percent and 25 percent of the total costs. This separated the projects desired from the projects deemed necessary. In addition, the civil-service statutes were bypassed in deference to the crisis times, and consequently those employed in the administration were not permanent. The same holds for the clients of the programs. The jobs were temporary. The method whereby wages were determined also provides a lesson. Although there were conflicting policies concerning prevailing versus security wages, practical compromises were reached either by shortening the number of hours worked or through local agreements.

Finally, we should note an appropriate caveat. In a 1939 public opinion poll, which asked people about the best and worst things done under the Roosevelt administration, the WPA won on both counts. In the final analysis, it is a question of one's perspective. In a present context this would come down to whether or not one favored massive government intervention to ameliorate employment problems. Those of us now in favor of this would likely have voted yes in 1939. The program was a product of the 1930s and must be judged in that light. We must take its wheat and apply it now, and leave the chaff in the history books.

THE POST-WORLD WAR II ERA: CYCLICAL
AND/OR STRUCTURAL UNEMPLOYMENT

Introduction

World War II kept America's industry and labor force fully utilized. As the war drew to a long-awaited close, Washington policy makers, remembering the 1930s, began to worry about economic prospects for the postwar period. A wave of postwar nationalism swept the United States and produced a host of strange bedfellows, from Harry Truman and Adlai Stevenson to Roy Cohn and Joseph McCarthy. The crest of that wave was reached in 1946 with the passage of the Full Employment Act. That act, which passed amidst much controversy and even more compromise, mandated the federal government to "promote maximum employment, production and purchasing power." However, it contains no mechanisms for accomplishing its rhetorical goals, nor does it define maximum employment (originally the act called for full employment, then defined at about 3 percent).

There were few who were against the rhetorical goals of the act, but equally few who were willing to include enforcement provisos in the legislation itself. In 1945, during the extensive hearings on the bill, Secretary of Labor L. B. Schwellenbach described full employment as "a condition in which all who are able and willing to work can find jobs under satisfactory conditions," a goal which has yet to come to fruition.[34] Herbert Stein, later chairman of the Council of Economic Advisers under President Nixon, described the situation in the following manner:

> Every phase in the [employment] act is a monument to the battle of the year long legislative war that preceded its passage. The biggest guns of ideology and pressure, conservative and liberal, business and labor, had been engaged in the fight. There has been in our generation no other confrontation on so massive a scale over the basic character of the American economy. When the smoke cleared it was impossible to tell who had won.[35]

The only really clear result of the act was that it committed the federal government to the concept of full employment, but the questions of how to carry it out, and for whom, remain unanswered. This section of the chapter discusses the methods and impacts of a series of modest federal attempts to address both structural and cyclical employment problems through accelerated spending on public-works projects.

The first attempt to put economic muscle behind the Full Employment Act was a bill introduced in the Eighty-first Congress by Senator James Murray and 14 other Democrats. The bill (S.281) was aimed at "the treatment of serious unemployment whenever it arises in any geographic or industrial area." The bill was ambitious, containing effective language that was later adopted in several important pieces of economic-development and countercyclical legislation. It would have committed $2.2 billion to aid depressed areas and had provisions for retraining and mobility allowances for those in certain depressed areas. As Sar A. Levitan pointed out, the bill "died a-borning" with the recovery in 1950.[36]

A certain amount of attention was given to areas of the country with labor surpluses during the Korean conflict, through the directives included in Defense Manpower Policy No. 4 of 1952 ("Placement of Procurement and Facilities in Areas of Current or Imminent Labor Surplus"). This policy was designed to give a disproportionate share of defense procurements to firms in labor-surplus areas. How well it worked is uncertain because no evaluations are available. Following the period of the Korean conflict, the Eisenhower administration took a stance that we could call the old federalism, since it assumed that high-level growth in the overall economy would pull up lagging areas. The *Economic Report of the President, 1955*, stated that programs for local areas "should be carried out by the local citizens themselves."[37] With this attitude from the administration, the battle lines were drawn as Senator Paul Douglas led those who favored aiding depressed areas of the country with special federal grants (during Douglas's previous campaign for the Senate, he had become acutely aware of the depressed-area problem as he observed the economic situation in southern Illinois). Because Douglas persuaded his fellow senators of the efficacy of aid, the Council of Economic Advisers reversed its position. The problem then became one of adjusting the scope of the assistance. Six years of legislative juggling began; one bill died in the House Rules Committee, another was pocket-vetoed by the president, and yet another was vetoed in 1960. A combination of the indefatigable Douglas* and the elevation of John F. Kennedy† in 1960 finally brought passage of the first major postwar economic-development legislation—the Area Redevelopment Act.

Levitan details the issues involved in the passage of the bill, noting both the practical and philosophical differences among the friends and foes. Not surprisingly, the issues were the same as those settled later by the President's Commission on Technology and the American Economy,[38] and much the same as issues raised during the legislative battles that followed (and are still going on) in reference to the Humphrey-Hawkins bill. The president's task force on aid to depressed areas, headed by Douglas, recommended special treatment for businesses in depressed areas, through targeting of government procurement; measures to increase the educational level of persons in depressed areas, and expansion

---

*Douglas was an economist in his own right. Indeed, he was elected president of the American Economic Association.

†Kennedy, while a senator, acted as floor chairman for the Douglas bill(s) in 1956.

of placement services; a comprehensive public-works program; tax incentives for new or expanding firms in depressed areas; the establishment of a youth conservation corps; and special regional programs to combat unemployment and underemployment in certain depressed areas.[39]

Only the last of the recommendations was passed into law by the Area Redevelopment Act. The remainder of the list saw legislative enactment in one form or another over the ensuing decade; for example, the Manpower Development and Training Act of 1962, the Accelerated Public Works Program of 1962, and the Special Impact Program.

The report of the Douglas task force represents the beginning of the modern-era use of public-works construction as a tool to combat cyclical and structural employment problems. The major pieces of legislation passed that specifically address these issues are the Area Redevelopment Act (1961), the Accelerated Public Works (APW) program (1962), the Public Works and Economic Development Act (1965), the Public Works Impact Program (1971), the Emergency Jobs Unemployment Assistance Act (1974), and the Public Works Employment Act (1976).

The program implemented under each of these acts will be discussed in turn, and special reference made to the costs, the allocation formulas, the characteristics of those employed, the speed of implementation, the aggregate impact, value of the output, wages paid, administrative arrangements, and the level of effort. Title X of the Public Works and Economic Development Act of 1965, as amended, and known as the Emergency Jobs Act, is discussed in more detail in subsequent chapters. At the outset it should be mentioned that there are no detailed evaluations of any of the programs prior to Title X, except for an in-house (Economic Development Administration) study done on the PWIP program.[40] Thus, specific conclusions concerning impacts and administration are often gleaned from impressionistic evaluations of the programs.

The Area Redevelopment Act

The Area Redevelopment Act was passed in 1961 with the enthusiastic endorsement of the administration.* A new agency, the Area Redevelopment Administration (ARA) was charged with carrying through its mandates. The funding for the ARA, however, was meager compared to the magnitude of the problems it was designed to address.

---

*While campaigning, Senator Kennedy had, some say, won the West Virginia primary because of his firm stand on, and commitment to, federal aid to depressed areas.

The ARA was supposed to design a program to alleviate conditions of substantial and persistent unemployment in certain economically distressed areas. Immediately, two problems emerged that were to plague not only the ARA, but all subsequent programs aimed at both structural and cyclical employment problems: the timing of grants and eligible-area designation. The economic-development mandate was to be implemented by encouraging new business ventures through loans or by tying public-facility construction to the development of a new business. The latter issue resulted from a practical problem within the ARA. Demand for public-facility construction funds was far outstripping supply. Demanding a link of the public facility with a new business was a convenient allocation tool. This led to problems as the economy was just then moving into a recession—clearly the hardest time to encourage new business ventures in any part of the country, let alone in depressed areas.[41] Secondly, the ARA officials depended on low-income and employment statistics to measure need and eligibility. These statistics simply do not allow for differentiating between cyclical and structural problems, nor between declining and depressed areas.[42]

Within the first two years of ARA's operation, it designated over 1,000 counties as eligible for assistance, nearly one-fifth of the counties in the entire country. Actual obligations from ARA totaled about $350 million—approximately $350,000 per eligible county. Of this amount, approximately $104 million went to public-facilities grants (40 percent) and loans (with the remainder allocated to industrial and commercial loans, technical-assistance projects, training courses, and research projects). The percentage given in grants to the eligible areas was directly related to the unemployment rate; areas with a rate above 12 percent received five-sixths of the total in the form of a grant.[43] The ARA investment per job under the public-facilities grants and loan program ranged from $600 for those projects with funding of under $250,000 to about $7,000 for those with over $1 million in funding. According to ARA documents, the average investment per job was $1,800.[44]

The public-facilities grants portion of the ARA program was highly controversial, with advocates defending grants on the basis of certain communities' inability to raise any money at all, and opponents claiming that grants would "rob communities of their initiative by making them more dependent on federal aid."[45] The compromise which came out of the debate allowed for as much as 100 percent of assistance in grants if the projects "fulfilled a pressing need" in the depressed area.[46] To accommodate this provision, the ARA covered about 86 percent of the total project costs during the first two years of operation.[47]

The popularity and subsequent demand for public-works grants had a tremendous impact on the ARA, which had too little money and experience and had promised too much. Project selection for allocations became an ad hoc process, and charges of political favoritism occurred (not unlike those facing the Economic Development Administration [EDA] in reference to present allocations of funds under the Local Public Works [LPW] Program).

Regionally, the disbursement of funds under the ARA seemed to favor the South. During the first two years of the program, 57 percent of public-facilities grants and loans went to southern states, even though only one-third of the eligible population lived in that area of the country.[48] Also, far-reaching promises of job creation and impact under ARA programs were somehow translated into overstated accomplishments in ARA publications and news releases. The image of the ARA was becoming tarnished by media charges of incompetence.

Soon after ARA began, the administrators realized that industry was unwilling to locate in the places where roads, sewers, and water lines were not satisfactory. This realization led to the increasing emphasis placed on public- and civil-works construction, which constituted a grant and selection process unfamiliar to ARA personnel (as indicated earlier, public-works grants had to be directly linked to a private business venture).

It should be kept in mind that public-facilities grants were not the major raison d'étre for ARA. The legislative debate centered on the simple, but severe problem of a lack of industrial jobs in rural America. To ameliorate this problem, the business-loan program was set up at the heart of ARA to offer low-interest startup capital to expanding firms. It was assumed that this would sufficiently lower operating costs and make the firms economically viable. The legislators also implicitly assumed that the areas had sufficient social overhead and infrastructure.* The legislative emphasis on loans is reflected in the actual allocations: 54 percent of total funds became industrial and commercial loans.[49] The legislation, however, did anticipate the need for training or retraining, and about 8 percent of the funds went to this end. However, the training program was later overshadowed by the Manpower Development and Training Act (MDTA) of 1962.†

One positive accomplishment of the ARA was the requirement that made the formulation of an overall economic-development program (OEDP) essential for grant or loan eligibility. Even though the original development documents were rather primitive by today's standards, they did facilitate discussion among local leaders regarding the future economic development of the area. This provision is retained by the successor agency—the EDA. The OEDPs were to provide a blueprint for development, and each project and loan request had to be appropriate to the medium- and long-run plans.

---

*It may well have been that the financial institutions were charging a premium interest rate in the areas to account for the higher risk of doing business in the region(s). Another possibility is that the track record (or lack thereof) of industrial establishments in the areas was poor, and other firms were afraid to move there.

†The MDTA was administered by the Department of Labor (and HEW in the early stages), and lack of interagency cooperation became a problem.

While the ARA was still trying to administer the multifaceted Area Redevelopment Act, the national economy was moving into a recession. Congress responded by passing new legislation with an explicit purpose: "to speed up and expand public works in communities with substantial unemployment, primarily to provide 'immediate useful' employment, but also to aid industrial development and make them better places in which to live and work."[50] Obviously, Congress and the president intended to combine a countercyclical policy with an economic-development strategy. The legislation is called the Public Works Acceleration Act of 1962. The ARA was designated as the administering agency, after the president rendered the allocated funds to the Department of Commerce.

Accelerated Public Works Program

Although the stated purpose of the APW program was to combine economic development and countercyclical job creation, the legislation did not require the formulation of an OEDP by a locality applying for funds. This facilitated the implementation of the program, but also gave rise to the criticism that the projects did nothing for economic-development goals. This criticism is a quizzical leap in logic, although it is clear that coordinated efforts for improving an area's infrastructure are more likely to enhance economic development than are uncoordinated efforts.

The ARA, with the assistance of the Community Facilities Administration (CFA) and the Public Health Service (PHS), managed to distribute nearly the full $900 million authorization in less than two years.* In fact, within five months of enactment the response to the program was so great that localities were urged to withhold further applications, but to attempt funding through the ARA (which still had some public-facilities funds). But even that source was exhausted by June of 1963.[51]

The ARA acted as the coordination center for the APW projects, with 14 different federal agencies using their existing networks to distribute the funds to localities. ARA functioned further as a watchdog to assure adherence to the statute in terms of project allocations, approvals, and progress reports on the grants. This proved to be a severe strain on the ARA staff, which was just becoming familiar with the problems and processes of the ARA program. The assignment of responsibility for administration to the ARA may well have been the straw that broke its back. It simply did not have enough time to set allocation and

---

*This compares favorably with the fact that ARA took almost three years to commit just over $100 million for public-facilities projects under the earlier act, where an OEDP was mandatory.

selection standards to satisfy both the economists and the politicians. The target areas for APW assistance remained the same as the areas previously determined by the ARA, in addition to areas designated by the secretary of labor to have had substantial (read over 6 percent) unemployment during the previous 9–12 months. As the national unemployment rate averaged 6.7 percent in 1961, it was virtually an all-inclusive eligibility rule. Thus, ARA efforts to allocate funds to those areas most in need were met with opposition, and "a fair share for all" became the basic watchword for fund distribution.[52] The allocation problem once again became a political decision with supposedly analytical foundations. There can be no question that the impact of cyclical unemployment is distributed unevenly across geographic areas and sociodemographic groups.[53]

The question of who should have been first in line for jobs under the APW program remained vague. The criterion was that the "jobs [on APW projects] were to be made available to the maximum extent feasible to the unemployed within the eligible communities."[54] There are no records of the employment status of persons hired under the APW program; thus, no conclusions on this issue can be drawn. However, there is clear evidence that the recession impacts to a greater extent on some labor-force cohorts than on others.[55] For example, lesser-skilled workers suffer more unemployment than higher-skilled workers. Although we do not have sociodemographic data on those hired for APW projects, a sample of 200 projects showed that nearly one-half of all those employed were unskilled or semiskilled. The federal projects run through government units (as opposed to subcontracting) showed the highest proportion of unskilled workers: one-half of the Department of Agriculture projects and two-thirds of the Interior Department projects employed over 80 percent unskilled and semiskilled workers. On the other hand, the construction of hospitals and administrative buildings, done primarily through subcontracting, showed "a preponderance of skilled workers."[56] These findings become very important in designing a countercyclical program that has certain skill groups as its target workers.

The guidelines for approval of APW projects involved the alacrity with which they could be implemented (or continued), whether they met an essential public need (that of subsequently reducing local unemployment), whether they could be completed within a year, and, if possible, accommodate the OEDP of the project area. In addition, the guidelines stressed that the federal money should not replace state or local funds that would have been spent on the project with or without the APW help. The locality had to contribute at least 25 percent of the total cost. In fact, the local and regular federal-agency contributions to the total expenditures were approximately 51 percent.[57] Thus, total outlays for the program were estimated to be $1.74 billion. Initially, the ARA estimated that the total outlays would generate 250,000 man-years of employment—a number that was later proven to be a gross exaggeration. On-site employment on APW projects peaked in June 1964, when 45,519 individuals were estimated to have been employed.[58] The ARA estimates of on-site employment generated were almost twice as large as those revealed by a General Accounting Office (GAO) study.[59] We have no numbers to indicate whether or not the APW projects did in fact substantially reduce local unemployment. On a national level, however, the impact is easily estimated. During any given month in 1962-63, there were approximately 4 million persons unemployed. At most, the APW program had one in a hundred on its payroll.

The types of projects to be funded under the APW program were not stipulated in the authorizing legislation, nor in the ARA regulations. Clearly, there are differences among project types in terms of the skills needed and labor-capital ratios, as evidenced in a 1977 Rand study. For a $1 billion expenditure, they show a range of 17,000 to 49,000 on-site jobs (depending on the project type), with the mean number of on-site jobs calculated to be approximately 33,000.[60] The project types also vary in terms of the skills they utilize; this too can be estimated with appropriate tools.* The distribution of project types funded under the APW breaks down as follows:

Type of Project	Percent of Total Allocation
Waste treatment, water, sewer, and other public utilities	48
Hospitals and other health facilities	13
Street and road construction	13
Public buildings	12
Wildlife and conservation	3
Other	11

The APW program analysis data seem to indicate that the mandates of speed of implementation and of completion were not met by most of the projects. Within a year of the first appropriation, 3,600 projects were completed or underway, and by June of 1964—21 months after the first appropriation—7,769 projects had been approved by the ARA and were either completed or in process.[62] The model level of employment under these projects was approximately 30,000 jobs per month and was reached within seven or eight months of funding. The recession had its beginning in the latter part of 1960 and hit bottom near the end of 1961. The APW program was criticized because of long delays in starting the projects, even after they had been approved by the ARA. Over three-fourths of all projects took place in FY 1965.[63] Had there been an ongoing program with triggers for startup, employment under the APW program

---

*Input-output analysis and econometric estimation are the most useful in this regard, and are discussed later.

would have peaked 12 to 18 months earlier, at the height of the recession. A strong argument for a triggered countercyclical program can be based on these findings.

Before summarizing the experiences under the ARA and APW programs,* it is worthwhile to note the level of effort vis-a-vis the federal budget that was put into the countercyclical program. The total allocations for APW were $400 million in 1962 and $450 million in 1963, representing approximately 6 percent and 9 percent of the total federal deficit of those two years.[64] If this ratio measures the relative willingness of Congress and the White House to go into debt to combat unemployment with countercyclical spending, we would presently have to spend between $4.5 billion and $7 billion on employment-generating programs to equal the 1962-64 effort. Further, we presently have almost twice as many unemployed as there were in the 1962-64 period. By any measure, be it GNP, federal receipts, or federal deficit, our present package of counter-cyclical employment programs is small. Compared to expenditures during the 1930s, the current figure is even more meager.

The ARA was functioning for almost four years, and during that time its function was not only to stimulate economic-development plans in nearly one-third of U.S. counties and to coordinate federal funding with these plans, but also to administratively implement the largest public works project since the 1930s. Its failures and accomplishments must be viewed in the light of these intentions.

Available information makes it unwise to conclude whether or not the ARA succeeded in stimulating economic development in lagging areas of the country. Its funding was small compared to the demand for aid. Applications for public-facilities grants soon assumed the central role in ARA program selection. The command given the ARA to carry through provisions in the law relating to business loans, training and retraining, public-facility construction, and technical assistance proved to be too much for a newly created agency to effectively handle. Even with the heroic administrative efforts extended by some in the agency, they were unable to overcome long delays in funding (as they often had to wait for several agencies to approve a project and an OEDP). Further, there was no experience in the Department of Commerce in allocating funds, nor in impartially designating areas as targets. In their enthusiasm, some of the ARA administrators overestimated what they could accomplish, espe-

---

*Note that the Appalachian Regional Development Act of 1965 was an additional program that was a specialized offshoot of the ARA. Through 1975 there has been $2.5 billion appropriated under this act, with over 60 percent going to highway construction and only 5 percent to public-facilities construction. I have been unable to find an evaluation of this program, and it is therefore not included in the analysis.

cially given that the nation was moving into a recession just as they were beginning to make some headway with loan programs.

On a more positive note, the ARA made great strides in getting local areas to think in terms of economic-development plans. (The OEDPs are still embodied in the work of the successor agency, EDA, and are becoming more and more sophisticated.) Further, the ARA learned the problems inherent in differentiating among areas without a specific and defensible allocation formula. No one appeared to be happy with the amount of help given by the ARA, because the politicians who had supported the Public Works Acceleration Act had told the folks back home to expect substantial help. The economic-development resources were simply spread too thin. Levitan summarized this point very well:

> A depressed area program can be effective only when the number of depressed areas is reduced to manageable proportions and only when areas with a potential for development at a reasonable economic cost are made eligible to participate in the program. In short, the program must recognize that some areas are more equal than others.[65]

In effect, Levitan is supporting a policy of regional economic triage. One would trust that Levitan is not advocating a policy of leaving the most depressed areas to decline even further, but is, rather, arguing for an overall economic situation in which only a few severely depressed regions would be in need of economic-development aid.

In sum, the economic-development efforts under ARA left much to be desired, but they did establish the fundamentals for the refinement of the presently operating EDA.

The efforts undertaken to implement the APW program are another story altogether. If one could point to a single cause of the downfall of the ARA, it was that the president turned over to the ARA the responsibility to implement the act. It then moved full tilt toward allocating money through a complicated and unspecified bureaucratic procedure, and was forced to turn attention away from the economic-development efforts in order to attempt to integrate the two programs. Surprisingly, the funds were handed out fairly quickly, and many were put to work under the program. This program was not the sole cause of recovery from the recession, but certainly contributed to the effort. Had funding been appropriated by a more expedient Congress or by a previously decided trigger mechanism, the jobs provided would have been more timely. The APW program proved to be very popular, with the demand for funding, even with the 50 percent-matching preference, far surpassing available resources. Priorities were not clear on which areas should be funded. As we shall see, this lesson has still not been learned.

By the end of 1964 the APW program's funding had expired and the nation was recovering from the recession. There was a consensus among both supporters and foes of the ARA that the agency and its mission should be restructured. This happened in 1965 with the passage of the Public Works and Economic Development Act and the creation of the Economic Development Administration within the U.S. Department of Commerce. The next section discusses the experience of the EDA with both economic-development and countercyclical public works programs.

The Economic Development Administration

As the national economy had almost completely recovered from the recession of the early 1960s, congressional attention turned once again to economic aid for lagging areas of the country, resulting in the creation of the Economic Development Administration, under authorization of the Public Works and Economic Development Act of 1965. The popularity of, and demand for, grants under the APW program was still fresh in the minds of congressmen, and the mandate stated in the legislation reads as follows:

> [The agency's mission] is to provide grants for public works and development facilities, other financial assistance and the planning and coordination needed to alleviate conditions of substantial and persistent unemployment and underemployment in economically distressed areas and regions.

Implicit in this mandate is a preference for the emphasis on public-works projects, but the priorities are unstated and left to the discretion of the administrators. The only indication the EDA got in terms of the level of effort expected by Congress was the size of the yearly funding level. Initially, Congress authorized $500 million for four years, but the annual level of funding varied. Total funding from 1966 to 1975 was $2.4 billion. The spending breakdown saw 74 percent go to public-works grants and loans, 17 percent to business loans, 5 percent to technical assistance, and 4 percent to planning and research.[66]

The mere existence of the EDA, and its use of public-works projects as an economic-development tool in certain depressed areas of the country, indicate a cognizance on the part of the federal government that there is uneven development in the United States, and that the normal budgetary expenditures on public-facilities construction are not equitably distributed. The total federal, state, and local public-construction budget in 1975 was $19.5 billion, representing 28 percent of total construction put in place that year. Of this, about half is funded by the federal government either through direct construction or grants to states and localities. Even a conservative estimate shows that the normal allocations are 20 times larger than annual appropriations for EDA's economic-development efforts.[67]

At the outset it must be mentioned that evaluation of the impact of EDA-run economic-development programs on the national economy is not a fruitful endeavor. Even with $500 million in annual appropriations, it would be difficult to find a noticeable impact on our $1.5 trillion economy. This is not to say that the impact in certain localities has not been substantial.

EDA has several program tools at its disposal: business loans, technical assistance, and public-facilities construction. Attention here is directed to the latter. In addition, there is a brief discussion later of EDA experiences in administering the PWIP, a countercyclical employment program initiated in 1971.

Although EDA retained the three major program tools developed by the ARA, it altered the emphasis in programs as well as the eligibility rules. The public-works program was given a greater role, and the county unit yielded to a larger multicounty area having a growth center where business activity could be stimulated. Rural areas remained top priority, but the new legislation allowed for aid to depressed urban areas with a population greater than 250,000.[68] Selection of areas for aid still was based primarily on the employment situation, although there were additional provisions for medium family-income levels. Indian reservations received special treatment.

The Public Works and Economic Development Act established broad goals for EDA but did not establish priorities. EDA chose, at least in its early years, never to set agencywide priorities, but rather, to evaluate each individual project in terms of the area's needs.[69] The need for specific policies soon became apparent (after the first-year review it was found that 110 of 364 projects funded were ineligible), and in December 1966 the assistant secretary of commerce for economic development announced a policy of "worst first." The returns and expected benefits are, of course, fewer under this policy, and the EDA administrators seemed to take this seriously until objections from the business-development staff emerged; they demanded that investments at least break even. The policy changed tacitly in 1968, when the "worst" areas were still funded, but with a smaller proportion of the total than in the previous two years.[70] In 1973 President Nixon tried to eliminate EDA altogether and transfer its funds to the Community Development Revenue Sharing Program. The logic behind this transfer was that the communities knew not only what was needed, but also how to plan it and carry it through—logic virtually identical to that behind the passage of CETA in the same year. Congress rejected this initiative as it felt that the redistributional aims of EDA were important, and would be unmet by the formulas for distribution of Community Development Revenue Sharing funds; EDA funding levels were, however, reduced. Further, there was no guarantee that localities would target the money as the legislation had intended.

The standard development approach of the EDA was to focus on facilities which directly created jobs; but in 1969 this changed to include more unconventional projects such as day-care centers, parking garages, theaters, and the like.[71]

The shift in project emphasis reflects a change in perspective on economic development; things which made the community a better place to live and which possibly attracted tourists were now acceptable.

The overall economic-development plans of the local areas remain a mainstay of EDA development efforts. The EDA, since 1965, has provided funds to local areas to hire professional planners to draw up an overall program. In many areas and states this document is the only economic plan available. In Massachusetts, for example, the CETA staff is making attempts to combine CETA planning with the local overall plans—clearly a step in the right direction, as CETA is indeed an economic-development tool.[72]

Given its broad, sometimes loosely interpreted goals and its frequently changing administration, what can be said about EDA's accomplishments over the years?

After years of running ARA and EDA like a pickup baseball game, the administrators decided to evaluate their programs. What immediately comes to mind is the problem of comparing a multimillion dollar project in Oakland with a ten-foot bridge in Downhome, Alabama. This simply cannot be done, and the administrators wisely chose to formulate a methodology whereby the projects could be evaluated on a case-by-case basis,[73] with certain measures developed that could be compared across projects. From the outset, EDA was aware that its program was aimed at only one aspect of economic development: the improvement of the infrastructure of the local area. EDA had long since been out of the labor-training business and had little to do with natural resources, technology, or the cultural characteristics of the area. Even with the most sophisticated tools for evaluation, the real answer to whether EDA aided the development or slowed the decline of certain areas will remain obscured for a long time to come. A sewer system has a life of at least 40 years, and a new hospital, city hall, or industrial park endures long after yearly congressional appropriations. Partially because of the impossibility of defining the process of economic change, and partially as a response to public and congressional demands to prove their worth, EDA evaluations have centered on computing impact measures of the projects funded (the number of jobs created, at what price, and so on). Very little has been done to evaluate the process of aiding depressed or declining areas, to obtain the maximum in equity and/or efficiency. In order to accomplish this, a case-study approach is the best method, although it is the most difficult to execute. EDA has in fact funded or directly conducted a number of case studies, but as indicated above, the outcomes are measured in terms of dollar and jobs impact, not in the context of area development itself.[74]

The direct-impact measures of EDA public works programs have been well summarized by Levitan.[75] He points out administrative problems that have accounted for delays in getting projects underway.

The blame is shared by local officials who have failed to get bond issues funded promptly or to obtain necessary user commitments and the very careful

TABLE 1.3

Economic Development Administration Public Works Projects, 1966 to 1975

Type of Project	Number	EDA Investment (millions of dollars)
General-industrial/commercial-development facilities	1,861	819
Industrial parks, site development	793	331
Recreation and tourism	279	154
Educational facilities	151	98
Port and harbor facilities	106	122
Airport facilities	55	29
Health facilities	89	64
Other public facilities	412	142
Total	3,746	1,759

Source: U.S. Department of Commerce, Economic Development Administration, *1975 Annual Report* (Washington, D.C.: Government Printing Office, 1976).

(and therefore slow) process of EDA approval itself. Even after approval, the data show that it takes nearly ten months to activate the project and another 73, on the average, to complete it.

Over the decade 1966-75, EDA's projects have continued to favor the building of industrial and commercial facilities, with indirect job creation being the major goal. A summary of the projects is shown in Table 1.3.[76]

One severe problem is that there is a low rate of utilization of industrial parks created under EDA programs. For non-Indian programs the utilization rate was 50 percent in 1974, and for Indian projects, only 16 percent.[77] Isolation of the parks, especially among the Indian projects, may be the determining factor, but this clearly suggests that careful medium- and long-run planning was not carried through. Building a useless industrial park is no worse than digging a hole and filling it later. The direct on-site jobs look impressive, but the contribution to economic development is small if anything.[78]

Levitan also makes an excellent point regarding EDA's investment in tourism projects. Not only are these projects very capital intensive, but the benefits from them usual inure to a small number of people in an area. The jobs provided in this industry are both seasonal and low paying. As such there is a serious question about public funding of this type of project.[79] The assessment of EDA's urban projects is mixed because of the enormous allocations that have been made for several of them. They are worthwhile, but they simply cannot be undertaken with the limited funding of the EDA.[80] The Indian projects represent a major investment of EDA's time and funding. The results are mixed, but a firm commitment to aid the most impoverished of minority groups continues.

During 1966-74, the EDA paid for approximately 60 percent of total costs of public-works projects, with the other 40 percent being supplemented by other federal agencies and the localities. For capital investments on industrial and commercial projects, the EDA's share was less than 5 percent. Levitan hints, and I agree, that this small proportion may not have been the determining factor in inducing private business to invest in projects, but rather, was simply a windfall. This issue is extremely important because the EDA funds are very limited and should be targeted to where they are more likely to "make the difference."[81]

The indirect jobs associated with public-works projects often tend to be low-skill and low-wage jobs, rarely lifting people above the poverty level. Indeed, the reason for the development in the first place was often the existence of a low-wage surplus labor force. On a more positive note, data collected on a sample of projects showed that 90 percent of the jobs went to area residents.[82] These findings are in sharp contrast to work-force characteristics of participants in PWIP, which is discussed in the following section.

An assessment of the long-term benefits of EDA projects is not available. The problems of following the development of an area and the impact of a specific project on that area over an extended period of time are formidable. However, it is worthwhile to carefully construct a longitudinal sample similar to the ongoing project at Ohio State University involving different labor-force cohorts. EDA has two longitudinal evaluations underway and should be encouraged to continue them.[83] Before summarizing the experience of the EDA's economic-development efforts, I will discuss the agency's experience and success in administering the Public Works Impact Program of 1971.

The Public Works Impact Program

In response to the recession in 1970-71, Congress allocated additional funds for EDA to implement a countercyclical employment program along with the regular economic-development, public-works projects. The funding for the Public Works Impact Program was limited to more than 25 percent but less than 35 percent of the total appropriated for public-works projects in the economic-development areas. Over its life span of three fiscal years, the PWIP program had total expenditures of $129 million, the smallest appropriation of any countercyclical program in U.S. history.* No matter how small the allocations, EDA had to go through with the full effort of establishing criteria for selection and approval. The experience gleaned under the APW program helped a great deal, but as we shall see, EDA did not appear to have learned from the problems encountered by the ARA during the APW program period.

The PWIP program had a single objective: the creation of employment opportunities for underemployed or unemployed residents of designated areas. The long-term development requirements that were present in the APW program were dropped, as was the pump-priming goal of the APW program and of the programs of the 1930s.† In addition, the EDA was to become the only federal agency involved in the administration of the program.

All of the areas eligible for EDA long-term assistance were able to apply for PWIP grants. Also able to apply were areas which were experiencing substantial unemployment (8.5 percent); areas which had more than 50 percent of families below the OEO poverty line; areas which were experiencing substantial out-migration; and/or areas which were experiencing, or were threatened with, an abrupt rise in unemployment. The substantial-unemployment criterion was the most important: over 70 percent of the projects went to areas with unemployment rates above 8.5 percent.

Like the APW, the PWIP was targeted at areas, and was designated to employ area residents to the maximum extent possible. Further, there were no provisions in the PWIP legislation that would disqualify a project that was not an addition to the funds which would be spent in the area on public works. There was no maintenance-of-effort provision. Wages on PWIP were to be area prevailing wages, as in the APW projects, and projects could be done either through contract bids or government-force accounts.

As a response to the lack of reliable detailed information on the previous programs operated within the Department of Commerce, EDA conducted a comprehensive evaluation of the PWIP.[84] The evaluation was done in-house, using a sample of 226 projects completed during the program's first two years. Curiously, EDA made no attempt in the evaluation to assess the long-term benefits, if any, of the PWIP projects, nor to assess their net costs, nor to give estimates

---

*Note that the funds for PWIP were, according to an EDA official, taken out of economic development and put into countercyclical jobs. He went on to say that EDA still had the same amount of money to allocate to public works, but had double the administrative problems.

†The easing of coordination with the OEDP was, according to congressional testimony, done so that the projects could get into operation faster. Further, pump priming would have been rather bold for the Congress to list as a goal, with only $50 million available in appropriations for the first year. The Nixon administration had previously vetoed a bill calling for a $2 billion program.

of indirect and induced employment, of income generated by program expenditures. The latter shortcomings are easy to understand, as these estimates are complicated and time consuming, but the fact that EDA did not assess the economic-development impact is somewhat ironic, given the mission of the agency (the net program cost calculations are also detailed and expensive, and the first attempt to do this is discussed in connection with the Title X program). Nevertheless, the evaluation conducted provides previously unavailable data on countercyclical employment programs.

Once again, the time which elapsed between congressional reaction to a cyclical downturn and the implementation of a program was too long for the program to aid employment at the depth of the recession. Further, the evaluation points out that PWIP was "proseasonal," and that it "was half a year too late to counteract the short-term rise in area unemployment that peaked in January 1973."[85] As in the APW program, the full impact came a bit too late. Further, the evaluation found that at least six months elapsed between an application receipt and the startup of a project. This delay could be eliminated by the maintenance of a backlog of approved projects within the EDA organization.

PWIP had no maximum limit on the federal share of project costs, although it had a goal of 50 percent, with supplementary funding up to 100 percent. Overall, EDA paid for 70 percent of the total costs of the projects; the average total cost was $334,000 and EDA's share was $234,000.

In assessing PWIP's ability to employ residents of underemployed project areas, the EDA evaluators found a rather distressing fact—only 22 percent of the jobs in sampled projects went to target-group workers. Further, they found that the non-Indian projects were only contributing an average of 21 percent of total costs to wages.[86] Only three of the 202 non-Indian projects had wage payments exceeding 50 percent of the total costs. Further, 48 percent of the man-months of employment went to skilled workers and 42 percent to unskilled. Almost two-thirds of the skilled positions went to nonresidents of the area, and on the average, nonresidents were paid more than the residents.[87] As the evaluators examined the actual program data further, they found few accomplishments in accordance with the mission of the program. Estimated man-months of employment to be generated by the projects turned out to be over 100 percent too high, while the estimates of the number of jobs turned out to be almost 100 percent too low. The discrepancy in the latter category is explained by the fact that the average duration of the job was slightly more than one man-month. Also, EDA and the project applicants estimated that 73 percent of the jobs would go to target-group workers; as mentioned before, the final number was 22 percent. And the funding level of the program was too low to affect the unemployment rate of the areas.

Perhaps one of the most interesting findings of the PWIP evaluation was the wide discrepancy between the employees and jobs on the government-run projects (force-accounts) versus those that were contracted under bids. (Note that in a government-run project, not all jobs are necessarily done with the governmental unit's labor force and employment facilities; some of the specialized work can be subcontracted.) On the government-run projects, the target group accounted for 59 percent of the employment, while only 22 percent employed on the bid projects were previously underemployed. Labor intensity on government-run projects was 33 percent, versus 18 percent on bid accounts, and the cost per man-month of employment was substantially higher on bid accounts ($4,559 versus $2,539). Overall, government-run projects were more labor intensive, more cost effective, and they came closer to meeting the mandate of a countercyclical employment program. A special evaluation of PWIP Indian projects was undertaken where it was found that over 80 percent of the jobs and 90 percent of the man-months of employment went to residents of the area; two-thirds of those who received jobs were previously unemployed or underemployed.

In sum, the PWIP program started too late, suffered delays in the processing of applications, and did not aid in significantly easing the employment situation in designated areas, as the projects appeared to move into the regular stream of construction activities in the areas. Force accounts, however, did better in meeting the goals than did the bid contracts. The EDA evaluators made a series of excellent recommendations on future programs of this type, and the extent to which they were incorporated into the Title X and the LPW programs is discussed later. In short, the framers of the PWIP legislation and of the regulations for implementation did not appear to have learned from the experiences under APW. Either that, or they were purposely attempting to operate the program with the employment and materials purchases designed to benefit the regular construction labor force and contractors. If any countercyclical impact was gained, it occurred in only a few locations and was very short lived.

It should be added here that during the spring of 1971, when Congress was debating the future of EDA, it proposed a $2 billion appropriation for a countercyclical public works program, in addition to continued funding of EDA's regular program. This bill was passed and then vetoed by President Nixon. The president gave his reasons in a message to the Senate that stated that the lead time was too long, and that the jobs would not go to those groups with the highest unemployment. He was absolutely right, as even the much smaller PWIP appropriations that came later were too late, too small, and incorrectly targeted. However, the questions of project selection and of enforcement of guidelines for those hired on the projects reflect administrative inadequacy rather than basic program weakness.

Throughout the previous discussion comments have been made on the efficiency of the programs implemented under the ARA and EDA. However, a few more general comments seem in order.

The economic-development efforts of the agencies have achieved mixed results. On a positive note, some of the special-area efforts have halted or at slowed economic decline. Thousands of jobs have been created and many still-utilized facilities have been built. At a very minimum, economic-development plans have brought together previously unconnected interest groups within communities to discuss their goals and priorities. At a maximum, the plans will aid in furthering smooth and coordinated economic change in the future.

In recent years, the EDA has taken a more serious and concerted approach to evaluation of its projects and processes. From these evaluations have come a series of constructive and critical comments about what was done and was not done. It would be unrealistic to think that each and every recommendation would be immediately implemented as policy, given that the agency has changed leadership so often, and that its mandate has changed with administrative and, sometimes, congressional whim. For endeavors in any area so heavily discussed and so little understood as economic development, it would be unwise to think in terms of dramatic quantum leaps. But it is realistic to view activities as making incremental changes in the areas served.

Finally, the fact that long-term benefits are really the cornerstone of economic-development efforts reinforces the notion that we cannot expect to see impact assessments beyond criticism. The goal of EDA is long-run results, and the demands put upon the agency are short run. The time frame for impact results is relevant for EDA's countercyclical efforts, but not for its economic-development mission.

The EDA experience with countercyclical job creation is an entirely different story and must be judged with stricter criteria and in a shorter time frame. In the use of countercyclical public works projects, the long-term economic-development benefits are a desirable (albeit peripheral) goal. The overall assessment of the large APW program is that it appears to be, on balance, reasonable. Funding was too late to meet the needs at the depth of the recession, but it did appear to go to useful projects. The selection criteria came down, in the final analysis, to a matter of providing a fair share for all; little attention was paid to the relative needs of one area versus another. We unfortunately do not have enough information of the sociodemographic groups served under the program, and therefore cannot assess whether its impact was felt by the groups that needed it the most. We do know that the force-account projects under both the APW program and PWIP had a more favorable labor-capital ratio than the bid contracts, and this is a valuable lesson for the future.

The results of the PWIP were somewhat disappointing. Although small in size and not expected to have influence on the national economic situation, the program did not really reach those in need. Only about 20 percent of the persons hired were either unemployed or underemployed prior to program hiring. Further, the allocation formulas failed to direct the limited money to the areas that, according to unemployment criteria, needed it the most.

SUMMARY

Almost five decades have passed since the United States plunged into the Great Depression. The belief that market mechanisms will equitably and efficiently allocate our human and natural resources is held only by a few academic and Wall Street scribblers. Full utilization of our labor force has occurred only sporadically over this period and has always been connected with a war effort. In response to the problem, various levels of government legislated programs that first and foremost guaranteed every citizen the right to income support of one sort or another. For those who are deemed members of the regular labor force and are idled temporarily because of recessionary problems, unemployment insurance is provided—a transfer program of incredible magnitude,[88] from which no directly useful product emerges. For those who are unable to work due to health problems, family responsibilities, or institutional barriers to their employment, other transfers are provided in cash or in kind—welfare payments. From these come no useful product, either.

Only occasionally over the five decades have we identified projects, financed by the federal, state, and local governments, that would offer employment to those who wanted to work while they waited for the market to provide them with regular employment. Even less frequently have we taken the position of targeting money for infrastructure enhancement in areas of the country deemed lagging or depressed. Sometimes we have combined the two strategies. Indisputable evidence on program performance in both equity and efficiency terms is lacking, while opinions are abundant.

Economic-Development Efforts

The special efforts of the federal government to provide aid to lagging areas, first through the ARA and then through the EDA, were aptly described by Levitan as "too little but not too late." It is virtually impossible to quantitatively assess the impact of the ARA and EDA programs, as they are by definition designed to have a longer-term impact on the chosen areas. One would be hard pressed to defend a position against the services and dollars offered by the EDA, as the areas served are clearly better off—how much better off remains unknown. One would be equally hard pressed to argue for the continuation of aid to certain areas in the same manner as we have done in the past. There are several major reasons against this argument, the majority of which were discussed earlier. However, several points are worth repeating here.

First, we have yet to carefully document the causes of economic depression and identify the most effective points of intervention. Indeed, some have even proposed a form of development triage where those areas which are the worst off will simply be left to fend for themselves, as the limited funding of EDA is already spread too thin. Although this is practical and possibly very efficient from a cost-benefit point of view, this position is indefensible. Instead, we must take a positive approach to ameliorate conditions in the areas of the country that share the least in our abundance. Equal hardship may exist in a town in West Virginia and in a slum in Boston. We cannot allow aid to be based simply on the visibility of need or on the power of political representatives. We must find out the causes of depression and assess the amount and type of intervention needed to give life to some of those still-needy citizens in Michael Harrington's *The Other America*.

The first step in this process is to determine what constitutes a lagging area. As they stand, the allocation and eligibility formulas please neither the economists nor the politicians. The economists should be satisfied first, followed by as few compromises as possible. Surely, this process will document the fact that the resources of EDA are totally inadequate for dealing with the enormous problems of uneven development. This must be stated loudly and clearly to Congress and the White House.

Secondly, consolidation of the federal economic-development efforts is essential. The variety of programs now in effect are spread out among Labor, HUD, Commerce, HEW, Interior, and so on. All have one basic purpose, although the target constituencies and areas of the country that are aided differ. Instead of competing for segmented congressional favor, effort should be put into dovetailing present programs as much as possible with future plans for totally coordinated economic development. EDA already has a start in this process because of its wise insistence on overall economic-development plans. Given the experience and history of the EDA, it may be the likely place for coordinated efforts.

Thirdly, the business of economic development does not have to focus exclusively on depressed areas. The problems of certain declining economic regions of the country lie clearly within the same purview. The causes of decline are different from those of depression; thus the solutions may also be different—one solution builds up and the other acts as a prop. Again, research is needed to identify the symptoms and causes of the decline. As elementary as this may sound, it has not yet been done.

The programs of the EDA should include parallel planning efforts in which socioeconomic plans are drawn up for both depressed and declining areas, in conjunction with visible projects of the public- and civil-works nature. There are certain obvious needs in both areas, and long waits are unnecessary—the parallel processes will add credibility to each other. This process will require more effective state and local coordination with EDA in the development and financing of an economic-growth strategy. Goals should be explicit, with targets laid out and the consequences of certain strategies outlined ahead of time (that is, target and indicative planning).

Moreover, the business-loan program pleases few. Lending institutions balk at the competition, existing businesses don't like to see subsidized competitors, and the default rate is high. A program with the public sector holding an equity position in the firms may be worthy of consideration.* Areas for expansion must be carefully selected so as not to compete with private businesses. Energy conservation and production might well be a good place to begin, with financing arranged in a manner similar to that of community development corporations.

Finally, the EDA must make a set of explicit goals for its development monies. It must enumerate the problems to which its programs are addressed and describe the kinds of assistance it should (and can) offer.

Insofar as there exists an uneven distribution of our economic wealth and of the growth rate in that wealth—whether that unevenness exists among areas or people—federal-government intervention is not only proper, but obligatory.

Countercyclical Jobs through Public Works Projects

Governmental responses to the problems of cyclical unemployment require a compromise to be worked out among three major objectives: net expansion of employment, the creation of useful output, and the provision of transfers for support. The bulk of our attention over the last two decades has focused on the third objective. Federal and state outlays for unemployment insurance and transfer payments dwarf those outlays that are directed toward employment expansion and the creation of useful output. During the 1930s concentration centered on work relief, resulting in vast increases in net employment and an incredible array of visible outputs. During the 1930s we had less patience with the dole. Now there is less concern with the moral need to work and far more concern with inflationary pressures that might be generated by increased spending.

Consequently, our commitment of resources to the public works and public-service employment programs has been less than full. Countercyclical public works programs have been instituted four times since 1960. Without exception, excess demand for program funds has occurred, along with delays in implementation, allowing the critics of the programs to mutter a series of "I told you so's." If a countercyclical program is implemented too late to provide jobs while the recession is at its worst, it may well generate the inflationary pressures its critics predict. And if the funds are not substantial enough to provide a fair share for all, even its political friends may turn against it.

---

*Massachusetts is preparing to experiment with this approach through its Community Development Finance Corporation. Also, the Canadian Local Employment Assistance Program (LEAP) fits this model.

The response must be one of substantial funds triggered for appropriation and released by early indicators of an impending downturn in the business cycle. Ideally, the funds should peak at the time when the recession bottoms out, and should then be expended in ever-lessening doses until recovery and expansion occur. A simplified method is illustrated by the following diagram:

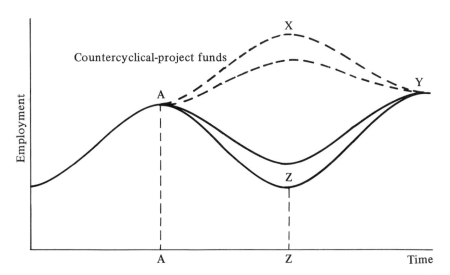

In the diagram, point A represents the first early-warning indicators of a coming recession,[89] which would trigger the release of funds by formula. For example, the line representing employment can be $E = a + bt + ct^2 + dt^3$. The broken line is the inverse of the employment equation and represents the funds to be released (expended) for countercyclical projects. It could be cited as: project money $= K(-bt - ct^2 - dt^3)$, where K is, say, a percentage of total employment. By this formula the maximum funds would correspond with the bottom of the recession (Z) and would trail off as employment became stable or expanded at the end of the recession (Y). The interior broken and solid lines in the diagram represent a possible compacting of the amplitude of recessionary employment changes and the countercyclical money expended. This method of triggering money would appease those who are most concerned with the inflationary aspects of the countercyclical projects and would compensate solely for the recession. If, on the other hand, the money were to be spent with the intention of spurring a change in private optimism (and hence investment), it should be released in a larger series of chunks at the beginning of the recession, thereby possibly reducing the amplitude of the employment drop that would have occurred without the injection. The choice here depends on the amount of concern with inflationary pressure, and the purpose of the program.

Moreover, explicit decision rules and regulations must be included for area designation and the target industries and workers, as the impact of a public-works program can vary widely. As pointed out earlier, the PWIP and the APW program provided stimulus and direct employment almost exclusively to the construction sector, while Title X (discussed in the following chapters) was far more widespread in its impact. The difference in impact resulted from congressional caveats concerning labor intensiveness, from the participation of the Labor Department in the Title X program, and the project selection priorities. The most recent program, LPW, is targeted at the construction industry. Thus, we cannot expect to see a large portion of the jobs going to disadvantaged persons, nor used in the provision of services. Moreover, LPW, following the tradition of public-works programs, has no provisions which would limit employment to those out of work and/or those receiving a transfer payment. Although area unemployment is mentioned in the legislation as a "factor which must be considered" in project selection, the only explicit reference to target groups is to "unemployment or underemployment in the construction and construction-related industries."[90]

One cannot criticize the LPW legislation for providing assistance to the ailing construction industry. But without comparable funds directed toward other groups of workers and industries, the allocation can be faulted on equity grounds. One possible solution to this equity problem is to provide in the legislation for a certain percentage of the projects to be run under force accounts, rather than by bid. In the latter case, history has shown that the labor costs are higher (as prevailing wages are used), and that the impact is lowest on the most needy unemployed. When units of government themselves hire workers for projects, we find a greater share of the jobs and the new income going to the needy. Indeed, as will be pointed out in the Title X net-cost calculations, the transfers saved constitute an important component of the adjusted cost of the programs. Congressional leaders might also consider allowing (asking) the military bases around the country to provide skilled assistance in the construction of public works. They have both the manpower and machinery, often idle, that are needed for many of the public-sector projects.

Another option to be considered for expansion of employment in recessionary times is based on the Canadian Local Initiatives Program (LIP). This program has been implemented on a trial basis in Massachusetts, and evaluation results indicate positive accomplishments, especially when matched with the regular PSE positions. LIP is quite simple in design. Any unemployed person or persons can propose to carry through a project of limited duration that will employ those in need and offer some benefit to the public either through rehabilitation, new business development, or provision of a needed service. All projects are visible (civil and public works projects) and initiated by those who will carry them through.[91] Another example of a locally needed and initiated public-employment program can be found in the Netherlands, where the right to work is taken seriously and addressed by a very large program called the Dutch Social Employment Program. This program also is worthy of serious attention by policy makers.

On the administrative side of both countercyclical and economic-development programs encompassing public works projects, there is much room for improvement. However, the administering agencies cannot be expected to accomplish what is only hinted at in legislative authorizations. Without exceptions, the series of recent laws has been vague and noncommittal, save in their reference to funding levels. Allowing those who write the regulations to steer the program in directions that they deem appropriate is no more or less than a congressional shirking of responsibility. Regulation hearings almost always become sessions where each interest group presents its most extreme case of need, hoping to have half its desired projects approved, rather than none. With clearly specified intentions, priorities, and goals, the administering agencies will no longer have to remain in the state of limbo so often observed in the last 15 years (witness the court battles impending over LPW allocations).

Present and past experiences with the utilization of public-works and related projects as a tool of economic development and countercyclical employment policy prove that, with careful planning and implementation, employment can be provided, growth and development fostered, and valuable and visible output produced.

NOTES

1. For an early definition, see John K. Galbraith, *The Economic Effects of the Federal Public Works Expenditures, 1933-38* (Washington, D.C.: Government Printing Office, 1940), p. 128; for a definition in a more modern context, see William J. Tobin, *Public Works and Unemployment: A History of Federally Funded Programs* (Washington, D.C.: Economic Development Administration, U.S. Department of Commerce, 1975).

2. The format of the federal budget does not allow for distributing the portion of federal expenditures directly spent on public works, although the figures for ownership indicate that the state and local governments "own" almost 85 percent of the total expenditures. Of course, this results from the large number of federal grants for the construction of schools, roads, and so forth. See Bureau of the Census, U.S. Department of Commerce, *Statistical Abstract of the United States, 1976* (Washington, D.C.: Government Printing Office, 1977), table 1244.

3. See for example, Thomas Oliphant, "Will Carter's Promises Become Economic Progress for the Northeast?" *Boston Globe (New England Magazine)*, January 30, 1977.

4. All of the programs discussed are assumed to be financed through government debt. There is little debate on whether this works in the sense of increasing employment and expanding output. See Alan Blinder and Robert Solow, "The Analytical Foundations of Fiscal Policy," in Blinder, Solow, et al., *The Economics of Public Finance* (Washington, D.C.: Brookings Institution, 1974), pp. 3-115. Also, on the question of the comparative efficacy of programs for countercyclical employment stimulation, see Congressional Budget

Office, *Temporary Measures to Stimulate Employment* (Washington, D.C.: Government Printing Office, 1975).

5. For a discussion of this question, see Sar A. Levitan and Joyce K. Zickler, *Too Little But Not Too Late: Federal Aid to Lagging Areas* (Lexington, Mass.: Lexington Books, D. C. Heath and Co., 1976), especially chap. 1.

6. Public-works and public-employment programs are usually distinguished by whether funds are appropriated for materials and equipment. For example, Michael Wiseman defines public-service employment under the Comprehensive Employment and Training Act (CETA) as a program "designed to preserve skills and maintain income during a cyclical downturn." Funds over and above those paid for subsidized wages and salaries of the PSE clients are usually earmarked for only administrative purposes. See Wiseman, *Achieving the Goals of the Employment Act of 1946–30th Anniversary Review Paper No. 1, On Giving a Job: The Implementation and Allocation of Public Service Employment*, U.S. Congress, Joint Economic Committee (Washington, D.C.: Government Printing Office, 1975). This problem of distinguishing public works and PSE is becoming increasingly difficult as the new regulations covering Title VI of CETA now explicitly call for PSE projects.

7. Paul Studenski and Herman Krooss, *Financial History of the United States*, 2d ed. (New York: McGraw-Hill, 1963), pp. 354-58. Part of the expedited construction program included the Hoover Dam.

8. Ibid., p. 357.

9. See Donald Watson, "The Reconstruction Finance Corporation," in *The Municipal Yearbook, 1937* (Chicago: International City Managers Association, 1937).

10. This program is discussed in some detail in Galbraith, op. cit.

11. This provision is very similar to a recently proposed program in the commonwealth of Massachusetts: former Governor Dukakis asked HEW Secretary Califano for a waiver of regulations to allow the state's Department of Human Services to force persons to work on public projects for a period of time necessary to earn their welfare payment. See Dukakis to Califano, with attached proposal, February 25, 1977.

12. A discussion of the CWA can be found in Committee on Social Security, *Work Relief Experience in the U.S.* (New York: Social Science Research Council, n.d.).

13. Arthur Burns and Edward Williams, *Federal Work, Security and Relief Programs*, WPA Division of Research, Monograph 24 (Washington, D.C.: Government Printing Office, 1941).

14. Jack Isakoff, "The Public Works Administration," *Illinois Studies in the Social Sciences* 33, no. 3 (Urbana: University of Illinois Press, 1938), p. 137.

15. Quoted in Anthony Sulvetta and Norman Thompson, *An Evaluation of the Public Works Impact Program* (Washington, D.C.: Economic Development Administration, Department of Commerce, 1975), app. C, p. 316.

16. As quoted in Lois Craig, "Beyond Leaf-Raking, WPA's Lasting Legacy," *City*, October–November 1970, p. 23.

17. See Alden F. Briscoe, "Public Service Employment in the 1930's: The WPA," in Harold L. Sheppard et al., *The Political Economy of Public Service Employment* (Lexington, Mass.: D. C. Heath and Co., 1972).

18. For an impressive list of the accomplishments of the WPA and other job-creation programs of this era, see Garth L. Mangum, "New Deal Job Creation Programs," in Subcommittee on Employment, Manpower and Poverty, Committee on Labor and the Public Welfare, *Emergency Employment Act Background Information*, Final Report (Washington, D.C., 1967).

19. The issues of administration are discussed in detail in Arthur W. MacMahon et al., *The Administration of Federal Work Relief* (Chicago: Public Administration Service, 1941). The authors point out further that WPA requests to Congress to establish a civil service within the WPA were turned down.

20. This and part of the following discussion of the WPA are taken from Briscoe's excellent piece on the WPA, op. cit.

21. Ibid., p. 100.

22. Ibid., p. 102.

23. This same technique has been utilized in certain rehabilitation projects funded under CETA-VI in Massachusetts, where the $10,000-per-year limit would be exceeded if prevailing (read Davis-Bacon Act) wages were paid. Thus, those working on some of the rehabilitation projects only worked part time or part year until the $10,000 maximum was reached. This is discussed in more detail in Thomas A. Barocci and Charles A. Myers, "An Evaluation of CETA in Eastern Massachusetts," mimeographed (Cambridge: Industrial Relations Section, Sloan School of Management, MIT, 1977).

24. Bureau of the Census, *Statistical Abstract of the United States, 1941* (Washington, D.C.: Government Printing Office, 1942), tables 409 and 416.

25. See William H. Miernyk, *Elements of Input-Output Analysis* (New York: Random House, 1965), especially chap. 3, or Michael K. Evans, *Macroeconomic Activity: Theory, Forecasting and Control* (New York: Harper and Row, 1969), especially chaps. 19 and 20.

26. These figures were derived from Congressional Budget Office estimates using 1976 dollars. See Congressional Budget Office, *Temporary Measures to Stimulate Employment* (Washington, D.C.: Government Printing Office, 1975). Note that the estimates cited are for the employment impact of the programs 12 months after enactment.

27. Briscoe, op. cit., p. 113.

28. The $2.2 billion figure is derived from a category in the federal budget called "Federal Works Agency," and includes several agencies. See tables 192 and 193 in Bureau of the Census, *Statistical Abstract of the United States, 1941* (Washington, D.C.: Government Printing Office, 1942).

29. For an expansion of this point, see Thomas A. Barocci and William Spring, "Jobs and the Management of the Economy," mimeographed (Boston: Boston University Regional Institute on Employment, Training and Labor Market Policy, 1975). Also, a fully detailed list of accomplishments is included in Committee on Social Security, op. cit.

30. U.S. Community Improvements Appraisal, *A Report on the Programs of the WPA* (Washington, D.C.: Government Printing Office, 1939), p. 7.

31. Ibid., as cited in Sulvetta and Thompson, op. cit., p. 343.

32. Cited in Sulvetta and Thompson, op. cit., pp. 319–20.

33. Galbraith, op. cit., p. 42.

34. *Hearings Before a Subcommittee of the Committee on Banking and Currency, U.S. Senate, 79th Congress, 1st Session, on S. 380* (Washington, D.C.: Government Printing Office, 1945), p. 572.

35. Herbert Stein, "Twentieth Anniversary of the Employment Act of 1946," statement in *Supplement to the Joint Economic Committee Symposium* (Washington, D.C.: Government Printing Office, 1966), pp. 143–52.

36. Sar A. Levitan, *Federal Aid to Depressed Areas: An Evaluation of the Area Redevelopment Administration* (Baltimore: Johns Hopkins Press, 1964), p. 21.

37. *Economic Report of the President, 1955* (Washington, D.C.: Government Printing Office, 1956), p. 57.

38. See President's Commission on Technology and the American Economy, *Technology and the American Economy*, vol. 1, Report of the Progress (Washington, D.C.: Government Printing Office, February 1966). A reading of this document is highly recommended for all those who are presently concerned with the employment problems of the American economy. The report was carefully and insightfully done. The series of recommendations could have been written last week, rather than a decade ago.

39. See Levitan, *Federal Aid to Depressed Areas*, especially chap. 8.

40. Sulvetta and Thompson, op. cit.

41. See Raymond Milkman et al., *Alleviating Economic Distress: Evaluating a Federal Effort* (Lexington, Mass.: Lexington Books, 1972), chap. 1.

42. Levitan and Zickler, *Too Little But Not Too Late*, p. 10.

43. Levitan, *Federal Aid to Depressed Areas*, pp. 150–51.

44. Levitan, in ibid., mentions the high-end project costs but offers no further explanation for this wide discrepancy. Also, there is no indication of the job tenure. This may have been due to several especially large capital-intensive projects on the high end.

45. Ibid., pp. 137–38.

46. Ibid., p. 138.

47. Ibid., p. 151.

48. The reasons for this disproportionate allocation to the South are not clear, although Levitan hints that southern support in Congress for this legislation was given in anticipation of obtaining a large part of the public-facilities money. See ibid., p. 149.

49. Levitan and Zickler, *Too Little But Not Too Late*, p. 9.

50. Quoted in Levitan, *Federal Aid to Depressed Areas*, p. 152.

51. Milkman et al., op. cit., p. 5. It is worth noting that President Kennedy had asked for "standby" authority to feed more money into the economy, as deemed necessary to fight the recession. However, conservative congressmen called this a "political slush fund," and it was dropped from the final version of the legislation. After the great demand for the original $900 million allocation, proponents went to Congress to ask for more and were refused. The president was by this time committed to the tax-cut strategy and did not push for an additional allocation for the APW. See Levitan and Zickler, *Too Little But Not Too Late*, p. 11.

52. Tobin, op. cit., p. 110.

53. See Andy Sum and Thomas P. Rush, "The Geographical Structure of Unemployment," *Monthly Labor Review*, March 1975, pp. 3–9.

54. Executive Order 11049 (Washington, D.C.), September 14, 1962.

55. See Edward Gramlich, "The Distributional Effects of Higher Unemployment," in *Brookings Papers on Economic Activity*, vol. 2 (Washington, D.C.: Brookings Institution, 1974), pp. 293–342.

56. Johannes U. Hoeber, "Some Characteristics of Accelerated Public Works Projects," *Redevelopment*, September 1964.

57. Ibid.

58. Ibid. There are no wage data available for APW employers.

59. House Report No. 92–92, pp. 100, 102, cited in Anthony Sulvetta et al., eds., *Alleviating Unemployment Through Accelerated Public Works in the United States: An Historical Perspective* (Washington, D.C.: Economic Development Administration, 1976), p. 27.

60. Georges Vernez et al., *Regional Cycles and Employment Effects of Public Works Investments*, Rand report to the Economic Development Administration (Santa Monica: Rand Corp., 1977), p. 128.

61. Hoeber, op. cit.

62. Ibid., cited in Tobin, op. cit., p. 110.

63. Nancy H. Teeters, "The 1972 Budget: Where It Stands and Whither It Might Go," in *Brookings Papers on Economic Activity*, vol. 1 (Washington, D.C.: Brookings Institution, 1971), p. 233.

64. *Economic Report of the President, 1976* (Washington, D.C.: Government Printing Office, 1977), table B-63.

65. Levitan, *Federal Aid to Depressed Areas*, p. 253.

66. Levitan, *Too Little But Not Too Late*, p. 19.

67. *Statistical Abstract of the United States, 1976* (Washington, D.C.: Government Printing Office, 1977), table 1245.

68. Consider the Special Impact Program (SIP), which has some characteristics in common with certain portions of the EDA programs. It was initiated under Title I of the Economic Opportunity Act (1965), to create federally subsidized projects in depressed inner-city and rural areas. The projects were initiated within the EDA, as well as through the FHA, the Office of Economic Opportunity (OEO), and the Department of Labor (DOL). The program never had public-facilities construction as either a major or minor goal. See Geoffrey Faux, *CDCs: New Hope for the Inner Cities* (New York: Twentieth Century Fund, 1971), and Abt Associates, *An Evaluation of the Special Impact Program*, vols. 1–4 (Cambridge, Mass.: Abt, 1973). Also, Harvey Gorn et al., *Community Development Corporations* (Washington, D.C.: Urban Institute, 1976).

The SIP's vehicle for economic development is the Community Development Corporation (CDC); as of 1976 there were 16 urban and 14 rural CDCs still operating under funding and administration of the Community Services Administration (CSA). The total level of funding is about $50 million, divided 60–40 percent in favor of urban centers. The basic format is that the CDCs are provided equity (not loan) grants to begin businesses in the designated areas. The evaluations conducted report a mixed success rate, with approximately 20 percent failures, 30 percent profitable ventures, and the remainder just at the border line. With careful coordination and sufficient resources, it appears that the CDCs can succeed in establishing a profit-making enterprise within the inner city or rural depressed area.

69. Economic Development Administration, *The EDA Experience in the Evolution of Policy: A Brief History, 1965-73* (Washington, D.C.: Department of Commerce, 1974), p. 13.

70. See ibid. This volume gives excellent insights into the problems and processes of EDA over the years. Elections bring changes both in definitions of economic development and in priorities.

71. Milkman et al., op. cit.

72. Thomas A. Barocci, "Planning and Economic Development Under CETA," *Adherent* 2, no. 2 (1976).

73. Economic Development Administration, *Developing Methodologies for Evaluating the Impact of the EDA Programs* (Washington, D.C.: Department of Commerce, 1972).

74. For example, see EDA, *Public Works Program: An Evaluation*, vols. 1 and 2 (Washington, D.C.: Department of Commerce, 1970).

75. Levitan and Zickler, *Too Little But Not Too Late*, especially chap. 6.

76. Ibid., p. 106.

77. Ibid., p. 107.

78. In fact, digging a hole and filling it might even be more cost effective since the entire bill would go to wages (with a little for shovels), and the project would have a more immediate stimulative impact on the area. Wage payments move through the economy faster than do material purchases. See Evans, op. cit.

79. For a more detailed discussion of this issue, see Bennett Harrison, "The Economic Development of Massachusetts," report to the Massachusetts Senate Commerce and Labor Committee (Boston, 1974).

80. For an interesting and informative assessment of the largest EDA urban project, see Jeffrey Pressman and Aaron Wildavsky, *Implementation: How Great Expectations in Washington are Dashed in Oakland* (Berkeley: University of California Press, 1973).

81. With respect to state tax incentives as an economic-development policy, a similar criticism is made in Bennett Harrison and Sandra Kanter, "The Political Economy of State Job Creation Business Incentives," in *The Declining Northeast* (New Brunswick: Rutgers University Press, forthcoming 1979).

82. Boise Cascade Center for Community Development, *An Evaluation of EDA Public Works Projects*, vol. 1 (Boise: Cascade Center, 1975), p. 136.

83. Centaur Management Consultants, *Re-Evaluation of the Impacts of Fifty Public Works Projects and EDA: An Updated Evaluation of EDA Funded Industrial Parks, 1968-74*, Project done for EDA, undated.

84. Sulvetta and Thompson, op. cit.

85. Ibid., p. 27.

86. Ibid., p. 272.

87. Ibid., p. 273.

88. The federal share of UI payments was $13.5 billion in 1975 and an estimated $19.5 billion in 1976, as noted in *Statistical Abstract of the United States, 1976* (Washington, D.C.: Government Printing Office, 1976), table 379.

89. See Vernez et al., op. cit.

90. Public Law 94-369, sec. 107, 1977.

91. See Thomas A. Barocci, *The Canadian Job Creation Program and Its Applicability to the U.S.*, study prepared for U.S. Congress, Subcommittee on Economic Growth, Joint Economic Committee, Paper no. 2, vol. 1 (Washington, D.C.: Government Printing Office, 1976). Also, see Abt Associates, *An Evaluation of the Massachusetts Local Initiatives Program*, vols. 1-3 (Cambridge: Abt, 1977). The original design of the Massachusetts LIP was to link those LIP projects that had the possibility of becoming financially self-sufficient with a new program designed to inject equity money into businesses which otherwise would be unable to expand. The public would take an equity position that could be retained or later sold out. Unfortunately, the state officials have not followed up this link with the LIP projects that might have qualified.

2

STRUCTURE OF
THE JOB OPPORTUNITIES
PROGRAM

The Job Opportunities Program has provided funds for 2,255 individual projects in metropolitan and nonmetropolitan areas throughout the country. Almost $500 million in Title X funds ($497.5 million) has been supplemented by monies from other federal, state, local, and private sources, to provide a total of over $758 million in support of these projects. An administrative evaluation of Title X, conducted by the Program Analysis Division of the Economic Development Administration, describes in detail the process of program development, project selection, and funding.[1] A study of the direct impacts of Title X, by the Program Analysis Division, analyzes the scale and composition of projects and their direct impacts upon employment and employees.[2]

This chapter parallels some of the analysis in EDA's direct-impact study. The data are derived from the same sources—EDA data bases for Title X application information, ED-110X payroll reports, and ED-736 project-completion reports. The purpose is to provide an overview of the Title X program, a frame of reference not only for interpreting data on the types of people employed under Title X (Chapter 3), and the net cost of Title X (Chapters 4 and 5), but for an analysis of Title X employment (Chapter 6), and a summary of long-term impacts (Chapter 8).

Table 2.1 summarizes the approved distribution of funds provided to projects under the Job Opportunities Program.

About 34.4 percent of funds for the Job Opportunities Program has come from sources other than the Title X allocation. Fully 18.2 percent has been provided by state, local, or private sources. The total federal investment, therefore, had an immediate leveraging impact of about 22 percent on other funds. The average Title X project received $220,600 from the Title X allocation and a total of $336,222 in funds.

TABLE 2.1

Approved Funding of the Job Opportunities Program

Funding Sources*	Funds
Title X	$497,452,928
Other federal	123,063,911
State	52,667,182
Local	65,182,156
Private	19,815,375
Total funds	758,181,552
Number of projects	2,255
Average Title X funds per project	220,600
Average total funds per project	336,222

*Approved totals are only available from EDA for Title X funds and total funds. Other figures are extrapolations from data submitted by projects in their applications, and in no case do they vary from the application data by more than 3 percent.

Source: Compiled by the authors.

Four classes of variables describing all Title X projects are available from EDA information systems. These include measures of project purposes (project type), project scale (estimated employees, total funds, estimated person-months of employment), project location (region, state, urban/rural), and labor intensity (cost per person-month, labor cost per total cost). A key measure is project type, a descriptive variable derived by EDA after analysis of the titles and textual descriptions of each Title X project. Three-digit codes were created for each project, distinct codes representing the major function of the project (for example, construction, repair, social service) and the type of facility or service receiving attention (for example, warehouses, sewers, recreation spaces, home-maker services). For purposes of analysis, Abt Associates aggregated these codes into seven project types defined as follows:

1. public-works construction: construction of new structures or expansion of existing structures, such as arenas, hospitals, municipal buildings, and schools;
2. civil-works construction: construction of new, or additions to existing, civil-works facilities such as water and sewer systems, streets, bridges, dams, and drainage ditches;
3. forestry, conservation, recreation: work in the development, protection, maintenance, or management of forests or recreational spaces that involves little or no construction-type activity;

TABLE 2.2

Distribution of Title X Projects by Type

Project Type	Number	Percent
Public works construction	192	8.5
Civil-works construction	170	7.5
Forestry, recreation	637	28.2
Rehabilitation, repair	708	31.4
Service	427	18.9
Training	86	3.8
Other	35	1.6
Total	2,255	100

Source: EDA.

4. maintenance, rehabilitation, renovation: work to maintain, repair, or improve existing structures or facilities;
5. public and social service: nonconstruction services for governments, quasi-governmental units, and needy target groups;
6. training: projects whose primary purpose is the provision of skills or job-related training;
7. other: remaining projects that are not easily categorized within the EDA three-digit code structure.

Using the seven project types,* the distribution of Title X projects is shown in Table 2.2.

The distribution of projects alone is of some interest. Only 16 percent of the projects are in the civil- and public works construction categories usually associated with EDA in the public image, while more than 20 percent are in the service or training categories usually associated with HEW and the Department of Labor. In fact, many of these are projects jointly sponsored by Title X and HEW or by Title X and DOL. The relative scarcity of construction projects and the relative abundance of service and training projects distinguish the Job Opportunities Program from previous employment-generating programs of EDA or ARA. The distinction is understandable. The countercyclical objectives of

---

*Because each type of project has a distinctive set of activities, pattern of employment, and occupational mix, other measures of Title X are presented in this chapter with reference to project type.

Title X, labor-intensity constraints, and the stipulation that project work be largely completed within one year ruled out most major construction proposals. Thus, rehabilitation activities (31.4 percent) and forestry-improvement activities (28.2 percent) have been undertaken most often, since they usually involve discrete, labor-intensive work that can be completed relatively quickly.

The location of Title X projects in different regions and states is a function of the extent of unemployment in different states and localities, and of project rankings established by EDA in the application-review process. Project location is also of particular relevance to estimates of net cost, since taxes, unemployment compensation payments, and other transfer payments vary considerably from state to state. Thus, the scale of returns to governments from labor and non-labor expenditures will be affected by the distribution of projects across states and regions. Table 2.3 presents the regional distribution of Title X projects.

Title X projects are concentrated in regions 01 (East/Northeast) and 04 (Southeast), which account for 46.8 percent of the projects. Service and training projects are particularly prevalent in region 01. Region 04 contains more public-works, civil-works, and forestry projects than the average, while region 01 is underrepresented by construction projects. Forestry projects account for a relatively consistent proportion of Title X activity in all regions except region 01, which is underrepresented.

Examination of the universe of Title X projects shows that the average number of projects per state or territory is 40. California (148), Michigan (136), Florida (106), New York (91), and Georgia (90) contain the most projects. The 13 top states account for 50.1 percent of the projects; the 13 states with the fewest projects account for only 4.0 percent. Notable, too, is the fact that over two-thirds (67.7 percent) of Title X projects are in nonmetropolitan areas. Service, training, and rehabilitation projects are most likely to be located in standard metropolitan statistical areas (SMSAs) (about 40 percent are located therein). Most construction and forestry projects (77 percent) are not located in metropolitan areas.

The distribution of total project dollars (including nonfederal funds) varies considerably from the distribution of projects shown in Table 2.4. Over 40 percent of total program funds has been allocated to projects in region 01, which average $584,000 in funding. In contrast, region 04 has received 14.9 percent of total funds, though it has 23.6 percent of the projects. Average project funding size in region 04 is only about $212,000. All other regions show a slightly lower proportion of total funds than would be suggested by their proportion of total projects. Multistate or multiregional projects receive more than regional projects, averaging $1,334,000 per project.

The distribution of funds by project type also varies from the distribution of projects. Public-works construction projects are larger than other types, averaging $508,000 in funding size, and construction projects in general are larger than average ($433,000 per construction project versus $336,200) across all

TABLE.2.3

Regional Distribution of Title X Projects

EDA Region	Total Number	Percent of Projects	Project Type (percent distribution)					
			Public Works	Civil Works	Forestry	Rehabili-tation	Service	Training
01	524	23.2	13.0	16.5	15.5	22.6	40.7	30.2
04	532	23.6	27.6	35.9	28.6	21.0	15.9	14.0
05	218	9.7	9.9	6.5	10.0	12.0	5.2	12.8
06	340	15.1	14.6	13.5	15.7	13.6	17.8	16.3
07	410	18.2	24.0	14.7	19.9	18.8	13.6	18.6
08	224	9.9	10.4	12.4	10.2	11.7	6.3	7.0
99*	7	0.3	.5	.6	—	.3	.5	1.2
Total	2,255	100.0	100.0	100.0	100.0	100.0	100.0	100.0

*99 designates multiregional projects.
Source: Compiled by the authors.

TABLE 2.4

Total Approved Funds of Title X Projects, by Region and Project Type
(in thousands of dollars)

EDA Region	Public-Works Construction	Civil-Works Construction	Forestry, Recreation	Rehabilitation	Service	Training	Other	Total	Percent
01	22,953	10,178	26,779	105,144	120,955	16,162	3,844	306,014	40.4
04	17,268	18,274	25,026	30,215	15,595	4,239	2,015	112,633	14.9
05	22,845	7,231	10,887	10,080	3,369	3,265	1,686	59,362	7.8
06	14,424	6,642	17,833	28,543	30,674	6,866	2,570	107,552	14.2
07	14,636	8,884	29,806	31,362	23,199	3,403	1,446	112,735	14.9
08	4,402	4,229	11,483	13,744	11,755	4,811	123	50,546	6.7
99	1,000	3,788	—*	2,113	1,190	1,250	—	9,341	1.2
Total	97,528	59,226	121,814	221,201	206,737	39,996	11,684	758,182	100.0
Percent of total	12.9	7.8	16.1	29.2	27.3	5.3	1.5	100.0	
Mean funding size (thousands)	$508,000	$348,400	$191,200	$312,400	$484,200	$465,100	$333,800	$336,200	

*Data not available.
Source: EDA.

49

TABLE 2.5

Distribution of Title X Projects by Total Approved Funds

Total Funds (in $000s)	Total Number	Percent	Project Type (percent distribution)					
			Public Works	Civil Works	Forestry	Rehabili-tation	Service	Training
Under 100	879	39.0	25.0	31.8	44.4	42.8	38.9	17.4
100–200	470	20.8	22.9	21.8	23.9	19.8	17.1	20.9
201–300	292	12.9	22.9	15.9	13.3	10.7	11.9	7.0
301–500	297	13.2	11.5	13.5	10.5	12.6	13.1	36.0
501–1,000	196	8.7	8.9	11.2	6.8	8.5	10.1	10.5
>1,000	121	5.4	8.9	5.9	1.1	5.6	8.9	8.1
Total	2,255	100.0	100.0	100.0	100.0	100.0	100.0	100.0

Source: Compiled by the authors.

TABLE 2.6

Planned Number of Employees on Title X Projects

Number of Employees	Projects		Public Works	Public Works	Forestry	Rehabili- tation	Service	Training
	Number	Percent						
1–10	607	26.9	17.2	20.0	28.1	27.1	34.4	17.4
11–25	702	31.1	26.0	34.1	37.0	32.6	24.1	16.3
26–50	504	22.4	35.9	28.8	22.3	20.1	20.6	9.3
51–100	280	12.4	10.9	12.4	9.7	12.7	10.3	37.2
101–200	97	4.3	5.7	4.7	2.4	4.5	5.2	8.1
>200	65	2.9	4.2	—*	.5	3.0	5.4	11.6
Total	2,255	100.0	100.0	100.0	100.0	100.0	100.0	100.0
Total employees	99,312	—	9,343	5,711	18,231	29,888	25,345	9,311
Percent	100.0	—	9.4	5.8	18.4	30.1	25.5	9.4
Mean employees per project	44.0	—	48.7	33.6	28.6	42.2	59.4	108.3

*Data not available.
Source: Compiled by the authors.

TABLE 2.7

Planned Person-Months of Employment on Title X Projects

Person-Months	Total		Public Works	Civil Works	Forestry	Rehabili- tation	Service	Training
	Number	Percent						
1–120	902	40.0	30.2	40.0	44.6	43.8	35.8	19.8
121–240	497	22.0	24.5	23.5	22.0	23.9	20.1	10.5
241–480	440	19.5	28.7	22.9	20.1	15.6	19.7	18.7
481–1,200	305	13.5	8.9	10.6	12.6	11.8	15.7	36.1
>1,200	111	4.9	7.8	2.9	.8	4.1	8.7	15.1
Total	2,255	100.0	100.0	100.0	100.0	100.0	100.0	100.0
Total Person- Months	854,524	—*	82,777	46,905	151,940	244,642	237,772	78,449
Percent	100	—	9.7	5.5	17.8	28.6	27.8	9.2
Mean Person- Months	379	—	431	276	239	346	557	912

*Data not available.
Source: Compiled by the authors.

52

Title X projects. Forestry and rehabilitation projects are smaller than the average, but service and training projects are considerably larger. Between them, the latter two types account for about one-third of total funds, further strengthening the distinction between Title X and previous EDA programs. The distribution of projects by funding level is presented in Table 2.5.

As shown in Table 2.5, nearly 40 percent of all projects have received less than $100,000 in total funds, and nearly three-fourths are under $300,000. Only 5.4 percent requested over $1 million. The median project funding size is approximately $152,000. Clearly, most projects have not performed large-scale building or other activities with their Job Opportunities Program funds. However, in some instances, Title X funds have been used to expand projects which were already ongoing, projects which may be of considerable scale.

Another measure of project size is the number of persons the projects planned to employ, as presented in Table 2.6.

In total, Title X projects planned to employ 99,312 persons, with funds of $758 million, an average of $7,634 per employee. Almost 60 percent of Title X projects planned to employ 25 or fewer persons over the life of the project. Only 7.2 percent planned on more than 100 employees. Although the median project planned 11–25 employees, the larger projects bring mean project size up to 44 employees. As would be expected, training projects are by far the largest, with almost one in five having planned to employ over 100 people and a mean size of 108.3 employees. Service and public-works construction projects are also relatively large, with civil-works and forestry projects having planned to employ substantially fewer persons.

Because projects vary in duration and in assumptions about turnover, planned person-months of employment provide a more precise indication of employment scale than do employees. Table 2.7 shows the person-months of employment planned under Title X.

The distribution of planned person-months differs very little from the distribution of planned employees, suggesting that most projects did not consider likely turnover in making their employee estimates. A total of 854,524 person-months of employment was planned by the 2,255 projects, an average of 379 person-months per project. The median project, however, plans substantially less employment, between 121 and 240 person-months. Again, training projects plan the most employment, with service and public-works construction projects also well above the mean. The typical forestry and civil-works projects plan the least employment.

Data from Tables 2.4, 2.6, and 2.7 provide two other descriptive measures of the Title X program—planned cost per person-year and planned duration of employment. These are presented in Table 2.8.

On the average, Title X projects planned to provide 8.6 months of employment (about 37 weeks) to each employee. Planned duration of employment varies somewhat by type of project, but the differences are not large. More

TABLE 2.8

Planned Costs per Person-Year and Duration of Employment

Project Type	Planned Person-Months	Planned Employees	Planned Duration of Employment (person-months)	Total Funds (thousands of dollars)	Planned Cost per Person-Year
Public works	82,777	9,343	8.9	97,528	$14,100
Civil works	46,965	5,711	8.2	59,226	15,100
Forestry	151,940	18,231	8.3	121,814	9,600
Rehabilitation	244,642	29,888	8.2	221,201	10,900
Service	237,772	25,345	9.4	206,737	10,400
Training	78,449	9,311	8.4	39,996	6,100
Other	11,979	1,483	8.1	11,684	'11,700
Total	854,524	99,312	8.6	758,182	10,600

Source: Compiled by the authors.

TABLE 2.9

Planned Labor Intensity of Title X Projects

Project Type	Planned Labor Cost (thousands of dollars)	Total Funds (thousands of dollars)	Planned Labor Intensity (percent)	Planned Labor Cost per Person-Year
Public works	67,149	97,528	68.9	$ 9,700
Civil works	44,318	59,226	74.8	11,300
Forestry	98,232	121,814	80.6	7,800
Rehabilitation	174,660	221,201	79.0	8,600
Service	184,676	206,739	89.3	9.300
Training	35,572	39,996	88.9	5,400
Other	9,353	11,684	80.0	9.400
Total	613,758	758,182	81.0	8,600

Source: Compiled by the authors.

interesting are differences in the planned costs per person-year. Across all Title X projects, $10,600 per person-year of employment was planned. This is higher than the person-year costs of CETA Title II and Title VI programs, which are estimated at $8,141 and $7,240, respectively.[3] This would be expected as a consequence of Title X nonlabor expenditures and of CETA's regulation that at least 90 percent of funds be spent on wages and fringes. Note, however, that Title X training projects, which are paying wages on the job (not training stipends), are projected to cost only $6,100 per person-year. In contrast, public-works construction and civil-works construction projects plan costs of more than twice as much per person-year, presumably because of nonlabor expenses for materials and equipment. This probability is investigated in Table 2.9, which presents planned labor intensity of Title X projects.*

Overall, Title X projects planned to spend 81.0 percent of their funds on wages and fringes, well above the 75 percent target for labor intensity mentioned in program regulations. As expected, construction projects are the least labor intensive, having planned to spend about 71 percent of funds on wages and fringes. Service and training projects have planned a higher level of labor intensity

---

*Planned labor intensity is equal to planned labor costs divided by planned total costs.

than other project types. If one calculates labor cost per person-year, Title X costs drop from $10,600 to $8,600 per person-year. This figure is still higher than the person-year costs of CETA and likely reflects the different wage structures of the programs. CETA sets a ceiling of $10,000 on salaries payable under the program. Title X does not set a ceiling and is more likely to pay the prevailing wage rate in the local area.

ACTUAL PERFORMANCE

Many of the preceding project measures are measures of project plans, based upon information provided by projects in their grant applications. Because this study has been conducted while Title X projects are still operating, data on actual performance are not yet available from many projects. However, as of April 15, 1977, some information was available to EDA on 691 projects that indicated that they had completed work. Completion reports (the ED-736 form)—containing full information on project employment and budget performance—had been received and processed on 543 projects, most of them funded in the first round of Title X allocations. Representing about 24 percent of all Title X projects, the completed projects are, on the average, smaller than the typical Job Opportunities project. Projection techniques, however, can be applied to the performance data for these projects to provide the best early estimates of performance under the Job Opportunities Program. The principal projections are summarized in Table 2.10, in comparison with project plans.

As shown in Table 2.10, the actual total expenditures of Title X projects are virtually identical to the planned total. However, the distribution of expenditures between labor and nonlabor costs varies considerably from that indicated on project applications. Approved applications show labor expenditures of almost $614 million, for an average labor intensity of 81 percent for Title X. Projected actual labor costs are only $521 million, bringing projected labor intensity down to 68.8 percent. Although substantially more labor intensive than the typical construction project, Title X appears to have fallen somewhat short of the 75-percent labor-intensity target of EDA.

Of considerable interest are the data on person-months of employment and number of employees under Title X. The program is projected to support slightly more than three-quarters of the employment months planned on applications, but will have employed 37.5 percent more persons than planned. Overall, over 655,000 person-months of employment (54,601 employment years) are being provided to almost 137,000 employees. The shortfall in person-months is partially a function of the shifting of expenditures from labor to nonlabor items. However, it is also a consequence of higher wages, the labor costs per person-year projected to be over 10 percent higher than planned. The increased number

TABLE 2.10

Performance of Title X Projects: Planned versus Projected Actual

Measure	Planned by Projects	Projected Actual Performance	Percent Difference
Total expenditures (thousands of dollars)	758,182	757,924	$< -.1$
Total labor expenditures (thousands of dollars)	613,758	521,267	-15.1
Labor intensity (percent)	81.0	68.8	-15.1
Person-Months of employment	854,524	655,211	-23.3
Number of employees	99,312	136,571	+37.5
Duration of employment (months)	8.6	4.8	-44.2
Labor costs per person-year	$ 8,619	$ 9,547	+10.8
Total costs per person-year	$10,647	$13,881	+30.4

Source: Compiled by the authors.

of employees probably reflects the fact that few projects considered likely turn-over when making their original estimates of employees served.

As a consequence of the projection of fewer person-months and more employees, the average duration of Title X employment is considerably shorter than originally anticipated. Project applications suggest an average duration of 8.6 months (37 weeks); projected duration is only 4.8 months (20.6 weeks). Moreover, since the Job Opportunities Program will have provided less employment than planned, while spending almost all of the approved funds, the total cost per person-year increases dramatically. From a planned figure of $10,647, person-year costs rise to $13,881, almost double the person-year costs of CETA Titles II and VI.

Departures from planned expenditures vary considerably by project type. Table 2.11 compares planned and projected actual expenditures of different types of projects.

Construction projects have spent far less on labor than planned, purchasing much higher amounts of materials, supplies, and services than initially anticipated. As a result, labor intensity for both public-works and civil-works projects is substantially below 50 percent. At the other end of the spectrum, service and training projects are the most labor intensive (over 80 percent), though actual labor expenditures are below the planned figure. Forestry projects have come closer to planned figures than any other type, with actual labor intensity only 3.1 percentage points below planned intensity.

TABLE 2.11

Planned versus Projected Actual Expenditures

Project Type	Planned			Projected Actual		
	Total Funds (thousands of dollars)	Labor Funds (thousands of dollars)	Labor Intensity (percent)	Total Funds (thousands of dollars)	Labor Funds (thousands of dollars)	Labor Intensity (percent)
Public works	97,528	67,149	68.9	99,391	44,297	44.6
Civil works	59,226	44,138	74.8	62,071	26,838	43.2
Forestry/recreation	121,814	98,232	80.6	123,624	95,804	77.5
Rehabilitation	221,201	174,660	79.0	211,797	140,304	66.2
Service	206,739	184,676	89.3	208,955	172,015	82.3
Training	39,996	35,572	88.9	40,425	33,133	82.0
Other	11,684	9,353	80.0	11,661	8,876	76.1
Total	758,182	613,758	81.0	757,924	521,267	68.8

Source: Compiled by the authors.

TABLE 2.12

Planned versus Projected Actual Employment

Project Type	Planned			Projected Actual		
	Person-Months	Employees	Duration (in months)	Person-Months	Employees	Duration (in months)
Public works	82,777	9,343	8.9	52,481	13,809	3.8
Civil works	46,965	5,711	8.2	29,447	5,962	4.9
Forestry/recreation	151,940	18,231	8.3	130,820	30,847	4.2
Rehabilitation	244,642	29,888	8.2	180,546	47,881	3.8
Service	237,772	25,345	9.4	189,266	25,831	7.3
Training	78,449	9,311	8.4	62,445	9,490	6.6
Other	11,979	1,483	8.1	10,206	2,751	3.7
Total	854,524	99,312	8.6	655,211	136,571	4.8

Source: Compiled by the authors.

As shown in Table 2.12, deviations from planned employment vary substantially in different kinds of projects. Public-works and civil-works construction projects, for example, provide only 63.1 percent of their planned person-months, in comparison with 79.1 percent on other project types. In contrast, unplanned turnover on construction projects has not been nearly as high as on forestry and rehabilitation projects. The latter project types employ fully 63.6 percent more persons than planned, in contrast to a 31.3 percent increase on construction projects. Unplanned turnover is negligible on training and social-service projects funded under Title X. For this reason, duration of Title X employment is longest on service projects (7.3 months, or 31.5 weeks) and on training projects (6.6 months, or 28.3 weeks). It is shortest on public-works construction (16.4 weeks), on rehabilitation projects (16.2 weeks), and other projects (16.0 weeks).

A comparison of planned and actual person-year costs is presented in Table 2.13.

All types of projects incur higher labor costs per year of employment than planned, with the single exception of civil-works projects, whose labor costs drop about 4 percent. Probably as a function of higher wages, the three types of projects that planned the highest labor cost per person-year (public works, civil works, and service) also incur the highest actual labor cost per person-year. Overall, the projected cost per person-year is about 10 percent greater than planned.

TABLE 2.13

Planned versus Projected Actual Person-Year Costs

Project Type	Planned		Projected Actual	
	Labor Cost per Person-Year	Total Cost per Person-Year	Labor Cost per Person-Year	Total Cost per Person-Year
Public works	$ 9,700	$14,100	$10,100	$22,700
Civil works	11,300	15,100	10,900	25,300
Forestry/recreation	7,800	9,600	8,800	11,300
Rehabilitation	8,600	10,900	9,300	14,000
Service	9,300	10,400	10,900	13,200
Training	5,400	6,100	6,400	7,800
Other	9,400	11,700	10,400	13,700
Total	8,600	10,600	9,500	13,900

Source: Compiled by the author.

Total costs per person-year are higher than planned for all project types, partially as a function of higher labor costs per person-year, but primarily as a consequence of higher nonlabor spending. Here, the differences among project types are more dramatic. The average cost per person-year in a civil-works construction project is $25,300, more than three times as great as that for a training project. Overall, a person-year costs almost $23,700 on construction projects, in contrast to $12,500 per person-year for all other types. Judged purely in terms of gross cost per employment-year, construction projects are a poor employment investment. Such a judgment, however, ignores the short-term value and possible long-term impacts of project output—which are likely to be greater in construction projects—and, thus, is unjustified. As expected, training projects cost the least per employment-year. Rehabilitation and repair projects also cost less than other types, with actual costs per person-year only slightly above planned costs.

It should be stressed that the preceding discussion of projected actual performance is based upon preliminary estimates. The projections are the most accurate possible from currently available data, but may require revision when full information from all projects becomes available after their completion. Moreover, the fact that the Job Opportunities Program will not have fully achieved all of its planned performance goals should be placed in context. A relevant comparison is the Public Works Impact Program funded by the Economic Development Administration in 1972-74.[4] A smaller program than Title X (approximately $134 million was spent, of which about $92 million was granted by EDA), PWIP also had a principal goal of providing immediate employment. PWIP, however, primarily funded civil- or public-works construction projects and, probably as a consequence, did not achieve nearly the employment impact of Title X. For example, PWIP was only 22 percent labor intensive, compared with 68.8 percent projected for Title X and 43.2 percent for civil-works construction projects (the least labor intensive) under Title X. PWIP provided 39,045 person-months of employment (approximately 63 percent of what was intended), while Title X will provide 655,211 person-months (about 77 percent of the planned figure).

Other comparisons between PWIP and Title X are even more notable. The total cost per person-year on Title X is projected to be $13,881. Under PWIP, costs per person-year were $41,052, which is $51,295 in 1976 dollars. Even civil-works construction projects under Title X, which cost $25,300 per person-year, provide employment with 51 percent less funds. The labor costs per person-year under PWIP were about $8,910. In 1976 dollars, this amounts to $11,133, 16.6 percent higher than the $9,547 estimate for Title X. Moreover, average duration of employment in PWIP was only 4.1 weeks, in comparison to 20.6 weeks in Title X. Finally, turnover in PWIP was extremely high, with projected actual employees exceeding estimated employees by 112 percent (41,243 versus 19,413). In contrast, projected turnover in Title X exceeds project estimates by only 37.5 percent.

This statistical perspective on the program structure of the Job Opportunities Program provides a context for the analysis of employees and jobs under Title X, which follows in Chapter 3.

NOTES

1. Program Analysis Division, Economic Development Administration, *Evaluation of the Administration of the Title X Program* (Washington, D.C.: Economic Development Administration, forthcoming).

2. Program Analysis Division, Economic Development Administration, *Evaluation of the Direct Employment Impacts of the Job Opportunities Program (Title X)* (Washington, D.C.: Department of Commerce, forthcoming).

3. Congressional Budget Office, *Employment and Training Programs*, Staff Working Paper (Washington, D.C.: May 4, 1976). Figures are for fiscal year 1975. If one presumed inflation to be 7.58 percent (the increase in hourly wages for production and nonsupervisory workers during 1976), the figures for Title II and VI would be $8,760 and $7,790 per person-year.

4. Data cited on the PWIP program are from Anthony J. Sulvetta and Norman Thompson, *An Evaluation of the Public Works Impact Program* (Washington, D.C.: Economic Development Administration, 1975).

3

TITLE X
EMPLOYEES AND JOBS

The characteristics of individuals employed by a job-creation program, and the attributes of the jobs provided are, in themselves, important to policy makers. They indicate the constituencies most served by the program and describe the occupational opportunities offered. Since data collection done by the Economic Development Administration on Title X employees and jobs is incomplete, a large-scale survey of employees was conducted in October-December 1976; it includes 1,969 completed personal interviews with employees at 195 Title X projects. This survey provides complete and valid data on these two important dimensions of the Job Opportunities Program, data which are presented here to complete the statistical description of the Title X program. Wherever possible, comparable data on the U.S. labor force and on the CETA program provide a point of reference to Title X.

TITLE X EMPLOYEES

Personal Characteristics

Title X terms and conditions for projects encourage employers to give preferential consideration to unemployed persons "who have exhausted unemployment benefits, ... are not eligible for unemployment benefits [or] ... have been unemployed for fifteen or more weeks."[1] This study suggests that most Job Opportunities projects have made a serious effort to reach the severely unemployed. The demographic characteristics of Title X employees are an indication. These are presented in Table 3.1, in comparison with

TABLE 3.1

Characteristics of Title X Employees as Compared with 1976 Labor-Force Data

Employee Characteristics	Title X Employees	Civilian Labor Force	Unemployed Labor Force	Unemployment Rate
White male	44.2	53.3	44.2	6.4
White female	11.3	35.2	36.1	7.9
Black and other Male	31.8	6.2	10.2	12.7
Black and other Female	12.7	5.3	9.5	13.6
Age: 16–17	1.1	3.9	10.8	21.1
18–19	8.0	5.6	12.6	17.4
20–24	27.4	14.7	22.9	12.0
25–34	29.3	24.8	22.8	7.1
35–44	13.9	18.1	11.6	4.9
45–59	14.5	25.2	14.6	4.4
60 or over	5.8	7.7	4.0	4.8

Source: Compiled by the authors. Labor-force data are from *Employment and Earnings* (Bureau of Labor Statistics, U.S. Department of Labor), and Abt Ass. Inc. and U.S. Dept. of Labor, B.L.S., 1976.

the characteristics of the 1976 civilian labor force and the unemployed labor force.*

Fully 44.5 percent of Title X employees are nonwhites, who historically have experienced a much higher rate of unemployment than whites. Almost four times as many nonwhites have been employed under Title X as would be expected from their share of the civilian labor force (11.5 percent). Half as many Title X employees are black (27.3 percent) as are white (55.5 percent), with Mexican-American, Puerto Rican, Oriental, and other ethnic groups having modest levels of representation (4.4 percent). The unusually high proportion of American Indians (12.8 percent) probably reflects the extremely high levels of reported unemployment on Indian reservations.

---

*The data presented in Table 3.1 and throughout this chapter are for the sample of 1,969 employees. Unlike data in Chapters 4 and 5, they are not adjusted or projected to the universe of all Title X employees. The funded scope of the study and the timing of analysis have not permitted such projections. However, analysis of the sample in relation to the projected employee universe shows that projections would not change significantly any of the findings presented herein. See Appendix D.

Second, Title X employees are younger than their counterparts in the civilian labor force. The median age of those who have worked on Title X is 27.5 years; the mean age is 32.8 years. Fully 36.5 percent of Title X employees are under 25 years of age, as compared with only 24.2 percent of 'the labor force. Since unemployment is inversely related to age in the United States, the relative focus of Title X on younger workers is also a focus upon a high-unemployment target population.

Third, about three-quarters (76.0 percent) of project employees are male. This predominance of males, in excess of the male proportion in the labor force (59.5 percent), is not unexpected for a program in which a majority of projects have performed outdoor manual labor in repair, construction, rehabilitation, or reforestation efforts (this point is discussed later in this chapter).

Fourth, the gross family income estimated by Title X employees for 1976 is exceedingly low, as shown in Table 3.2 below. Almost 30 percent of employees reported 1976 family income of less than $4,000; 59.9 percent received less

TABLE 3.2

Gross Family Income of Title X Employees

Income Range	Percent of Employees
$0–4,000	29.2
4,001–6,000	30.7
6,001–8,000	16.5
8,001–10,000	10.3
10,001–15,000	8.5
15,001–20,000	2.5
Over 20,000	2.3
Mean income	$6,300

Source: Compiled by the authors.

than $6,000. The median income is in the upper portion of the $4,000–6,000 range, substantially below the median family income of $9,867 recorded in the United States for 1969.* The mean for total family income of Title X employees

---

*Although national figures are not available, the median family income in 1976 was substantially higher. A rough estimate is $15,000, based upon increases since 1969 in weekly earnings of production and nonsupervisory workers.

TABLE 3.3

Prior Employment Status and Duration of Unemployment: Title X Employees and Noninstitutional Population

Employment Status at Time of Hire, and Duration of Unemployment for the Unemployed	Title X Employees	Noninstitutional Population
Employed	18.3	56.8
Unemployed	71.1	4.7
Not in labor force	10.6	38.4
Unemployed as percent of labor force	79.5	7.7
Duration of Unemployment for the unemployed (weeks)[a]		
1–4	17.7	38.3
5–14	25.7	29.6
15–26	19.9	13.8
27–39	8.8	18.3[b]
40–52	11.2	—[c]
53–65	4.6	—
Over 65	12.1	—

[a]BLS duration-of-unemployment figures are based upon continuous nonworking status while actively looking for work. Title X figures are derived from two separate items: labor-force status and the number of continuous weeks of unemployment. We cannot be certain that responses by workers in regard to "continuous weeks unemployed" always meant they were "not employed and actively looking for work." Thus, in a few instances, the weeks "officially unemployed" may be overstated by respondents. We do not, however, judge this possible overstatement to be frequent or to at all alter the duration-of-unemployment data here.

[b]27 weeks or over.

[c]Data not available.

Source: Compiled by the authors.

is approximately $6,300.* Clearly, a significant number of employees in the Job Opportunities Program are below the poverty level, regardless of family size or labor market area. Research has shown that the burden of a recession falls disproportionately on the lower-income groups in our society. Thus, a program which was designed as a countercyclical strategy, and has also focused on lower-income groups, has achieved a degree of both employment efficiency and distributional equity.[2] Although redistributive equity is not an explicit goal of programs such as Title X, this is prima facie evidence of Title X's positive distributive effects.

Unemployment

Given the demographic profile of Title X employees, one would expect a high proportion of them to have been unemployed prior to their Title X hire. This expectation is confirmed by employment data, shown in Table 3.3. When hired for their Title X jobs, more than four-fifths (81.7 percent) of Title X employees were not employed. Of these, 88 percent (71.1 percent of all Title X employees) were actively looking for work, satisfying the Bureau of Labor Statistics (BLS) definition of "unemployed." The remaining 10.6 percent of Title X employees were technically not in the labor force, most frequently because they could not find work (3.2 percent), were in school or a training program (1.6 percent), were keeping house (1.6 percent), or were laid off, expecting recall (1.2 percent). In an economist's terms, these 10.6 percent represent formerly "discouraged" workers.†

In comparison with the noninstitutional population in the United States, Title X workers were severely unemployed prior to hire. As would be expected, a higher proportion of them were part of the labor force (employed plus unemployed). However, the proportion of labor-force-attached Title X workers who were unemployed is more than 10 times the national unemployment rate for 1976 (79.5 percent versus 7.7 percent).

The average unemployed Title X employee had been out of work for a considerable length of time prior to hire. Fully 56.6 percent of previously unemployed Title X workers (40.2 percent of the entire Title X work force) had been unemployed, prior to hire, for at least 15 weeks, the preference level cited

---

*Mean income figures in this chapter are estimates, since data were collected in the ranges shown in Table 3.2. Estimates were calculated using the midpoint of the income range reported by each repondent.

+The discouraged-worker hypothesis is derived from the income and substitution effects that operate on individuals' decisions to enter the labor force, and is determined, in part, by the availability of work.

in Title X terms and conditions. Moreover, 36.7 percent had been unemployed for more than half a year. This 26-week duration of unemployment is the maximum period of unemployment compensation benefits provided by most states, before the payment of special unemployment insurance and federal supplemental benefits. It is also the standard used by the Bureau of Labor Statistics to define "long-term unemployed." Unemployment for at least a year was reported by 16.7 percent of respondents, with 12.1 percent having been unemployed for more than the 65-week maximum period for receiving unemployment compensation from any source.

Table 3.3 shows further that the duration of unemployment experienced by Title X employees was substantially greater than that of the U.S. unemployed work force. Whereas 38.3 percent of the unemployed work force experienced unemployment for less than five weeks, only 17.7 percent of Title X employees were unemployed for this brief period of time. Only about four in every ten formerly unemployed Title X workers were out of work for less than 15 weeks, in comparison to almost seven out of every ten unemployed in the work force. Across the United States, only 18.3 percent of the unemployed were long-term (over 26 weeks) unemployed persons, while 36.7 percent of unemployed Title X participants were out of work for at least 27 weeks. Clearly, the Title X program

TABLE 3.4

Prior Labor-Force Status and Unemployment of Title X Employees

Employee Group	Employed	Unemployed	Not in Labor Force	Mean Weeks Unemployed[a]
White	17.5	71.6	10.7	30.1
Black and other	19.3	70.3	10.4	26.7
Male	17.9	73.6	8.5	25.5
Female	19.2	62.8	18.0	39.4
Ages 15–19	20.1	72.6	7.3	20.2
20–24	16.0	72.9	11.1	23.2
25–34	18.8	71.0	10.2	30.3
35–44	17.5	70.4	12.1	30.3
45–59	17.9	71.9	10.2	35.3
60 and over	24.6	54.8	20.8	41.1
Total	18.3	71.1	10.6	28.7

[a] Data on mean weeks persons were unemployed are conservative, since data instruments limited prior unemployment responses to two digits. Thus the maximum length of unemployment recorded is 99 weeks, and persons unemployed for longer periods are counted as having been unemployed for 99 weeks.

Source: Compiled by the authors.

hired an unusually high number of persons who were long-term or, possibly, structurally unemployed persons.

Within the Title X work force, there are few major distinctions in prior labor-force status of selected demographic groups, as shown in Table 3.4. Whites and nonwhites are similar in this regard, while females are less likely to have been unemployed than males, and more likely to be entering the Title X program from outside the labor force. Age patterns are mixed, with older workers (over 60) being more likely to have been employed or out of the labor force, and less likely to have been unemployed.

Duration of prior unemployment varies considerably with personal characteristics. The most noticeable distinction is between men and women. Male employees in Title X jobs, if previously unemployed, had been out of work for an average of 25.5 weeks. Their female counterparts under Title X had experienced an almost 55 percent longer duration of unemployment, averaging 39.4 weeks. Fully 51.7 percent of previously unemployed Title X females were long-term unemployed persons, having been out of work for more than 26 weeks, in comparison to 32.2 percent of males. Whites had experienced a slightly longer spell of unemployment prior to Title X than had nonwhites (30.1 weeks versus 26.7 weeks), and 38.8 percent were long-term unemployed persons, in contrast to 34.4 percent of nonwhites. Finally, duration of prior unemployment is directly related to age. Youthful Title X workers averaged 20.2 weeks, compared to 35.3 weeks for those aged 45-59, and 41.1 weeks for employees 60 or older. This is consistent with expectations drawn from the total labor-force experience of these groups.

Transfer Benefits

The low family income and high unemployment among Title X employees would imply that, prior to Title X, a substantial number were receiving transfer benefits. This, too, is borne out by the data. Table 3.5 shows the percentage of Title X employees who were receiving various transfers prior to hire, in comparison with estimates for the general population of the United States.

For most transfers, a substantially higher proportion of Title X employees had received benefits than would be expected in the general population. For example, Title X employees were almost four times as likely to have been receiving unemployment compensation as the general population, and almost twice as likely to have been receiving Aid to Families with Dependent Children (AFDC), or Supplementary Security Income (SSI), or General Relief. Nearly three times as many Title X employees were getting food stamps as would be expected in the general population. This high incidence of transfer receipts is even more striking when one realizes that the Title X figures represent benefits received during the month prior to hire, while the general-population data are

TABLE 3.5

Transfer Benefits Received: Title X Employees
and U.S. Population

Transfer Benefit	Title X Employees (receiving benefit prior to hire)	General Population[a]
Unemployment insurance	27.4	7.4
AFDC	6.6	2.8
SSI	2.2	2.8
General Relief	4.5	1.8
Social Security	10.0	21.1
Food stamps	20.9	7.8
Medicaid eligibility	20.4	N.A.[b]
Public housing	10.9	N.A.

[a] Data in this column are taken from the University of Michigan's Panel Study of Income Dynamics (PSID). The PSID has employed personal interviews with heads of households as its major data-collection technique, supplemented with environmental information from other sources. The primary focus of the research is short-run changes in the economic status of families and individuals. Beginning in 1968, heads of households were interviewed every spring for eight years about attitudes, behavior, and economic status. Newly formed families containing 1968 panel-family members were added to the sample each year, making the number of families in the sample, after the 1975 interview year, approximately 5,200.

The original sample design is a merging of a national probability (clustered) sample of approximately 2,900 families, with 1,900 families drawn from the Census Bureau's Survey of Economic Opportunity (SEO). All households included in the SEO had incomes of less than twice the poverty level. Hence, merging the SEO data with the probability sample results in a stratified sample in which lower-income families are overrepresented. The sample can be made representative by employing the probability weights provided by the Survey Research Center.

[b] Data not available.

Sources: University of Michigan, Panel Study of Income Dynamics, Ann Arbor, Mich.

based upon benefits received any time during the preceding year. The one exception to the general trend is Social Security, which is received about twice as often by the general population. However, most Social Security is collected by persons over 55 years of age, a group which is substantially underrepresented in the Title X work force.

When one includes all benefits listed in Table 3.5, there were 1.03 benefits claimed prior to Title X for each employee. Fully 60.1 percent of Title X employees were receiving one or more benefits prior to Title X, with the average transfer recipient receiving benefits from 1.7 sources. In general, the likelihood of having received one or more benefits increases with the age of the Title X employee and is slightly higher among nonwhites (64.3 percent) than among whites (56.8 percent). Sex is not a significant indicator of prior receipt of transfers, but employment status is, with 63.6 percent of the unemployed receiving benefits, versus 45 percent of the employed. Curiously, there are regional patterns that are not explained by any obvious external or internal factors. The incidence of claiming is higher in EDA region 1 (the Northeast)—67 percent; region 4 (the Southeast)—61.7 percent; and region 5 (the Plains and Rocky Mountain States)—63.4 percent. It is substantially lower in region 8 (the Southwest)—49.4 percent; region 7 (the West Coast)—53.2 percent; and region 6 (the Midwest)—54.6 percent.

The characteristics of claimants vary considerably with the benefits received. For example, all benefits except unemployment compensation are more likely to have been received by employees with relatively low family incomes. Likewise, the previously unemployed do not claim a disproportionate share of any transfer except unemployment compensation. Moreover, the only benefit which has been claimed more often by males than by females is unemployment compensation. These three patterns distinguish the earned transfer of unemployment compensation from all other transfers.

Other patterns among Title X employees are distinct for each benefit. The likelihood of having collected Social Security increases if the Title X employee is over 60 or under 20, female, and a long-term unemployed person. Food stamps and AFDC are claimed most often by females over 25, nonwhites, and persons with a long spell of unemployment. Supplemental Security Income is most often received by females and persons over 60. Medicaid eligibility and residence in public housing are more likely among females and nonwhites, but are not related to age. General Assistance is not related to any demographic characteristic except income.

The preceding discussion shows that Title X has employed persons who are generally from low-income families, a substantial portion of which are minority families. A majority were unemployed at the time of hire and, on the average, had been unemployed for a considerable period of time. Over 60 percent had been receiving transfers from one or more sources, with total prior transfers averaging slightly more than one per employee.

TABLE 3.6

Characteristics of Title X Employees and 1975 Adult CETA Participants

Characteristic	Title X Employees	All Adult CETA Participants	CETA PSE Participants	Other Adult CETA Participants
White	56%	57%	66%	52%
Black, other	44	43	34	48
Male	76	61	68	56
Female	24	39	32	46
Under 18	1	2	1	3
18-21	19	24	22	27
22-29	36	41	42	39
30-44	24	20	22	19
45-54	10	8	8	7
55 and over	10	5	5	5
Mean age	32.8	29.7*	31.2*	29.02*
Income of $0–4,000	29%	36%	28%	41%
4,001–6,000	31	18	18	19
6,001-10,000	27	22	25	20
10,001-15,000	8	13	16	11
Over 15,000	5	11	13	9
Mean income	$6,300	$7,200*	$8,100*	$6,500*

*Exact means are unavailable since data are in ranges. Means are calculated from range data and are intended to be illustrative, not exact measures.

Note: CETA adult activities include employability development, public-service employment (PSE), and direct placement, but exclude specifically designated youth activities such as youth-work experience and summer youth programs. CETA PSE accounts for about 41 percent of new 1975 adult enrollees. Other CETA adult activities account for 59 percent and include the functional activities of employability development (classroom training, on-the-job training, adult work experience) and direct placement.

Source: Information presented here and in Tables 3.7 and 3.8 are from CETA data from Westat, Inc., Continuous Longitudinal Manpower Survey Report No. 4: Characteristics of Enrollees Who Entered CETA Programs During Calendar Year 1975, prepared for the Office of Policy, Evaluation and Research of the Employment and Training Administration (Washington, D.C.: Department of Labor, November 1976).

Title X Employees and CETA Participants

The profile of Title X employees is strengthened when compared with national data on persons supported under the Comprehensive Employment and Training Act of 1973.[3] As the nation's principal program for employment and training, CETA places emphasis on serving the disadvantaged, and its constituencies are more urban based than those of Title X. In general, CETA focuses more upon the structurally unemployed than was intended under Title X, though CETA Title VI is an explicitly countercyclical jobs program authorized by the same legislation as that which authorized Title X. Thus, one would expect CETA participants to be at least as disadvantaged as Title X employees and show high incidences of prior unemployment and receipt of transfers.

Table 3.6 presents selected demographic characteristics of Title X employees in comparison with those of new enrollees in CETA adult activities. Characteristics of CETA PSE participants are also shown, since this is a countercyclical public-employment program with which Title X can be fruitfully compared.

Table 3.6 shows a significantly higher proportion of males in Title X than is the case for CETA adult activities or CETA PSE. This is not unexpected, considering the types of jobs provided under Title X. Similarly, the typical Title X employee is substantially older than the typical CETA adult participant, and slightly older than the PSE employee. Note that in both jobs programs (Title X and PSE), participants are older and more likely to be male than are

TABLE 3.7

Incidence and Duration of Unemployment: Title X Employees and Adult CETA Participants

Employment Status, and Duration of Un-employment among the Unemployed	Title X Employees	All CETA Participants	CETA PSE Participants	Other Adult CETA Participants
Employed	18%	26%	30%	24%
Unemployed	71	52	53	51
Not in labor force	11	22	17	25
0–4 weeks of unemployment	18	20	21	19
5–13 weeks	24	33	37	30
14–26 weeks	21	24	22	25
27–39 weeks	9	10	8	11
40 weeks or over	28	13	12	15

Source: See Table 3.6.

TABLE 3.8

Transfer Benefits Received: Title X Employees
and Adult CETA Participants

Transfer Benefit	Title X Employees	All Adult CETA Participants	CETA PSE Participants	Other Adult CETA Participants
Unemployment insurance	27%	5%	1%	7%
AFDC	7	13	8	16
Food stamps	21	24	21	27
SSI	2	2	2	2
Public housing	11	4	4	4
Other public assistance*	15	7	6	7
One or more benefits	49	31	26	35
No benefits	51	69	74	65
Benefits per person	83	.55	.42	.63

*For Title X, other public assistance includes General Relief or General Assistance, and Social Security (but excludes Medicaid). CETA data are presumed to cover the same benefits. However, other public assistance is not defined in the CETA evaluation reports.

Note: The CETA figures are not perfectly comparable with the Title X data, since they include all persons who received a benefit during the year prior to entry into CETA. The Title X data include only those who received a benefit during the month before Title X hire. The one exception is unemployment-compensation data, which, for both programs, are the proportion of persons receiving the benefit at the time of program entry.

Source: See Table 3.6.

regular CETA participants. Of particular interest are the ethnic and income data. By these variables, Title X resembles the regular CETA program (with its emphasis on structural unemployment and the disadvantaged) more closely than it does PSE (a countercyclical program). The proportion of white Title X employees is slightly less than the white participation in CETA adult activities and substantially lower than that in PSE. Total family income of Title X employees is, on the average, lower than income of adult CETA participants, and is substantially lower than that of PSE employees.

Title X employees are also more likely than adult CETA participants to have been unemployed prior to Title X hire or CETA enrollment, as seen in Table 3.7.

Prior unemployment among Title X employees is substantially higher than among adult CETA participants. Fully 71 percent of Title X employees were unemployed prior to hire, compared with only 52 percent prior unemployment for CETA participants. Similarly, a lower proportion of Title X employees were employed, and appreciably fewer entered the labor force upon taking the job. Clearly, attachment to the labor force is greater among Title X employees, with 89 percent having been in the labor force at the time of hire. In comparison, 83 percent of PSE employees and only 75 percent of other adult CETA participants were labor force-attached.

Accompanying the greater incidence of unemployment is a longer duration of prior unemployment among Title X employees. Long-term unemployment (greater than 26 weeks) is reported by more than one-third (37 percent) of previously unemployed Title X workers, in comparison to only one-fifth of PSE participants and 23 percent of all adult CETA participants. Duration of unemployment experienced by Title X employees is more similar to that of the structural-unemployment-oriented CETA programs than to that of the CETA PSE countercyclical jobs program. And, the fact that both incidence and duration of unemployment are greater for Title X than for CETA lends credibility to the program's achievement of its objective to hire the long-term unemployed.

Since Title X employees are more likely to have been unemployed, and, in general, report a lower family income than CETA participants, one would expect that a higher proportion of Title X employees have received transfer and in-kind benefits prior to entering the program. This expectation is confirmed in Table 3.8.

Including all benefits except Medicaid, almost one-half of Title X employees were receiving some form of benefits during the month prior to hire. This is much higher than the proportion of adult CETA participants, and almost twice as high as the proportion of PSE participants, who received benefits during the year prior to program entry. Title X employees average 50 percent more prior benefits per person than do adult CETA participants (.83 versus .55) and almost 100 percent more than their counterparts in PSE. And since Title X figures are for the month prior to hire, while CETA data encompass the entire year prior to entry, the differences are probably greater than implied in Table 3.8.

One should be cautious, however, in drawing conclusions from this contrast. Table 3.8 shows that the incidence of prior receipt of most benefits by Title X employees is similar to, or only somewhat higher than, that for CETA PSE participants. For example, the proportions of Title X employees who were receiving AFDC, food stamps, or SSI are almost identical to those for CETA PSE participants. In contrast, it appears that Title X employees have received public housing and other public assistance benefits much more frequently than have their adult CETA counterparts. The differences, however, may be partially due to particular demographic differences in their populations. A substantial portion of those who reported that they lived in public housing prior to Title X are American Indians, who make up a much larger portion of the Title X sample than of the CETA samples. The higher level of other public assistance received prior to Title X is largely attributable to Social Security, which a number of workers were eligible to collect; the Title X population is older than either of the CETA populations, among whom very few are eligible for Social Security benefits. If data were adjusted to account for these demographic differences, Title X employees would still show a higher incidence of prior claims. However, the differences would be smaller.

The one dramatic difference in prior transfers received by Title X employees and CETA participants is in unemployment compensation. More than one out of every four Title X employees had been receiving unemployment compensation prior to hire, compared with only 5 percent of CETA participants who had received it prior to entry. Only 1 percent of CETA PSE employees had received unemployment compensation prior to entry, a remarkably small percentage for a jobs program, 43 percent of whose participants had been unemployed for 26 weeks or less. The comparatively high frequency of unemployment compensation claims by Title X employees is the primary difference in prior-benefits status between Title X and CETA participants. It alone accounts for most of the difference in the proportion of participants who received one or more benefits.

Different Title X Projects

The general characteristics of Title X employees, and comparisons of these employees with the adult CETA population, create a profile of the Title X constituency as being largely male, low income, overrepresented by minority groups; as experiencing a high incidence and duration of prior unemployment; and receiving a large number of transfers. It is reasonable to inquire whether this profile is consistent for different types of Title X projects and for projects aimed at different population groups.

For example, the project sample for the Title X employee survey includes 28 projects among Indian tribes or organizations (14.4 percent of sampled projects), accounting for 252 (12.8 percent) of sampled employees. If the employee composition for these projects differs greatly from the norm, it could affect the overall Title X employee profile. Similarly, Title X projects were funded in both urban and rural areas.* It is possible that the employee profile varies by urban-rural location and that such differences may be important to policy makers in targeting programs similar to Title X. Moreover, since the urban emphasis of CETA is greater than that of Title X, urban-rural differences could affect the comparisons drawn in the previous section. Finally, different types of projects were funded under Title X, and project type is an important stratifying element in the sample. If the characteristics of persons employed on different types of projects vary greatly, this could affect the design of future counter-cyclical jobs programs.

Each of these hypotheses is examined in this section. As an overall generalization, the differences between Indian and non-Indian projects, or between urban and rural projects, are not (with a few exceptions) great enough to affect the overall Title X employee profile. There are, however, patterns of difference across project types that could be of interest to policy makers.

Except for ethnic composition, the demographic characteristics of Title X employees on Indian projects do not differ substantially from those of other Title X employees, as seen in Table 3.9.

Not unexpectedly, 90.4 percent of employees on Indian projects are American Indians, while 9.2 percent are white and 0.4 percent, other races. If Indian projects were considered separately, the ethnic composition of the Title X work force would shift from 55.5 percent white to 62.3 percent nonwhite. However, the ratio of white to black employees is still two to one, and minority participation in Title X is far greater than the minority percentage of the civilian labor force.

On other demographic measures, there are few important differences between employees on Indian and on non-Indian projects. The mean ages of employees are almost identical, and median income of each group falls in the same $4,000-6,000 range. Mean income is slightly lower on Indian projects, and a somewhat higher proportion of employees are female. However, none of these differences substantially affects the general profile of the Title X employee.

Somewhat surprising is the fact that a higher proportion of employees on Indian projects report that they were employed prior to Title X hire. A greater proportion were also not in the labor force. The average duration of unemployment, however, is quite similar to that reported by the unemployed on non-Indian projects.

---

*The distinction between urban and rural areas used in this analysis is based upon information provided by projects on their Title X applications. The urban-rural code on second-round applications includes six response categories: urban areas with over 250,000 population, with 50,001 to 250,000 population, and with 5,000 to 50,000 population; rural communities; rural areas outside communities; and rural-public works areas.

TABLE 3.9

Characteristics of Employees on Indian
and Non-Indian Projects

Characteristic	Employees on Indian Projects	Employees on Non-Indian Projects
Age		
16–24	33.6%	36.8%
25–44	50.4	42.2
45+	16.0	21.0
Mean age	32.4 years	32.9 years
Sex		
Male	70.5%	76.4%
Female	29.5	23.6
Race		
White	9.2	62.3
Total black and other	90.8	37.7
Black	—	31.3
American Indian	90.4	1.4
Other	0.4	5.0
Total family income		
$0–6,000	58.6	60.1
6,001–10,000	27.2	26.7
10,001–15,000	10.9	8.2
Over 15,000	3.3	5.0
Mean income	$6,000	$6,300
Employment Status		
Employed	28.2%	16.7%
Unemployed	56.9	73.2
Not in labor force	14.9	10.1
Mean weeks unemployed	27.3	29.1

Source: Compiled by the authors.

TABLE 3.10

Transfer Benefits Received by Employees on Indian and Non-Indian Projects

Transfer Benefit	Employees on Indian Projects	Employees on Non-Indian Projects
Unemployment compensation	15.5%	29.2%
AFDC	3.6	7.0
SSI	2.4	2.2
General Relief	8.4	4.0
Social Security	5.6	10.6
Food stamps	11.6	22.2
Medicaid eligibility	18.3	20.7
Public housing	24.6	8.9
Benefits per employee	.90	1.05

Source: Compiled by the authors.

In general, employees on Indian projects are somewhat less likely to have been receiving transfer benefits prior to Title X employment, as seen in Table 3.10.

The incidence of prior receipt of unemployment compensation is substantially lower for Indian-project employees. Among the means-tested transfers, food stamps, AFDC, and Social Security are much less frequently claimed by employees on Indian projects; in contrast, General Relief and public housing are more likely to have been received. Overall, the incidence of prior benefits is .90 benefits per employee on Indian projects, and 1.05 benefits per employee on other projects. It should be noted that, if Indian projects were considered separately, the effect would be to slightly increase Title X estimates of prior transfers received and of returns to government from transfer savings. However, the effects would be relatively minor, as suggested by the fact that the non-Indian-project figures in Table 3.10 are not greatly different from the Title X figures in Table 3.5. Differences of more than one percentage point are noted only for unemployment compensation (up 1.8 percent), food stamps (up 1.3 percent), and public housing (down 2.0 percent).

Of the 195 projects included in the Title X employee survey, 84 (43.1 percent) are classified as urban, accounting for 804 (40.8 percent) of the surveyed employees. Examination of the characteristics of Title X employees in urban and rural areas reveals several slight and several substantial differences, as seen in Table 3.11

TABLE 3.11

Characteristics of Employees on Rural
and Urban Projects

Characteristic	Employees on Urban Projects	Employees on All Rural Projects	Employees on Rural Non-Indian Projects
Age			
16-24	38.8%	34.9%	35.5%
25-44	42.3	43.8	42.0
45 or over	18.9	21.3	22.5
Mean age	32.3 years	33.1 years	33.3 years
Sex			
Male	78.0%	74.1%	75.3%
Female	22.0	25.9	24.7
Race			
White	52.6	57.4	69.9
Total black and other races	47.4	42.6	30.1
Black	35.6	21.6	27.2
American Indian	2.5	20.0	1.6
Other	9.3	1.0	1.3
Total family income			
$0-6,000	52.5	65.0	66.7
6,001-10,000	29.4	24.9	24.3
10,001-15,000	10.7	7.1	6.1
Over 15,000	7.4	3.0	2.9
Mean income	$7,100	$5,700	$5,600
Employment status			
Employed	16.5%	19.4%	16.8%
Unemployed	74.2	68.9	72.4
Not in labor force	9.3	11.7	10.8
Mean weeks unemployed	29.3	28.4	28.6

Source: Compiled by the authors.

TABLE 3.12

Transfer Benefits Received by Employees on Urban and Rural Projects

Transfer Benefit	Employees on Urban Projects	Employees on All Rural Projects	Employees on Rural Non-Indian Projects
Unemployment compensation	28.9%	26.4%	29.3%
AFDC	6.8	6.5	7.2
SSI	1.4	2.8	2.9
General Relief	3.6	5.2	4.5
Social Security	8.3	11.2	12.5
Food stamps	20.3	21.3	24.0
Medicaid	20.7	20.3	20.6
Public housing	11.3	10.6	7.0
Benefits per employee	1.01	1.04	1.08

Source: Compiled by the authors.

In Table 3.11, two sets of data for rural projects are presented, the first set representing all rural projects, and the second excluding Indian projects (which are primarily rural). Using either data set, one observes only slight differences in the age and sex of urban and rural employees. Prior employment status and duration of unemployment are also relatively similar. However, if one excludes rural Indian projects, other rural projects are seen to employ a substantially larger proportion of whites than do urban projects. Almost one-half of urban employees are minority-group members, compared with about three out of every ten rural employees on non-Indian projects.

The other notable difference is in total annual family income. The mean for urban-project employees is about $7,100; it is only about $5,600 for rural non-Indian-project employees. Two-thirds of rural non-Indian-project employees report less than $6,000 in earnings, compared with only about half (52.5 percent) of urban employees.

Table 3.12 compares the prior benefits received by urban and rural Title X employees.

There are few notable distinctions in the proportions of urban- and rural-project employees who were receiving benefits prior to Title X. The number of prior benefits per urban-project employee is 1.01, compared with 1.04 for all rural-project employees and 1.08 for rural employees on non-Indian projects. A higher proportion of employees on rural non-Indian projects were receiving General Relief and Social Security; a lower proportion were living in publicly-supported housing. Overall, however, the differences in prior benefits are not striking.

TABLE 3.13

Characteristics of Employees by Project Type

Characteristic	Employees					
	Public Works	Civil Works	Forestry	Rehabilitation	Service	Training
Age						
16–24	13.1%	26.6%	45.9%	33.5%	29.4%	40.3%
25–44	49.6	46.7	41.6	42.6	45.5	34.4
45 or over	17.3	26.7	12.5	23.8	25.1	15.4
Mean age	34.5 years	36.0 years	29.7 years	34.2 years	35.8 years	33.6 years
Sex						
Male	74.8%	91.9%	92.9%	87.7%	41.5%	44.8%
Female	25.2	8.1	7.1	12.3	58.5	55.2
Race						
White	22.3	37.4	74.0	54.7	57.4	28.3
Total black and other	77.7	62.6	26.0	45.3	42.6	71.7
Black	2.9	25.2	18.9	24.3	37.6	61.4
American Indian	74.1	15.4	5.0	14.0	3.5	8.7
Other	0.7	22.0	2.1	7.0	1.5	1.6
Total Family Income						
$0–6,000	66.9	71.9	67.3	47.2	56.6	67.4
6,001–10,000	21.6	21.5	23.7	31.4	29.4	25.0
10,001–15,000	7.2	5.0	5.8	13.9	8.5	4.5
Over 15,000	4.3	1.6	3.2	7.6	5.5	3.1
Mean income	$5,500	$5,100	$5,600	$7,500	$6,500	$5,400
Employment status						
Employed	28.8%	22.6%	13.2%	19.8%	18.0%	17.9%
Unemployed	56.1	66.6	79.4	71.1	65.0	69.5
Not in labor force	15.1	10.8	7.4	8.5	17.0	12.6
Mean weeks unemployed	24.6	25.5	28.4	26.1	36.3	32.2

Source: Compiled by the authors.

It should be recalled that, when compared with CETA, Title X employees were shown to resemble the adult participants of structural CETA programs more closely than they did the CETA PSE participants in racial composition and family income. Moreover, Title X employees have experienced a higher incidence of prior unemployment, have averaged a longer period of prior unemployment, and have received more prior transfers than any adult CETA group. It might be argued, however, that, since CETA targets more upon urban areas than does Title X, the difference among participants may be a function more of locality than of program.

The urban/rural analysis of Title X employees does not support this argument. If one focused only upon projects in urban areas, Title X employees would still be more similar to structural CETA programs in ethnic composition and, to a lesser degree, family income. They are also more likely to have been unemployed, to have experienced a longer period of prior unemployment, and to have received more transfer payments.

Project type is a third variable by which title X employees could systematically differ. The characteristics of employees on different types of projects are shown in Table 3.13.

Differences in age across project types are relatively minor, with forestry and recreation projects tending to attract employees of a slightly younger age than other project types. Differences in other employee characteristics across project types are substantially more pronounced. Women, for example, are much more likely to have found employment on service or training projects than on other types of projects, This finding is quite expected, given the relative scarcity of women in construction-related occupations and the predominance of outdoor and/or manual work being pursued by construction, forestry, and rehabilitation projects. Somewhat surprising is the fact that over one-quarter of

TABLE 3.14

Ethnic Characteristics by Project Type, Non-Indian Projects

Project Type	White	Black	Other
Public works	86.1%	11.1%	2.8%
Civil works	44.2	29.8	26.0
Forestry	77.8	19.9	2.3
Rehabilitation	63.6	28.3	8.1
Service	59.5	39.0	1.5
Training	31.0	67.2	1.8
Total	62.3	31.3	6.4

Source: Compiled by the authors.

TABLE 3.15

Transfer Benefits Received by Employees, by Project Type

Transfer Benefit	Employees, by Project Type						
	Public Works	Civil Works	Forestry	Rehabili- tation	Service	Training	Total
Unemployment insurance	18.0%	25.8%	31.9%	32.7%	20.9%	15.7%	27.4%
AFDC, SSI, General Relief	10.9	8.0	11.5	10.8	17.2	23.9	13.3
Social Security	5.8	7.3	6.5	7.4	17.9	19.4	10.0
Food stamps	10.1	25.0	20.3	18.2	23.6	26.1	20.9
Medicaid eligibility	16.5	15.3	21.7	15.7	23.7	33.7	20.4
Public housing	17.3	12.1	7.6	10.6	10.7	14.6	10.9
Percent receiving one or more benefits	52.2	55.9	60.1	61.9	61.0	60.4	60.1
Benefits per employee	.77	.97	.99	.96	1.14	1.31	1.03

Source: Compiled by the authors.

public-works construction employees are women. This is a function, however, of the fact that Title X has funded a substantial number of clerical and administrative-support positions on these projects.

Curiously, total family income is reported to be quite low by public- and civil-works construction employees. Yet, these employees are somewhat more likely to have been employed prior to Title X. The highest family income is reported by rehabilitation-project workers (mean income, $7,500), followed by service employees ($6,500). Duration of prior unemployment is longest among service and training employees.

The ethnic characteristics of employees on different types of projects require some further examination, since the figures in Table 3.13 are skewed by the distribution of Indian projects in the sample. Indian projects account for a very high proportion of public-works construction projects in the sample and a higher than average proportion of civil-works construction projects.* Thus, it is more meaningful to examine ethnic composition without the Indian projects, as in Table 3.14.

White employees are most represented on public-works and forestry projects. Civil-works projects show relatively few white employees, due partly to a concentration of Chicano employees on several such projects in the sample. Black employment is highest on training and service projects. Together, these two project types provide 47.1 percent of their positions to minority employees, compared to 30.6 percent for other types of projects.

Patterns of prior receipt of benefits are also apparent for different project types, as seen in Table 3.15.

Employees on Title X public-works projects are least likely to have received transfers prior to hire. Only 52.2 percent were receiving one or more benefits prior to Title X, and the average number of prior benefits per public-works employee was only .77. In contrast, employees of training projects and, to a lesser degree, service projects have received a substantially greater number of transfers prior to Title X. The average number of prior benefits was 1.31 per training-project employee and 1.14 per service-project employee.

Patterns of prior claiming vary with the type of transfer. A substantially higher proportion of employees on training projects have received means-tested benefits (AFDC, SSI, General Relief, Social Security, food stamps, Medicaid), and service-project employees have also claimed such benefits more frequently than employees on other types of projects. However, service- and training-project

---

*It could be hypothesized that the skewed distribution of Indian projects by project type will distort other findings in this study. However, Indian employees are reasonably similar to other employees on all characteristics except race. Sensitivity analysis of the net-cost results presented in Chapter 4 does not indicate that Indian projects substantially affect net-cost estimates.

employees are less likely to have been receiving unemployment compensation than other employees. The incidence of prior unemployment compensation claiming is highest among forestry- and rehabilitation-project employees.

Overall, broad profiles of the work forces on different types of projects are apparent. Public-works-project employees are usually male and white, have lower-than-average family income, are most likely to have been employed, and least likely to have been receiving transfers prior to Title X employment. Civil-works-project employees are relatively similar, except that they are less likely to be white and have received an average number of transfers. Service- and training-project employees are relatively similar to one another and most different from employees on other types of projects. They are much more likely to be female, often are nonwhite, have experienced a longer period of unemployment, and are most likely to have been receiving transfers, particularly those which are means tested.

Regardless of project type, Title X employees are relatively disadvantaged in comparison with the general U.S. population and even adult CETA participants. Whether working on construction, rehabilitation, service, forestry, or training projects, Title X employees are highly attached to the labor market, have low incomes, have experienced unemployment of long duration, and have received a large number of publicly funded transfers.

Summary

Examination of the characteristics of Title X employees leads to several conclusions. First, Title X has provided short-term employment opportunities to people who, by any standard, are poor and are the long-term unemployed, many probably for structural reasons. However, the Title X constituency tends to consist of the working poor, those who have been in the labor force and suffered a considerable period of unemployment. Although a higher proportion of them were receiving public benefits than is the case for the general population (or CETA PSE participants), substantial numbers of Title X employees had enough work experience to earn unemployment compensation; in addition to the 27.4 percent receiving unemployment insurance, another 14.1 percent had exhausted their benefits.

Second, the characteristics of Title X employees suggest a phenomenon important to policy makers in the designing of a countercyclical employment-generation program: Countercyclical programs such as Title X tend to employ not only those persons who are temporarily out of work for frictional or reasonably short-term cyclical reasons. They also attract large numbers of persons who, by most definitions, are structurally unemployed, whose skills and education are less in demand, and who have been unemployed for a considerable period. The concept that countercyclical programs primarily serve the cyclically unemployed may, in fact, be a misconception. Employment programs intending to stimulate the economy tend to provide jobs in unskilled or low-skilled occupations, partly to minimize the possible inflationary impacts caused by high demand for scarce skilled resources, partly as an administratively practical way to implement a quick-startup, quick-phaseout program. These are the occupations for which the long-term and/or structurally unemployed can compete, and which they are willing to accept. The program may be countercyclical and may achieve its objective of providing an immediate, short-term stimulus to demand, helping the country out of an economic downturn. It may also, directly or indirectly, create more opportunities for the cyclically unemployed. However, the means for achieving these objectives may be a program in which a majority of the direct jobs are aimed, intentionally or not, at the structurally unemployed. This appears to be the case in the Job Opportunities Program.

JOBS PROVIDED UNDER TITLE X

Occupations

The jobs provided under Title X may be described in terms of type of occupation, compensation (wage/salary, average weekly income), and duration of employment. In order to define occupation type, descriptive answers by employees were postcoded utilizing a two-digit code structure developed for the study. The code structure was an adaptation of the two-digit structure utilized by the Economic Development Administration on its ED-110X payroll-reporting form for Title X. Adaptation was necessary to accommodate the variety of occupations cited under Title X, and the respondents' usual or prior jobs, and because preliminary analysis of the ED-110X data base showed that more than 60 percent of all Title X jobs were classified within only four of 84 available EDA codes. (See Appendix E for a presentation of the two-code structures used by Abt and the ED-110X, and their relationships to the *Dictionary of Occupational Titles*, prepared by the U.S. Employment Service.)

An overview of the types of jobs provided under Title X is presented in Table 3.16, which aggregates occupational codes into 12 categories. As might be expected from the types of projects funded under Title X, many of the jobs are in construction-related occupational categories. The most frequent type of job was in the construction trades, accounting for 17 percent of all Title X jobs. In addition, 12.3 percent of respondents described their job as that of a construction laborer or worker, without designating a particular trade or function. Another 10.1 percent called themselves laborers, not indicating whether or not they were working in a construction-related job. A further 10.6 percent were foremen or supervisors, more than half of them in construction work, and another one-quarter not mentioning the supervisory setting. Thus, about one-half of the Title X jobs appear to have involved construction-related occupations.

TABLE 3.16

Title X Occupational Categories

Occupational Category	Percent of Employees
Managerial/administrative	2.2
Professional/technical	4.4
Supervisory/foreman	10.6
Service	16.9
Government/social service	2.9
Clerical	8.6
Forestry, parks, and recreation	13.1
Operative/technician	1.7
Construction trade	17.0
Construction laborer	12.3
Miscellaneous laborer	10.1
Other	.2

Source: Compiled by the authors.

Given the substantial number of forestry and parks projects, it is not surprising that 13.1 percent of jobs involved such work. About six-tenths of these jobs were as a tree cutter or brush clearer. Clerical jobs accounted for 8.6 percent of Title X jobs, while service jobs (including government/social service) were reported by 19.8 percent of respondents. Managerial and administrative work encompassed only 2.2 percent of the jobs. Professional and technical jobs (in law, education, engineering, accounting, medicine) were cited by 4.4 percent of surveyed employees.

The most frequently mentioned individual jobs are displayed in Table 3.7.

Twelve types of Title X jobs were each held by at least 3 percent of Title X employees. Together these jobs account for about 70 percent of Title X workers. As suggested earlier, construction-related jobs dominate. Five of the 12 most frequently held jobs, accounting for about 40 percent of total jobs, are related to construction. Moreover, nine of the jobs (covering 58 percent of the Title X work force) are of the sort which usually require physical labor, often out of doors. Leaving aside questions of right or wrong, this probably accounts for the high proportion of men in Title X. This observation is carried a step further in Table 3.18.

Men clearly dominate in all construction, labor, and forestry/recreation jobs under Title X. Women are predominant in clerical, government/social-service, and professional/technical jobs, the latter being mainly in education.

TABLE 3.17

Frequent Title X Jobs

Job	Percent of Employees
Construction worker or laborer	12.3
Miscellaneous laborer	10.1
Tree cutter or sawyer	7.8
Carpenter or other construction woodworker	7.5
Construction-industry supervisor or foreman	5.9
Typist, stenographer, file clerk	4.9
Miscellaneous personal-service occupation	4.3
Cement worker, concrete laying, paving, or finishing	4.1
Building maintenance (exclusive of janitorial)	3.7
Miscellaneous forestry, parks, or recreation occupation	3.5
Truck or bus driver	3.4
Miscellaneous supervisor or foreman	3.0

Source: Compiled by the authors.

TABLE 3.18

Male/Female Participation in Title X Jobs

Occupational Category	Percent of Employees	
	Male	Female
Managerial/administrative	76.7	23.3
Professional/technical	29.1	70.9
Supervisory/foreman	95.7	4.3
Construction trade	98.5	1.5
Construction laborer	95.4	4.6
Miscellaneous laborer	95.4	4.6
Operative/technician	79.4	20.6
Forestry, parks, recreation	91.4	8.6
Government/social service	17.9	82.1
Service	52.4	47.6
Clerical	15.6	84.4
Total Title X	75.7	24.3
Percent of civilian labor force	59.5	40.5

Source: Compiled by the authors.

Women also are more represented in service jobs than in the Title X work force as a whole. Of note is the fact that women have received managerial/administrative positions in about equal proportion to their representation in Title X.

Other demographic patterns within the Title X work force are less pronounced or consistent. Forestry and miscellaneous laborers tend to be quite young (under 25), while service workers are older than the norm. Managers are mostly between 25 and 44 years of age. Nonwhites are underrepresented among the managers, operatives, and technicians, and in the forestry jobs. They are overrepresented among service workers, professional/technical personnel, and construction laborers. They are not underrepresented in the construction-trade or supervisor/foreman positions of Title X.

Of considerable importance to the entire evaluation is the relationship between the Title X occupational categories and a particular project type. The project type represents one of the very few important data items available on the entire universe of 2,255 Title X projects. It was used as a stratifying element in selecting the sample of projects for this study and in using net-cost results from the sample to generalize about the universe. The project type was chosen because it is an important descriptive measure of Title X projects and because preliminary analysis of early ED-110X data showed strong relationships between the project type and occupational categories. These relationships are confirmed in our study—which uses a different occupational-category structure—as shown in Table 3.19.

In this table, the 12 occupational categories used earlier in this chapter have been collapsed into five. As illustrated, among all projects, the construction and laborer (primarily construction-related) categories contain more than one-half of the employees. When one examines the occupational distribution by the project type, several relationships are clear. Civil-works construction projects have work forces concentrated almost entirely (91.1 percent) in construction and laborer categories, with a negligible number of persons employed in other types of work. This same distribution pattern is also strongly evident among rehabilitation, maintenance, and renovation projects, where more than seven out of every ten employees perform structural work. One would expect the same pattern for public-works construction projects, except perhaps that there would be slightly higher proportions of professional and clerical employees. This is the case, with 64.8 percent of the work force of such projects reported in construction and laborer categories.

A second, and totally distinct, distribution of employment is evident in service and training projects. For these project types, about 80 percent of the work force is reported to be in professional, clerical, or service categories; much fewer employees are in construction or forestry categories. The distribution of service-project employees among professional, clerical, and service categories is somewhat different from the distribution of training-project employees. However, the concentration of employees of both project types in these

TABLE 3.19

Occupational Distribution by Project Type

| Project Type | Occupational Categories (percent distribution) | | | | | |
	Managerial Professional, and Technical	Service, Govern- ment	Clerical	Forestry	Construction and Laborer	Total
Public works	8.6	15.8	9.4	1.4	64.8	7.1
Civil works	1.6	2.4	4.8	0.0	91.1	6.3
Rehabilitation	2.1	12.2	5.0	7.7	72.9	26.3
Forestry	1.4	3.9	3.7	35.1	55.9	28.8
Service	16.4	52.3	15.9	7.2	8.2	20.4
Training	18.7	36.6	21.6	1.5	21.6	6.8
Other	7.0	20.9	9.3	5.8	57.0	4.3
Total	6.6	20.3	8.6	13.1	51.4	100.0

Source: Compiled by the authors.

categories is about equally intense and contrasts sharply with the employment distributions of other project types. In fact, over 65 percent of managerial, professional, service, and clerical positions are found in service and training projects, even though these projects account for only 27.2 percent of the jobs.

A third employment pattern is distinguished for forestry, conservation, and recreation projects. Not surprisingly, this is the only project type reporting a high proportion of employees (39.1 percent) in forestry-related categories. Although forestry and recreation projects encompass only 28.8 percent of all employees, they provide over 70 percent of forestry-related jobs. In addition, many employees are listed as performing structural work (55.9 percent), with very few in other occupational groups. This dual concentration of the work force in forestry and construction categories is characteristic only of the conservation-type project.

Wages, Hours, and Weekly Earnings

In general, Title X has provided full-time work. The mean hours worked per week is 38.6, as shown in Table 3.20. The median is 40 hours. Over 80 percent of employees report that they work an average of 40 hours. Less than 2 percent of employees work an average of less than 20 hours per week, while about 3 percent average more than 40 hours weekly. There are no significant differences in the average number of weekly hours worked in different types of Title X jobs or by different demographic groups. Likewise, hours vary very little across different regions or types of projects.

The average weekly earnings from Title X jobs have been $135.57. This is well above the minimum wage and equivalent to $3.39 per hour for a 40-hour

TABLE 3.20

Hours, Wages, and Weekly Earnings of Title X Employees

Measure	Title X Employee Sample
Mean hours per week	38.6
Median hours per week	40.0
Mean hourly wage	$ 3.54
Median hourly wage	3.14
Mean weekly earnings	135.57
Median weekly earnings	123.00

Source: Compiled by the authors.

TABLE 3.21

Average Weekly Earnings on Title X Jobs, by Employee/Project Categories

Category	Average Weekly Earnings	Category	Average Weekly Earnings
Age		Project Type	
16–19	110.01	Public-works	
20–24	129.30	Construction	130.57
25–34	144.57	Civil-works	
35–44	146.47	Construction	126.14
45–59	146.17	Forestry/recreation	133.66
60 and over	152.61	Rehabilitation	162.33
Sex		Service	122.33
Male	147.84	Training	99.48
Female	108.53	Other	128.39
Race		Occupation	
White	141.81	Manager	185.11
Total black and other	128.34	Professional/technical	130.94
Black	113.65	Supervisor/foreman	177.74
American Indian	153.35	Construction trades	153.90
Other	150.55	Construction laborer	128.53
Estimated 1976 Family Income		Other laborer	152.29
$0–4,000	121.66	Operative/technician	128.98
4–6,000	122.51	Forestry	142.35
6–8,000	141.82	Goverment/social	
8–10,000	148.46	service	112.76
10–15,000	194.66	Service	104.91
15–20,000	207.48	Clerical	116.57
Over 20,000	223.21	EDA region	
Prior employment status		1	144.18
Employed full time	183.98	4	114.32
Employed part time	132.75	5	131.15
Unemployed	132.53	6	144.96
		7	209.63
		8	123.87
		All employees	$135.57

Source: Compiled by the authors.

week, or $7,050 per year. Given that Title X employees work slightly less than 40 hours per week, the effective hourly wage is $3.54. If it is assumed that hourly workers receive time and a half for more than 40 hours per week, average weekly earnings increase very slightly, to $135.80, or $7,062 per year. The vast majority of employees do not work overtime in Title X jobs.

Average weekly earnings are highest for managers ($185.11) and supervisors/ foremen ($177.74). They are lowest in the service (104.91), government ($112.76), and clerical ($116.57) occupations, as shown in Table 3.21.

There are also substantial differences in average weekly earnings among employees with different demographic characteristics. As shown in Table 3.21, average weekly earnings increase with age, from $110.01 for 16-19-year-olds to $146.17 for those 45-59 and to $152.61 for persons over 60. Men earn substantially more per week than women in Title X jobs ($147.84 versus $108.53), and whites have been in jobs paying slightly more than those filled by nonwhites ($141.81 versus $128.34). Interestingly, the mean Title X weekly earnings for American Indians and other minority-group workers (including small numbers of Orientals, Mexican-Americans, and Puerto Ricans) are higher than the mean for whites. With comparatively low weekly earnings received by blacks ($113.65), the nonwhite mean drops below the white mean.

As would be expected, Title X weekly earnings are directly related to total family earnings. Moreover, those who were employed full time prior to Title X receive more per week under Title X ($183.98) than those who were employed part time ($132.75) or those who were unemployed ($132.53). Interestingly, average weekly earnings are substantially higher in EDA region 7 ($209.63) than in any other region, with weekly earnings lowest in region 4 ($114.32) and region 8 ($123.87). Rehabilitation projects have paid the most ($162.33) per week, with training projects paying the least ($99.48). Weekly earnings on all other types of projects are very close to the mean.

The average weekly earnings on Title X jobs reported in Table 3.21 are simple group means for participants with various socioeconomic characteristics, and for project types, occupations, and regions. As such, they may overstate or understate relationships between various characteristics and weekly earnings. For example, Table 3.21 shows that men earn substantially more per week than women on Title X jobs ($147.84 versus $108.53). However, it is possible that substantially more men than women are older, are white, were employed full time prior to Title X, and are employed on rehabilitation projects. The independent influence of these socioeconomic characteristics, other than sex, may account for the finding that men earn more per week than women.

In order to control for the independent influence, on average weekly earnings, of socioeconomic characteristics, project type, and project region, a multiple regression has been estimated. The dependent variable in the estimate is average weekly earnings on Title X jobs. The independent variables are sex,

TABLE 3.22

Average Weekly Earnings on Title X Jobs:
A Multivariate Analysis

Independent Variable	Regression Coefficient	Standard Error	T-Value Statistic
White	16.95	2.69	6.29*
Male	25.71	3.26	7.88*
Age	5.66	.52	10.92*
Age squared	− .06	.006	10.43*
Part time	1.96	4.67	0.42
Full time	22.25	3.86	5.76*
Funded	2.21	3.45	0.64
Rural	− 8.00	2.73	2.93*
Public works	6.45	5.39	1.20
Civil works	− 5.64	5.51	1.02
Rehabilitation	22.45	3.49	6.43*
Service	− 1.77	3.99	0.44
Training	−10.04	5.64	1.78
Other	10.25	6.62	1.54
EDA region 1	16.37	3.30	4.96*
EDA region 5	12.81	5.46	2.34*
EDA region 6	17.80	4.29	4.15*
EDA region 7	56.11	4.47	12.56*
EDA region 8	.76	4.28	0.18
Small project	−12.71	2.74	4.63*
Large project	− .53	6.01	0.09

*Statistically significant at the 1-percent level or better.

Note: Constant = −7.61; $\bar{R}^2$ = .304; F-value = 39.4; N = 1,841. The unemployed-workers category is omitted from the list of variables, since it is the benchmark for analyzing the prior-to-Title X employment status categories; forestry/recreation is omitted as it is the benchmark for project-type categories; EDA region 4 is omitted as it is the benchmark for regional categories; and medium-size projects are omitted—the benchmark for size categories.

Source: Compiled by the authors.

race, age, prior employment status, project type, region, whether the prior job was publicly subsidized, whether the project location is urban or rural, and the size of the project.

The results of the multiple-regression estimation are reported in Table 3.22. The independent variables account for 30 percent of the variation in average weekly earnings under Title X, as measured by the adjusted coefficient of determination. The F-value, 39.4, indicates that the overall equation is statistically significant at the 1-percent level. The estimated regression coefficients for socioeconomic characteristics measure the impact on average weekly earnings, once the effects of the remaining independent variables are taken into account. The estimated regression coefficients for prior employment status, project type, region, and project size are differential-intercept terms. That is, they measure the influence on average weekly earnings relative to a benchmark category. The benchmark categories used are the unemployed-workers category, for prior employment status; forestry/recreation, for project type; EDA region 4, for region; and medium-size projects, for size.

The results of the multiple regression generally substantiate the simple group means reported in Table 3.21. Average weekly earnings increase with age, but at a decreasing rate. Men earn $25.71 more per week than women under Title X, and whites earn $16.95 more than nonwhites. These estimated differences in average weekly earnings, based on sex and race, are substantially smaller than those in Table 3.21. This suggests that the earlier estimates are altered by the effect of project type, region, and socioeconomic characteristics other than sex and race. Those workers who were employed full time prior to Title X experienced higher average weekly earnings (in the amount of $22.25) than those workers who were unemployed; again, this supports the group means reported earlier, although the $22.25 regression estimate is substantially below the $51.45 difference reported in Table 3.21. Workers who were employed part time prior to Title X had average weekly Title X earnings similar to workers who were unemployed prior to Title X, as indicated by the statistically insignificant regression coefficient.

Title X participants in rural projects received $8.00 a week less than those workers in urban projects. With regard to project type, rehabilitation projects paid substantially more than forestry projects, while weekly wages paid in the remaining projects are not statistically larger or smaller. The regression results on EDA regions also support the earlier findings. Controlling for the independent influence of socioeconomic characteristics and project type, however, lowers the differences in average weekly earnings paid across regions. With regard to size, small projects are estimated to pay less than large or medium-size projects.

Duration of Title X Employment

The typical Title X employee works almost a full 40-hour week and receives about $136 a week in wages. Moreover, the average employee in the Abt

TABLE 3.23

Duration of Title X Employment, by Employee/Project Categories

Category	Average Duration (weeks)	Category	Average Duration (weeks)
Age		Occupation	
16–17	26.2	Manager	44.3
18–19	29.0	Professional	40.1
20–24	34.0	Supervisor	39.5
25–34	36.3	Construction trades	32.3
35–44	36.6	Construction laborer	31.7
45–59	37.4	Other laborer	31.9
60 and over	36.8	Operative/technician	32.8
Sex		Forestry	31.9
Male	34.2	Government/social	
Female	38.5	service	39.9
Race		Service	38.4
White	35.0	Clerical	37.4
Total black and other	35.7	EDA region	
Black	37.1	1	34.5
American Indian	31.4	4	36.6
Other	39.1	5	36.3
Prior employment status		6	36.1
Employed full time	35.5	7	32.3
Employed part time	34.1	8	34.8
Unemployed	35.3	All employees	35.2
Project type			
Public-works construction	30.3		
Civil-works construction	36.3		
Forestry, recreation	32.8		
Rehabilitation	34.1		
Service	39.8		
Training	35.3		
Other	37.4		

Source: Compiled by the authors.

sample has stayed in the Title X job for a full eight months. Duration of employment, of course, varies greatly, from less than one week to 72 weeks. The mean duration of Title X employment is 35.2 weeks, with a median duration of 36 weeks.* Length of tenure varies directly with the age of the employee (see Table 3.23), from 26.2 weeks for those under 18 to 37.2 weeks for employees over 55. Women remain on the Title X job somewhat longer than men (38.5 weeks versus 34.2 weeks), but there are no significant differences in employment duration among either ethnic groups or the categories of prior employment status. Managerial, professional, supervisory, and government jobs under Title X are held somewhat longer (an average of 40 weeks) than other jobs, with construction and laborer positions showing a shorter employment duration (32 weeks). Similarly, the average employee on a public-works construction project is employed for 30.3 weeks, in contrast to 39.8 weeks on service projects. Duration of Title X employment does not differ significantly from region to region.

Gross Earnings

As a function of weekly earnings and duration of Title X employment, the gross earnings from the Title X jobs average $4,753 per employee (see Table 3.24). The median Title X earnings are $4,403. Gross earnings are highest in the 25-59 age ranges, with younger and older Title X workers receiving less. Male employees earn substantially more than female employees ($4,934 versus $4,191),

---

*The 35.2-week average duration of Title X employment observed for the employee sample is considerably longer than the 20.6-week average employment duration projected in Chapter 2 for the entire Job Opportunities Program. The difference could be caused by two factors. First, the 20.6-week projection could be skewed downward, being based upon reports from completed projects, which may be inaccurate or unrepresentative of the program. This is a possibility particularly because the completed projects are smaller, on the average, than most Title X projects and describe a different project-type distribution. However, project type is controlled for in the projection, and analysis of completed projects by size (see Appendix E) does not reveal any major likelihood of bias. While there may be some technical problems in the data, the 20.6 week estimate is probably very close to correct.

Second, the sample estimate of 35.2 weeks is likely to overstate duration of Title X employment. Abt's survey was conducted in October–December 1976, when many projects were finishing up their work. Since turnover on almost any type of project tends to be greater in its early stages than in its later stages, it is quite likely that the Abt sample includes a substantial number of project persisters and is underrepresented by employees with short periods of project employment. Moreover, seasonal factors may affect Abt's estimates of employment duration. The survey was conducted in the fall and early winter and, in several regions of the country, may have been too late to include workers whose jobs were confined to the summer months of temperate weather. For these reasons, the 35.2 week duration average observed for the sample is likely to be an overestimate.

TABLE 3.24

Gross Earnings from Title X Jobs, by Employee/Project Categories

Category	Average Gross Earnings	Category	Average Gross Earnings
Age		Occupation	
16–17	1,971	Manager	8,276
18–19	3,284	Professional	5,449
20–24	4,371	Supervisor	6,866
25–34	5,265	Construction trades	4,327
35–44	5,213	Construction laborer	3,943
45–59	5,335	Other laborer	4,678
60 and over	3,863	Operative/technician	4,275
Sex		Forestry	4,618
Male	4,934	Government/social	
Female	4,191	service	4,549
Race		Service	4,063
White	5,073	Clerical	4,409
Total black and other	4,371	Region	
Black	4,274	1	4,954
American Indian	4,153	4	4,278
Other	5,686	5	4,924
Previous employment status		6	5,275
Employed full time	5,459	7	5,727
Employed part time	4,402	8	4,124
Unemployed	4,688	All employees	$4,753
Project type			
Public-works			
construction	4,092		
Civil-works			
construction	4,419		
Forestry, recreation	4,645		
Rehabilitation	5,277		
Service	4,964		
Training	3,569		
Other	4,849		

Source: Compiled by the authors.

despite the fact that the average duration of Title X employment is longer for women. The notably higher average weekly earnings of men account for the difference. Similarly, whites earn more under Title X than nonwhites ($5,073 versus $4,371), with American Indians and blacks having lower gross earnings than any other ethnic group. And, as one might expect, persons who were employed full-time prior to Title X earn more than those who were unemployed or working part time ($5,459 versus $4,402 and $4,688, respectively).

Gross earnings for certain Title X occupations are substantially higher than for others. Managers ($8,276), supervisors and foremen ($6,866), and professionals ($5,449) average the highest gross income. Construction laborers ($3,943) and service workers ($4,063) average the least gross income. In the former case, a comparatively short duration of employment accounts for the lower earnings; in the latter, low weekly income is the critical variable. Employees in training projects, where weekly earnings are low, receive lower total earnings ($3,569) than employees in other types of projects. Gross income on public-works projects is also relatively low ($4,092), a function of shorter project duration. The average income on a rehabilitation project ($5,277) or a service project ($4,964) is the highest gross income under Title X.

Finally, there are significant regional differences in gross Title X earnings. An average Title X employee in region 7 receives $5,727, fully 39 percent more than an employee in region 8 ($4,124). Average gross earnings are also notably high in region 6 ($5,275), notably low in region 4 ($4,278). Substantial regional differences in average weekly Title X earnings account for most of the variation.

NOTES

1. "Terms and Conditions of Title X Projects," *Federal Register* 40, no. 250 (December 30, 1975), p. 52765.

2. Edward M. Gramlich, "The Distributional Effects of Higher Unemployment," *Brookings Papers on Economic Activity*, vol. 2 (Washington, D.C.: Brookings Institution, 1974); Thomas Barocci, "The Recession as a Regressive Tax," mimeographed (Cambridge: Sloan School of Management, MIT, 1976).

3. CETA data presented here and elsewhere are reported in Westat, Inc., *Continuous Longitudinal Manpower Survey Report No. 4: Characteristics of Enrollees Who Entered CETA Programs During Calendar Year 1975*, prepared for the Office of Policy, Evaluation and Research, of the Employment and Training Administration (Washington, D.C.: Department of Labor, November 1976).

4

THE NET COST OF
TITLE X

INTRODUCTION

Government programs such as Title X create financial, economic, social, and environmental benefits and costs that may accrue to project employees, the federal government, state and local governments, and the private domestic economy. A total program evaluation would consider each of these benefit and cost components. In the Title X indirect-impact evaluation, however, attention is focused strictly upon the financial effects of the program, the cash expenditures by government, and the returns to government that accrue from these expenditures. The purpose is to develop accurate estimates, for the Job Opportunities Program, of the net cost to governments, a concept which is not new but has not received careful attention. It is important because policy makers generally make investment decisions based upon the gross outlays for alternative programs, without considering the returns to government that reduce the actual financial costs of the program. Since the returns to government vary greatly with different kinds of investments, funding decisions are often made with incomplete information.

Simply put, net program cost is more accurate than gross expenditures as a measure of the actual costs of a program to taxpayers. Gross expenditures—actual outlays—should be reduced by the amount of primary and secondary cash returns to government, to arrive at net program costs. Primary returns originate from the earnings of Title X workers and the nonlabor expenditures incurred by the projects. The government receives personal income taxes, contributions to FICA, and excise- and sales-tax revenue from earnings of Title X workers. Moreover, transfer payments, such as unemployment compensation and food stamps, received by Title X employees prior to the program may be reduced. Other budget savings result from sales and corporate income tax revenue generated by nonlabor purchases of goods and services by Title X projects. (A more complete discussion of the net-cost methodology on direct returns is given later in this chapter and in Appendixes A, B, and C.)

Secondary, or indirect, returns occur because the expenditures made by individuals employed under Title X, as well as the outlays on program administration and on nonlabor project expenditures can have multiplier effects within the economy. These expenditures can affect employment in producing, wholesale, and retail industries; hence, secondary income-tax, sales-tax, and FICA effects may be traced to Title X projects (secondary effects are discussed in Chapter 5).

Careful consideration of the direct and indirect financial effects of programs such as Title X is particularly important, because the principal program objective is to provide a short-term employment and economic stimulus to impacted local areas. The returns to government reduce the real costs of the program and similarly affect its overall employment and income-generating impacts. Accurate estimates of returns, therefore, can substantially affect an assessment of program impact. Moreover, to the extent that returns accrue to state and local governments in excess of their proportional investments in the program, there are positive distributional effects. Money flows to state and local governments as a result of the program, a result which is consistent with the program objective of providing a local stimulus.

The estimation of net program costs (as noted above) is not an altogether new idea, and several program simulations have been carried through for policy purposes. For example, the Congressional Budget Office (CBO) has employed computer-simulation techniques to estimate the increase in jobs, the reduction in the national unemployment rate, and the net budget costs for a variety of employment generating programs.[1] None of these programs resembled Title X, but the APW program, on which a simulation was done by CBO, is more similar to Title X than the others. Taking into account the taxes generated and transfers saved (using a $1 billion expenditure), the CBO estimated that the net costs for the initial impact of the public-works expenditures ranged from 79.3 percent to 91.5 percent of gross costs, and after 12 months they dropped to between 51 and 53.7 percent. This means that for each $1 billion public expenditure for accelerated public works, various government levels would have experienced a net return (saved transfers plus additional taxes) in the range of $463 million–$490 million.[2] The net budget costs drop even further after 24 months. The CBO estimates have generated some controversy, as have other efforts to estimate net costs and related measures of displacement.[3]

All prior studies have been based upon simplified assumptions and aggregate data, with the intention of yielding rough estimates of net cost. The Abt Associates study provides the first opportunity to develop a precise net-cost methodology and apply it to empirical data on participants of a current employment-generating program. Data from samples of participants and projects funded under the auspices of Title X allow for a valid estimate of the net costs of the Title X program. The Abt study is carefully designed to generate data which can be combined with additional program data to arrive at net-cost estimates generalizable for the entire universe of Title X projects.

A central question in the calculation of net Title X program costs is whether to attribute the cause of any measured increase in earnings and employment to Title X or to other economic forces. There are two plausible approaches. The first is to assume that all labor and physical resources employed in the Title X projects would have remained idle in the absence of the program. This approach implies that all earnings from Title X should be used in the calculation of tax returns and the reduction in transfer payments that accrue to government. Consider, for example, a Title X employee who earns $100 a week and is employed for 20 weeks in the program. The total earnings from Title X, $2,000, would be used as a base for the calculation of tax revenues to the government. If this individual was previously unemployed and receiving unemployment compensation, the full reduction in unemployment compensation (20 weeks of payments, or a lesser amount if the person was about to exhaust benefits) would accrue to the government.

In general, the assumption that all estimated returns are attributable to the program will overstate returns (and understate net cost) simply because many Title X employees would have earned income if they had not worked under Title X. However, estimates based upon the full-return assumption are useful because they show the literal flow of dollars that results from Title X investments. Such estimates are presented in this chapter as unadjusted returns.

A more realistic and conservative assumption is that a portion of Title X employment (and earnings) would have occurred in the absence of the program. A participant in Title X might have been employed for some length of time in the private or public sector during the period of Title X. Title X employment (and earnings) must, therefore, be discounted by the estimated number of weeks of employment and estimated earnings that each program participant would have received in the absence of Title X. The discounting of employment and earnings will reduce the returns from the program and increase its net cost.* Thus, if the employee in the previously noted example would have worked ten weeks at a weekly wage of $100, regardless of Title X, earnings used as a base for the calculation of tax revenues would be $1,000 rather than $2,000. The reduction in unemployment compensation would accrue for the government for a maximum of ten rather than 20 weeks.

---

*In one instance, there is an opposite effect. Previously employed Title X workers would likely have been unemployed for a brief period in the absence of the program. If one assumes that these workers would have been eligible for unemployment compensation, then a modest amount of additional savings in unemployment compensation is attributable to Title X.

Employment in the absence of Title X, as seen by the individual enrollees, should have been estimated through the use of a control group of persons with similar sociodemographic characteristics and employment histories. However, timing and cost considerations precluded the use of a control group. Instead, we adapted a statistical control group, which is detailed in Appendix B.

Estimates of employment in the absence of Title X have been made in this study for each individual in the employee sample. Estimates are generated with a model developed by Charles Holt, Ralph Smith, and others, working at the Urban Institute on a grant from the Department of Labor. When adapted for the Title X study, the model is capable of producing estimates of weeks worked for 16 age/race/sex cohorts, estimates varying with prior labor-force status (whether a person had been employed, unemployed, or not in the labor force) and the month of the year. The model thus provides a statistical control for the Title X employee sample.[4]

Estimates using this discounting methodology are presented in this chapter as adjusted returns from Title X. Adjusted returns are more accurate than unadjusted returns, since they account for employment and earnings in the absence of Title X. However, they are conservative, somewhat understating the real cost impact of the Job Opportunities Program. The reason for this is that in areas of high unemployment, such as those at which Title X has targeted, there is likely to be a queue of persons seeking available jobs resulting from Title X investments.

This chapter discusses in detail each facet of Title X net cost: unadjusted returns from Title X labor expenditures; adjusted returns from labor spending; returns to governments from Title X nonlabor expenditures; and the net direct costs of, and returns from, Title X.

UNADJUSTED RETURNS TO GOVERNMENT FROM TITLE X LABOR EXPENDITURES

Projections of unadjusted returns to governments from Title X labor expenditures are based upon sample data from a total of 1,969 questionnaires completed at 195 projects during the Title X employee survey. The projects that were chosen are roughly proportional to the universe of 2,255 Title X projects, by project type and regional location. Employees were selected to be representative of the current project work force, by occupation and wage. A brief summary of the key sample data appears in Table 4.1.

Sampled employees earned approximately $9,354,000 from their Title X jobs, or about $4,751 per employee. The total wages and salaries of these 1,969 workers are estimated to bring returns to government of about $3,322,000. In other words, for each dollar of wages expended on the employees, governments get back almost 36 cents in increased tax revenues and reduced transfer payments,

TABLE 4.1

Total Unadjusted Returns from Labor Expenditures: Employee Sample

Measure	Total	Tax Revenues	Reductions in Transfer Payments
Employee earnings	$9,354,000	–	–
Unadjusted returns	3,322,000	$2,237,000	$1,085,000
Percent of earnings	35.5	23.9	11.6
Percent of returns	100.0	67.3	32.7
Savings per employee	$ 1,687	$ 1,136	$ 551
Federal share of savings	2,459,000	1,665,000	794,000
State share of savings	864,000	572,000	292,000
Net wage/salary cost to government	6,032,000	–[a]	–

[a] Data not available.

Source: Compiled by the authors.

prior to multiplier effects of indirect and induced returns. The net wage/salary cost to government is $6,032,000, or 64.5 percent of gross wage/salary costs.*

Increased direct-tax revenues account for a majority (67.3 percent) of unadjusted labor returns on the sample. The typical Title X employee pays $737 in income, FICA, sales, and excise taxes on $4,753 of earnings, an effective overall tax rate of 15.5 percent. Other taxes of $400 per employee are paid by the employer for FICA and unemployment insurance (UI) contributions. Overall, about 24 cents on every dollar of Title X wages is returned to federal and state coffers from taxes. Transfer-payment reductions return $1,085,000 to governments, or about $551 per employee. This is almost 12 cents for every dollar expended on Title X wages.

The federal government's share of returns on labor expenditures is $2,459,000, or 74.0 percent of total returns on labor. More than two-thirds of returns are in the form of taxes, primarily income tax and FICA. The federal share of tax revenues represents about 74.4 percent of total tax revenues.

---

*Note that returns on the sample are presented here as a proportion of wages, not of total labor cost. Complete data on fringes paid to employees were not available; so total labor costs for the sample are not known. Estimates of total labor cost have been made for the universe. Thus, as shown later, projections of returns do yield an accurate estimate of net labor costs.

Transfer-payment savings accruing to the federal government amount to $794,000, or 73.2 percent of total transfer savings.

Whereas returns to the federal government account for about 26 cents per dollar of Title X wages, returns to state governments are about 9.2 cents on the wage dollar. Fully 33.8 percent of state returns on labor are in the form of transfer savings, principally on unemployment compensation, General Relief, and Medicaid payments. State sales, income, and excise taxes account for 66.2 percent of state returns on labor and 25.6 percent of total tax returns.

Sample estimates of returns on labor expenditures can be used to make projections for the entire Job Opportunities Program by considering each sampled project (and the employees on that project) as representative of a larger number of Title X projects (and employees) in the program. Estimates for sampled employees are weighted first to the sampled project. Individual project estimates are then weighted (within project-type strata) to the full project sample and ultimately to the universe (stratified by project type).

Two variables are critical to the calculation of projection weights: labor expenditures and person-months of employment.* As presented in Chapter 2, the Job Opportunities Program is projected to spend a total of $757,924,000 in federal, state, local, and private funds to support 2,255 projects. Of these monies, $521,267,000 is estimated to be labor expenditures, providing about 655,211 person-months of employment to an estimated 136,571 persons. Based upon the employee-sample data, estimates of the unadjusted returns and net labor cost of the entire Job Opportunities Program can be made. These estimates are summarized in Table 4.2.

The $521,267,000 in Title X labor expenditures generate direct unadjusted returns of about $155,310,000. Thus, almost 30 cents out of every dollar expended on Title X wages and fringes is returned directly to government in tax revenues on transfer savings. The net direct labor cost to government is $365,957,000, or 70.2 percent of gross labor outlays.

A majority of returns ($110,211,000, or 71 percent) are in the form of increased taxes, which return more than 21 cents to federal, state, and local governments for each Title X labor dollar (see Figure 4.1). Transfer savings account for approximately 9 cents per dollar of Title X expenditures on wages and fringes. The bulk of returns (71.9 percent) accrue to the federal government, which is estimated to receive $81,391,000 in additional tax revenues and to save $30,299,000 in transfer payments. The federal government's share of

---

*For weighting purposes, person-months of employment are preferable to number of employees, because of the long duration of employment observed in the sample.

TABLE 4.2

Total Unadjusted Returns from Labor Expenditures:
Job Opportunities Program

Measure	Total	Tax Revenues	Reduction in Transfer Payments
Total Title X Labor Cost (in thousands of dollars)	521,267	—[a]	—
Unadjusted returns (in thousands of dollars)	155,310	110,211	45,099
Percent of labor cost	29.8	21.1	8.7
Percent of returns	100.0	71.0	29.0
Savings per person-month	$237.04	$168.21	$68.83
Savings per employee	1,137.21	806.21	330.22
Federal share of returns (in thousands of dollars)	111,690	81,391	30,299
State share of returns in thousands of dollars	43,620	28,820	14,800
Net unadjusted labor cost of Title X (in thousands of dollars)	265,957	—	—

[a] Data not available.
Source: Compiled by the authors.

total increased tax revenues (73.9 percent) is higher than its share of transfer savings (67.2 percent).

The summary of unadjusted returns on labor presented above aggregates estimates of many different tax and transfer items. A more detailed examination of these returns, and the ways in which they were calculated, provides a comprehensive sense of the dynamics of government investments in job-creation programs.

Increased Taxes

Considering taxes first, the earned income of Title X employees generates increases in tax revenues to public treasuries via several tax streams: personal income taxes, sales taxes, excise taxes, Social Security taxes or other retirement contributions, and employer contributions to unemployment insurance funds. The general procedure used to calculate personal income tax revenue is to apply the appropriate federal and state effective income tax rate to the Title X earnings

FIGURE 4.1

Unadjusted Net Labor Cost of Title X

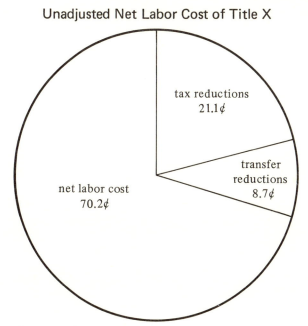

Source: Constructed by the authors.

of each employee. Effective rates vary with the gross family income and family size of each individual. Social Security and unemployment insurance taxes are calculated by multiplying the FICA and UI rates by the Title X wages that are subject to the taxes. The first $15,300 of earnings, for example, is subject to Social Security taxes at a rate of 5.85 percent for both the worker and the employer.

Sales- and excise-tax revenues are based upon the proportion of increased disposable income from Title X that is spent on goods and services subject to sales or excise taxes. Disposable income is Title X earnings minus personal income taxes, FICA, and any reduction in cash-transfer payments that occurs during Title X employment. It is assumed that the short-term increases in disposable earnings from Title X employment are spent, not saved, a reasonable assumption considering the low family earnings and the duration of employment of Title X employees. Sales- and excise-tax returns are based upon the distribution of spending, reflected in the Consumer Expenditure Survey (CES),[5] according to the median family income of the Title X employee sample. Thus, excise taxes encompass state and federal taxes on gasoline and tobacco, but not those on alcoholic beverages (which are not included in the CES). To this extent, estimates of excise taxes are conservative, probably understating by a modest amount the actual excise-tax returns.

The following equations summarize the procedures used to calculate tax revenues generated by Title X earned income for each individual:

$$\begin{bmatrix} \text{Earned income} \\ \text{from Title X} \end{bmatrix} = \begin{bmatrix} \text{Average weekly earnings} \\ \text{from Title X job} \end{bmatrix} \times \begin{bmatrix} \text{Estimated duration of} \\ \text{Title X employment} \end{bmatrix}$$

$$\begin{bmatrix} \text{Personal income-} \\ \text{tax returns} \end{bmatrix} = \begin{bmatrix} \text{Earned income from} \\ \text{Title X job} \end{bmatrix} \times \begin{bmatrix} \text{Effective federal and state} \\ \text{income tax rates} \end{bmatrix}$$

$$\begin{bmatrix} \text{Sales- and excise-} \\ \text{tax revenue} \end{bmatrix} = \begin{bmatrix} \text{Consumption expenditures} \\ \text{from disposable income earned} \\ \text{from Title X, subject to sales} \\ \text{and excise tax} \end{bmatrix} \times \begin{bmatrix} \text{State sales tax rate,} \\ \text{state and federal} \\ \text{gasoline tax rate,} \\ \text{state and federal} \\ \text{tobacco tax rate} \end{bmatrix}$$

$$\begin{bmatrix} \text{Social Security and} \\ \text{unemployment} \\ \text{insurance tax} \\ \text{returns} \end{bmatrix} = \begin{bmatrix} \text{Earned income from} \\ \text{Title X, subject to} \\ \text{sales and excise tax} \end{bmatrix} \times \begin{bmatrix} \text{FICA tax rate,} \\ \text{state UI tax rate,} \\ \text{federal UI tax rate} \end{bmatrix}$$

Application of the tax-return equations to unadjusted estimates for the Job Opportunities Program produces the returns presented in Table 4.3.

Increased taxes paid to government account for about 70 percent of direct unadjusted returns on labor expenditures. For each Title X employee, an average of $806.98 is returned to federal and state treasuries in income, sales, excise, FICA, and unemployment insurance taxes. The largest single source of tax returns is federal personal income tax, which accounts for 24.5 percent of increased taxes. State income taxes increase the total personal income tax returns to over $30 million, or 28.6 percent of taxes.

FICA payments by Title X employers and by employees are also substantial, estimated at almost $25 million from each source. More than 99 percent of Title X earnings are subject to FICA, with very few employees having Title X earnings greater than the $15,300 maximum subject to Social Security taxes.* Together, employees' and employers' FICA payments account for 44.6 percent

---

*Theoretically, Title X employees with other earnings during 1976 could, with their Title X earnings, exceed the $15,300 maximum. Thus, when they filed their income tax returns, they might have gotten back some of the FICA withheld from Title X earnings. However, data limitations do not allow us to identify this possible phenomenon. And, since only 4.8 percent of the sample reported total family income (including nonearnings and earnings of other family members) in excess of $15,000, overwithholding of FICA by Title X employers is at best a rare phenomenon.

TABLE 4.3

Unadjusted Tax Revenues from Title X Labor Expenditures: Job Opportunities Program

Type of Tax	Increased Tax Revenues (in thousands of dollars)	Percent of Total Tax Return	Federal Share (in thousands of dollars)	State Share (in thousands of dollars)	Taxes per Employee
Income	31,482	28.6	26,983	4,499	$230.52
FICA—Employees	24,589	22.3	24,589	—	180.04
FICA—Employers	24,589	22.3	24,589	—	180.04
Sales	8,980	8.1	—[a]	8,980	65.75
Excise, on gasoline	4,283	3.9	955	3,328	31.36
Excise, on tobacco	5,045	4.6	2,867	2,178	36.94
Unemployment insurance	11,243	10.2	1,408	9,835	82.32
Total increase in taxes	110,211	100.0	81,391	28,820	806.98

[a] Data not available.

Source: Compiled by the authors.

of increased taxes on Title X labor expenditures. With personal income taxes, FICA payments are the principal source of tax returns to the federal government.

Employers' payments to unemployment insurance funds are the third largest source of tax returns, comprising 10.2 percent of the total. Most payment ($9,835,000, or 87.5 percent) are to state funds, and unemployment insurance payments are the largest source of returns to states. The other major source of increased taxes is sales tax ($8,980,000).

The average Title X employee is estimated to earn approximately $3,180 in wages from the Job Opportunities Program. Of these wages, about $198, (or 6.2 percent) is paid in federal personal income taxes and another $33 goes for state income tax (see Figure 4.2). FICA withholding takes another $180; sales taxes ($66) and excise taxes ($68) reduce earned income after taxes to about $2,635 per employee. Thus Title X employees are subject to an effective total tax rate of 17.1 percent, bringing earnings after taxes down from about $138 to $114 per week.

FIGURE 4.2

Taxes on Employees' Earned Income

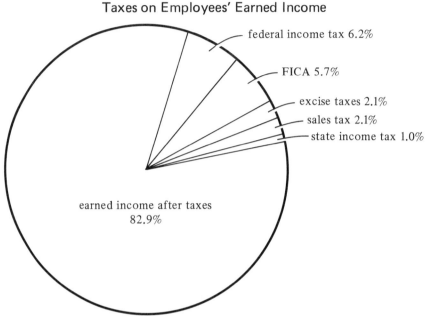

Source: Constructed by the authors.

Transfer Savings

Reductions in transfer payments comprise the other major component of financial benefits to governments stimulated by Title X labor expenditures. The following eight different transfer programs are considered in our analysis. Each is designed to meet different needs and provides benefits according to different formulas.

Unemployment Compensation. Unemployment compensation is a social-insurance program paying benefits to unemployed individuals on the basis of jobs covered under the program. Weekly benefit amounts are computed from base-period earnings and/or weeks of employment.

Social Security. Social Security is a social-insurance program providing old-age, survivors', and disability benefits to those who have paid in FICA contributions. Benefit amounts are based on contribution and current benefit schedules.

Aid to Families with Dependent Children (AFDC). AFDC is an income-mainten-ance program paying needs-based, means-tested benefits for dependent children in amounts varying according to state standards of need and state supplemen-tation (if any) of federal benefits.

Supplemental Security Income (SSI). SSI provides income-maintenance benefits to the aged, blind, and disabled, according to state standards of needs and pay-ment formulas, akin to AFDC.

General Relief or General Assistance (GA). GA is provided in 44 states for needy persons who do not receive adequate benefits from other programs.

Food Stamps. Food stamps provide a food-purchase subsidy based on need.

Medicaid. Medicaid provides medical insurance, based on need, to AFDC recipi-ents and other eligible persons.

Subsidized Housing. The primary form of directly subsidized housing is public housing in which rent payments are based on ability to pay, rather than on value. Other forms, including Section 8 rent subsidies, are still of minor impor-tance.

In general, estimated transfer savings are based on data provided by workers in the sample on the types and amounts of transfer payments received prior to and during Title X employment. The underlying assumption is that transfer payments received during Title X employment that are lower than those re-ceived prior to it represent a reduction in transfer payments due to Title X employment. Title X participants receiving unemployment compensation prior to Title X employment, for example, will not be eligible to receive payments during Title X employment. Any reduction in transfer payments is a return to government for the estimated duration of Title X employment, or, in the case of unemployment compensation, until the benefits expire.* The following equation expresses the general form of the calculation of reductions in each of eight transfer payments for each employee:†

---

*The possibility that income from Title X employment may have reduced means-tested benefits for a longer period of time, by bringing employees and/or their families over the income maximum for benefit eligibility, cannot be explored. Thus, estimates of means-tested transfer-payment reductions may be conservative.

†In calculating transfer savings and federal/state shares, possible reductions in federal and state costs of administering the transfer programs were ignored. Such reductions are, at best, conjectural, due to the minor impact of Title X on the overall caseloads of programs. Moreover, it is not altogether clear that a reduction in caseloads would produce significant administrative savings. Thus, all calculations are based upon changes in payments to claimants.

$$
\begin{bmatrix}
\text{Reduction in} \\
\text{transfer pay-} \\
\text{ments attrib-} \\
\text{utable to} \\
\text{Title X}
\end{bmatrix}
=
\begin{bmatrix}
\text{average weekly} \\
\text{benefits for} \\
\text{each transfer} \\
\text{prior to Title X} \\
\text{employment}
\end{bmatrix}
-
\begin{bmatrix}
\text{average weekly} \\
\text{benefits for each} \\
\text{transfer after} \\
\text{Title X employ-} \\
\text{ment}
\end{bmatrix}
\times
\begin{bmatrix}
\text{estimated} \\
\text{duration of} \\
\text{transfer} \\
\text{reduction}
\end{bmatrix}
$$

Unadjusted reductions in transfer payments are estimated at $45,099,000, or 29.0 percent of total direct returns from labor expenditures. This is an average of about $330 per employee, about two-thirds of which (67.2 percent) is returned to the federal government. The composition of transfer returns is presented in Table 4.4.

Reduced unemployment compensation benefits account for the highest proportion of transfer savings, 37.9 percent. For every labor dollar spent on Title X, more than 3 cents is returned via reduced unemployment compensation. The savings in unemployment compensation amount to $124.85 per Title X employee. Table 4.4 shows that most of the unemployment compensation return (79.8 percent) accrues to the federal government. This surprising

TABLE 4.4

Unadjusted Reductions in Transfer Payments: Job Opportunities Program

Transfer Payment	Reduction in Payments (in thousands of dollars)	Percent of Total Transfer Savings	Federal Share (in thousands of dollars)	State Share (in thousands of dollars)	Benefit Savings per Employee
Unemployment compensation	17,052	37.9	13,607	3,445	124.85
Social Security	1,256	2.8	1,256	—[a]	9.20
AFDC	4,546	10.1	3,579	967	33.29
General Relief	7,522	16.7	—	7,522	55.08
SSI	446	1.0	429	17	3.26
Food stamps	7,709	17.1	7,709	—	56.45
Medicaid	6,100	13.5	3,251	2,849	44.66
Public housing	468	1.0	468	—	3.43
Total reductions in transfers	45,099	100.0	30,299	14,800	330.22

[a] Data not available.

Source: Compiled by the authors.

TABLE 4.5

Unadjusted Labor Returns by Project Type
(thousands of dollars and percent of returns on labor expenditures)

Project Type	Total Labor Expenditures	Increased Taxes	Transfer Savings	Total Returns on Labor
Public works	44,297	8,118.0	2,468.9	10,586.9
		18.3	5.6	23.9
Civil works	26,838	4,767.5	1,955.0	6,722.5
		17.8	7.3	25.1
Forestry	95,804	17,962.0	10,107.3	28,069.3
		18.7	10.6	29.3
Rehabilitation	140,304	29,486.2	12,966.9	42,453.1
		21.0	9.3	30.3
Service	172,015	41,925.0	13,607.8	55,532.8
		24.4	7.9	32.3
Training	33,133	6,149.8	3,219.0	9,368.8
		18.6	9.7	28.3
Other	8,876	1,802.4	773.7	2,576.1
		20.3	8.7	29.0
Total	521,267	110,210.9	45,098.6	155,309.5
		21.1	8.7	29.8

Source: Compiled by the authors.

distribution of returns is partly a product of the fact that a number of Title X workers had been unemployed for many weeks and were drawing either Supplemental Unemployment Assistance (SUA) or food-stamp benefits. It is also a function of our methodology.*

Among means-tested transfers, reductions in government cost are substantial for food stamps ($7,709,000), General Relief ($7,522,000), Medicaid ($6,100,000), and AFDC ($4,546,000). Savings are less for Social Security,

---

*Lacking information on benefit weeks claimed prior to Title X, we assumed (only for purposes of allocation of returns to the federal and state governments) that employees were eligible for SUA and food stamps. Thus, returns to the federal government are overstated, and returns to states equally understated. This is another instance of being conservative with the net-cost methodology, since it tends to understate the redistribution of returns from the federal to the state and local governments. This redistribution is of policy relevance and is discussed later in this chapter.

Supplemental Security Income, and publicly supported housing. In the first two instances, very few employees experienced a change in benefit status during Title X employment; in the case of public housing, the modest return is more a function of small reductions in monthly rent subsidies or housing-assistance payments. Overall, means-tested cash-transfer payments account for 30.5 percent of transfer savings ($100.83 per employee). In-kind transfers are 31.6 percent of the savings, amounting to a cash value of $104.54 per employee.

It is notable that the direct returns on Title X labor expenditures vary for different types of projects. Table 4.5 shows the increased taxes and transfer savings received by governments from different Title X project types.

Labor expenditures on construction projects (public works and civil works) generate the lowest proportion of direct returns to government from transfer savings and increased taxes. Whereas Title X nonconstruction projects return an average of 30.7 cents per dollar to government from labor expenditures, construction projects return an average of only 24.3 cents per dollar. Transfer savings are particularly low (6.2 percent, versus 9.1 percent for nonconstruction projects), reflecting the lower incidence of transfer receipts by construction workers prior to Title X.

The rate of return on labor expenditures is highest for service and rehabilitation projects. On these two project types, increased taxes, particularly personal income taxes, account for a substantial proportion of returns. This is consistent with the fact that employees on service and rehabilitation projects average a higher total family income and higher Title X earnings than do employees on other types of projects.

ADJUSTED RETURNS TO GOVERNMENT FROM TITLE X LABOR EXPENDITURES

Adjusted labor returns take into consideration the likelihood that a portion of the employment and earnings derived from Title X would have occurred in the absence of the program. If they had not been hired under Title X, most employees would have had at least a brief spell of employment, earning income that would generate increased taxes and saving some of the transfer-payment costs to governments. Thus, in order to estimate the returns on labor that are directly attributable to the Job Opportunities Program, the likely employment and earnings in the absence of Title X must first be estimated. Then, previous calculations of increased taxes and transfer savings must be adjusted downward to reflect the earnings and weeks of employment projected for Title X employees in the absence of the program. A comparison of employment and earnings under Title X with those projected as likely in the absence of the program is shown for the sample in Table 4.6.

TABLE 4.6

Comparison of Actual and Adjusted Title X
Employment and Earnings: Employee Sample

Measure	Mean	Total
Weeks worked on Title X	35.44	69,777
Estimated weeks worked in the absence of Title X	10.41	20,506
Adjusted weeks worked	25.03	49,271
Title X earnings	$4,751.00	$9,354,219
Estimated earnings in the absence of Title X	$1,429.00	$2,813,117
Adjusted earnings	$3,322.00	$6,541,102

Note: The weeks-worked-on-Title X figure includes an estimate for 13 participants on whom there were no data from the survey instrument. The weeks-worked figure presented here is thus slightly different from the actual figure for the sample, excluding the 13 missing cases—35.2 weeks. Title X earnings presented here are also slightly different—$4,751, compared with $4,753.

Source: Compiled by the authors.

Sampled employees average 35.44 weeks of work on Title X projects. It is estimated, however, that on the average, they would have worked 10.41 weeks during the same period in the absence of the program. Thus, the additional number of weeks of work attributable to Title X is 25.03 weeks per sampled employee. This adjustment primarily affects the calculation of transfer-payment savings to government, which are a function of weeks employed under Title X. Whereas estimates of unadjusted returns are based upon total weeks worked (35.44, on the average), adjusted returns are estimated only on the basis of individual employment attributable to Title X (25.03 weeks, on the average).

Similarly, total Title X earnings of sampled employees are $9,354,219, or $4,751 per employee. However, these same employees are estimated to have been likely to earn $2,813,117 in the absence of the program, reducing adjusted earnings attributable to new employment from the Job Opportunities Program to $6,541,102 ($3,322 per employee). Adjusted tax revenues from Title X wages and salaries will, therefore, be lower than unadjusted estimates, since they are based upon adjusted employee earnings, not upon total employee earnings, from the program.

Table 4.6 suggests that, for sampled employees, about 71 percent of the person-weeks of employment, and 70 percent of the earnings, provided by Title X were new employment and earnings that would not have occurred

TABLE 4.7

Total Adjusted Returns from Labor Expenditures: Job Opportunities Program

Cost/Return Item	Total Returns	Tax Revenues	Reduction in Transfer Payments
Total Title X labor costs (in thousands of dollars)	521,267	_a	—
Adjusted returns (in thousands of dollars)	122,204	77,649	44,555
Percent of labor cost	23.4	14.9	8.5
Percent of returns	100.0	63.5	36.5
Returns per person-month	$186.51	$118.51	$68.00
Federal share (in thousands of dollars)	83,784	57,366	26,418
State share (in thousands of dollars)	38,420	20,283	18,137
Net adjusted labor cost (in thousands of dollars)	399,063	—	—

a Data not available.
Source: Compiled by the authors.

naturally in the absence of the program. Since the probram placed a priority upon hiring the unemployed, these figures provide a very rough index of the efficiency of Title X in achieving this objective.

As discussed in Chapter 2, the Job Opportunities Program is projected to spend about $737,924,000 in Title X, other federal, state, local, and private funds to support 2,255 projects. Of these monies, $521,267,000 is estimated to be labor expenditures, providing about 655,211 person-months of employment to 136,571 persons. However, it is estimated that $154,178,000 in salaries and fringes would have occurred in the absence of the program. The earnings attributable to Title X employment are $367,089,000, based on 459,631 person-months of new employment. Based upon these projections, estimates of the adjusted returns and the net labor cost of the Job Opportunities Program are presented in Table 4.7.

Labor expenditures of $521,267,000 generate adjusted primary cash returns to government of $122,204,000. Thus, the net adjusted labor costs of the Job Opportunities Program are $399,063,000. The actual returns to government are 23.4 percent of gross labor expenditures. In other words, for each dollar spent on wages and fringe benefits, almost 24 cents is returned directly

FIGURE 4.3

Net Labor Cost of Title X

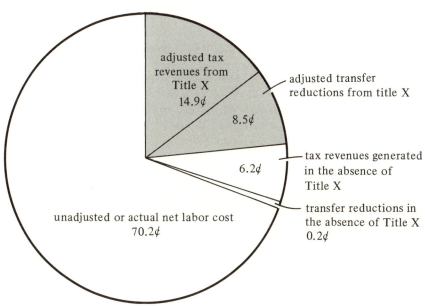

adjusted tax
revenues from
Title X
14.9¢

adjusted transfer
reductions from title X

8.5¢

tax revenues generated
in the absence of
Title X

6.2¢

unadjusted or actual net labor cost
70.2¢

transfer reductions in
the absence of Title X
0.2¢

Source: Compiled by the authors.

to the governmnent in tax revenues and reductions in transfer payments. Almost $84 million (about 68.6 percent of returns) accrues to the federal government, including 73.4 percent of increased taxes. State governments receive $38.4 million, with returns about evenly divided among taxes and transfer savings. Adjusted returns—those attributable to the Job Opportunities Program—and unadjusted returns—those representing the actual costs of the program—are contrasted in Figure 4.3.

The unadjusted net labor cost constitutes 70.2 cents for each dollar spent. Actual tax revenues generated from Title X earnings amount to 21 cents per dollar of labor expenditure. However, a portion of this tax revenue, 6.2 cents, would have accrued to the government in the absence of the program, due to normal economic activity. Hence, only 14.9 cents of the actual tax revenues can be attributed exclusively to the Job Opportunities Program. The actual reduction in transfer payments from Title X employment is much less, 8.7 cents for each dollar of labor expenditure. However, only .2 cents per dollar of labor expenditure would have accrued in the absence of Title X. Thus, almost all of the actual reduction in transfer payments (8.5 cents) is directly attributable to the Job Opportunities Program. The portion of tax revenues and transfer savings likely to have occurred in the absence of Title X can be added to the actual net labor cost to arrive at the adjusted net labor cost per dollar of labor expenditure, 76.6 cents.

Increased tax revenues account for 63.5 percent of adjusted labor returns. On the average, $569 is returned to government in income, sales, excise, FICA, and unemployment insurance taxes for each Title X employee. A breakdown of these adjusted tax returns is presented in Table 4.8.

Personal income tax revenue constitutes 29.1 percent of the total adjusted tax revenue, with 84.6 percent of income taxes accruing to the federal government. The largest single source of adjusted tax returns is FICA payments made by the employee and the employer. Together, the FICA contributions account for 44.6 percent of the total adjusted tax savings. All of the FICA contributions accrue to the federal government. Sales and excise taxes, in total, constitute 16.0 percent of adjusted tax revenue. Overall, 73.9 percent of increased tax revenues return to the federal government, principally from FICA and income taxes. The state-government share of adjusted tax revenue is 26.1 percent, with sales and unemployment insurance taxes being the major sources of state tax returns.

TABLE 4.8

Adjusted Tax Revenues from Labor Expenditures: Job Opportunities Program

Type of Tax	Tax Revenues (thousands of dollars)	Percent of Total Tax Revenues	Federal Share (thousands of dollars)	State Share (thousands of dollars)	Taxes per Employee
Income	22,578	29.1	19.097	3,481	$165.31
FICA—employees	17,330	22.3	17,330	—	126.89
FICA—employers	17,330	22.3	17,330	—	126.89
Sales	6,078	7.9	—[a]	6,078	44.50
Excise, on gasoline	2,906	3.7	639	2,267	21.28
Excise, on tobacco	3,402	4.4	1,918	1,484	24.91
Unemployment insurance	8,025	10.3	1,052	6,973	58.76
Total tax revenues	77,649	100.00	47,366	20,283	568.54

[a] Data not available.
Source: Compiled by the authors.

TABLE 4.9

Adjusted Reduction in Transfer Payments:
Job Opportunities Program

Type of Transfer	Reduction in Transfers (thousands of dollars)	Percent of Total Reduction	Federal Share (in thousands of dollars)	State Share (in thousands of dollars)	Savings per Employee
Unemployment compensation	22,243	49.9	13,172	9,071	$162.87
Social Security	1,128	2.5	1,128	–	8.26
AFDC	3,622	8.1	3,038	584	26.52
General Relief	6,477	14.5	–a	6,477	47.42
SSI	351	0.8	343	8	2.56
Food stamps	5,985	13.4	5,985	–	43.83
Medicaid	4,391	9.9	2.394	1,997	32.15
Public housing	358	0.8	358	–	2.62
Total Reduction in Transfers	44,555	100.0	26,418	18,137	326.24

a Data not available.
Source: Compiled by the authors.

The reduction in transfer payments, adjusted for the estimated employment in the absence of Title X, totals $44,555,000, or 36.5 percent of total adjusted labor returns. The federal-government share of the reduction in adjusted transfer payments is 59.3 percent, or $26,418,000. The composition of transfer returns is presented in Table 4.9.

Savings in unemployment compensation benefits account for the largest proportion of adjusted transfer-payment savings, almost 50 percent of the total. In fact, unemployment compensation is the only case in which the adjusted return to government is greater than the unadjusted return. The reason is that those Title X employees who were employed prior to Title X employment would have been unemployed for several weeks if they had not obtained Title X employment. Moreover, it is assumed that these employees would have been eligible for unemployment compensation when unemployed. The first reason is a function of the discount model. Just as persons unemployed prior to Title X are likely to have been employed for a certain number of weeks if they hadn't been hired under Title X, so also are previously employed persons likely to have been unemployed for a portion of time, if they hadn't accepted Title X employment. The second assumption is reasonable, given the fact that the persons were employed prior to Title X and are projected to have been employed for most of the period of Title X employment, even if not hired for a Title X project. These employees are assumed to have been eligible for the average weekly unemployment compensation benefit for their state of residence, a conservative assumption in light of their recent employment experience.*

It should be noted that the same assumptions do not apply to the means-tested transfers. Employed persons who were not receiving such transfers cannot be assumed to have been eligible for transfers as a result of projected unemployment. In general, such persons were employed prior to Title X, and would have worked for 16.6 of 20.6 weeks in the absence of Title X employment. Since they did not qualify for benefits prior to Title X and would have continued to earn income during the period of Title X, it is not plausible to assume that such persons would have become eligible for means-tested transfers during the four weeks of projected unemployment.

Thus, adjusted savings in means-tested transfers are lower than unadjusted savings to government. However, due to the increase in unemployment compensation, total adjusted transfer returns decline by only $544,000, or 1.2 percent. Unemployment compensation savings encompass more than $22 million of the $44.5 million in returns. Other principal sources of savings are General Relief ($6,477,000), food stamps ($5,985,000), Medicaid ($4,391,000), and AFDC ($3,622,000). Means-tested cash transfers account for 26.0 percent of returns; in-kind transfers account for 24.1 percent.

As was the case with unadjusted returns, the adjusted returns from Title X labor expenditures vary with different types of projects, as illustrated in Table 4.10.

As with unadjusted returns, construction projects generate lower adjusted returns per dollar of labor expenditures than do nonconstruction projects. The net direct labor cost of public-works and civil-works construction projects is 82.2 percent of labor expenditures, in comparison with only 75.7 percent for nonconstruction projects. Service projects bring the highest adjusted returns on labor, yielding 28.8 percent of returns (for a net cost of 71.2 percent of labor expenditures). Increased taxes from employees on service projects are

---

*An example illustrates these assumptions. The average Title X duration of employment is 20.6 weeks, and roughly speaking, previously employed Title X workers are projected to average about four weeks of unemployment in the absence of Title X. In other words, they were employed prior to Title X and would have worked for 16.6 out of 20.6 weeks during the period of Title X employment. Almost certainly, they would have earned benefits to cover the brief period of projected unemployment. At a 1976 national average of $68 per week of unemployment compensation, the 18.3 percent of workers employed prior to Title X would claim about $6,798,000 in UI. This additional return to governments is reduced by about $1,617,000, as a result of applying the employment-discount factor to those Title X workers who were unemployed and receiving benefits prior to Title X.

TABLE 4.10

Adjusted Labor Returns by Project Type
(thousands of dollars and percent of returns on labor expenditures)

Project Type	Total Labor Expenditures	Increased Taxes	Transfer Savings	Total Returns on Labor
Public works	44,297	5,072.1	2,704.4	7,776.5
	100.0	11.5	6.1	17.6
Civil works	26,838	2,976.1	1,915.4	4,891.5
	100.0	11.1	7.1	18.2
Forestry	95,894	12,316.0	10,102.0	22,418.0
	100.0	12.9	10.5	23.4
Rehabilitation	140,304	16,706.5	10,950.5	27,657.0
	100.0	11.9	7.8	19.7
Service	172,015	35,006.1	14,487.1	49,493.2
	100.0	20.4	8.4	28.8
Training	33,133	4,346.3	3,642.4	7,988.7
	100.0	13.1	11.0	24.1
Other	8,876	1,225.8	753.5	1,979.3
	100.0	13.8	8.5	22.3
Total	521,267	77,648.9	44,555.3	122,204.2
	100.0	14.9	8.5	23.4

Source: Compiled by the authors.

particularly high, as a function of the fact that these employees are projected to experience the least employment in the absence of Title X. Thus, the reduction in taxes due to this expected employment is less than for employees on other types of projects.

At the opposite extreme are employees of rehabilitation projects. These employees are projected to have the most employment in the absence of Title X, slightly more than construction-project workers. In addition, higher average family income, and lower expected unemployment compensation in the absence of Title X, combine to make adjusted returns, particularly taxes, from rehabilitation-project workers much lower than the unadjusted returns shown in Table 4.5. As a consequence, the net adjusted returns from labor expenditures of rehabilitation projects are below the Title X mean (19.7 percent versus 23.4 percent), even though unadjusted returns were slightly above the mean.

The foregoing presentation and analysis of returns on labor expenditures adopts the perspective of government, since net cost is essentially an estimation of the true government balance sheet for a program, after the effects of the tax

TABLE 4.11

Net Title X Earnings of Employees

Measure	Amount	Percent
Average gross Title X earnings	$3,180	100.0
Forgone net earnings in the absence of Title X	730	23.0
Income taxes	165	5.2
FICA	127	4.0
Sales and excise taxes	91	2.9
Lost transfer benefits	326	10.2
Net Title X earnings	1,741	54.7

Source: Compiled by the authors.

and transfer dynamics are projected. As a final observation, it is relevant to examine the effects of these dynamics on the net earnings of employees. As shown in Table 4.11, the impacts of forgone earnings, taxes, and lost transfers on the Title X earnings of employees are considerable.

Of the $3,180 earned by the average Title X employee, it is projected that almost 30 percent ($940) would have been earned from other employment in the absence of Title X. However, these forgone earnings would have been taxed and also accompanied by lost transfers. If one assumes, for purposes of illustration, approximately the same rates of taxes and transfer loss that are applied to Title X, the net forgone earnings are $730, 23 percent of Title X earned income. Title X earnings are subject to an effective total tax rate of 12.1 percent. In addition, it is estimated that the average employee loses another 10.2 percent of earnings in forgone transfer benefits. Only $1,741, or 54.7 percent of gross Title X earnings, remains after all taxes and forgone earnings and benefits are calculated. Average gross weekly earnings of about $138 are reduced to a net of approximately $75.50 per week.

TAX RETURNS FROM TITLE X NONLABOR EXPENDITURES

Most Title X projects were designed to be labor intensive, and the returns from labor expenditures have been detailed in the previous section. Almost all projects, however, have made nonlabor purchases. In fact, some projects have devoted a majority of their total funds to nonlabor items, the bulk of them being purchased with non-Title X funds. Nonlabor purchases range from construction materials (sand, stone, cement, lumber, steel) to medical equipment, from air and automobile travel to legal and architectural and engineering services, and include utilities, space rental, and office equipment and materials.

Returns to governments from nonlabor expenditures are in the form of extra taxes. However, there are literally thousands of federal, state, and local business- and sales-tax rates, making calculation of these taxes infeasible. Moreover, the use of published tax rates and schedules to apply to before-tax business profits would be inaccurate, since tax systems are now replete with incentives, allowances, and other so-called loopholes encouraging higher profits. What are needed are effective tax rates applicable to different industries, that is, the actual taxes paid by producers as a proportion of the value of their total output.

Our methodology utilizes readily available published data, by industry, in the Commerce Department's monthly *Survey of Current Business*. Tables in this publication provide data, at the two-digit SIC (Standard Industrial Classification) Code level, on total direct corporate tax payments to all levels of government, on total indirect taxes—sales, excise, property—paid to all levels of government, and on gross domestic product (GDP).* Effective direct and indirect tax rates can be calculated for each industry as the ratio of taxes paid to the market value of the industry's net output (GDP). Thus, tax returns to government from each industry as a result of nonlabor expenditures can be expressed as follows:

$$
\begin{array}{l}\text{Net} \\ \text{additional} \\ \text{tax returns}\end{array} = \begin{pmatrix}\text{Nonlabor} \\ \text{expenditure} \\ \text{in an industry}\end{pmatrix} \times \left[\left(\dfrac{\text{Direct}}{\text{taxes}} \right) + \left(\dfrac{\text{Indirect}}{\text{taxes}} \right) \right]
$$

It should be noted that the tax and GDP data used in these calculations are from 1975, the most recent year for which complete data were available at the time of this study. Moreover, all nonlabor expenditures are subject to tax returns; no discounting done, as in the labor-return computations.

A problem in estimating returns from nonlabor Title X expenditures is that projects are not required to submit to EDA an ongoing record of expenditures. A data base containing accurate information on the projects' nonlabor purchases, by industry, does not exist. Faced with this problem, we examined the project records at all projects visited for the purposes of estimating long-term impacts. Data at the two-digit SIC Code level were obtained from 50 projects—a combination of actual nonlabor-product expenditures incurred by each project and

---

*Identification of nontax items in the indirect-tax data is based upon unpublished data supplied by the Bureau of Economic Analysis (BEA) of the Department of Commerce. These data also allow allocation of indirect taxes to the federal or the state/local governments.

TABLE 4.12

Project Expenditures: 50 Projects

Project Type	Number of Projects	Total Expenditures	Nonlabor Expenditure	Labor Intensity
Public-works construction	6	$1,146,108	$447,445	61.0
Civil-works construction	6	1,043,235	565,027	45.8
Forestry, recreation	12	2,697,520	536,281	80.1
Rehabilitation, repair	12	3,434,962	710,776	74.3
Service	9	1,830,984	113,608	93.8
Training	3	1,256,229	37,302	97.0
Other	2	334,460	111,330	66.7
Total	50	11,743,498	2,521,769	78.5

Source: Compiled by the authors.

planned nonlabor expenditures cited by the project director and/or responsible agent.

The remainder of this section is based upon the data from the 50 projects. Understandably, estimates of returns to government from nonlabor expenditures of 50 projects are less precise than the estimates presented earlier on returns from labor dollars. This is a necessary limitation of the study, a concession to the limited resources and time available. The relative focus in the labor returns, however, is consistent with the employment goals of Title X and with the methodological complexities of estimating returns on labor.

Project expenditures are presented in Table 4.12. In the sample of 50 projects, nonlabor items worth over $2.5 million were purchased, compared with a total expenditure of more than $11.7 million. Labor intensity is 78.5 percent. However, because the sample has an overrepresentation of construction projects, these figures should not be considered as an exact indication of the expenditures pattern of the universe of projects. More interesting are the distinctions in expenditures among project types. As would be expected, construction projects are far less labor intensive than other types of projects. Civil-works construction projects are the least labor intensive (45.8 percent), followed by public-works construction projects (61.0 percent). Forestry and rehabilitation projects are about equally labor intensive (80.1 percent and 79.3 percent, respectively). Service (93.8 percent) and training (97.0 percent) projects are considerably more labor intensive than other types of projects.*

---

*These labor-intensity figures are higher than those projected for the entire universe (in Chapter 2) and are a product of the small sample. The relative patterns of labor intensity across different project types, however, are very similar for both the sample and universe.

TABLE 4.13

Title X Nonlabor Expenditures: by Project Type, and Industry, for 50 Projects
(thousands of dollars)

SIC Code	Industry	Project Type							
		Public-Works Construction	Civil-Works Construction	Forestry, Recreation	Rehabilitation, Repair	Service	Training	Other	Total
10–14	Mining	—*	5	8	5	—	—	—	18
15–17	Contract construction	—	1	46	110	—	—	—	165
20–23, 26–31, 19, 24,	Nondurable goods	10	32	12	6	16	2	8	86
25, 32–39	Durable goods	140	264	155	186	1	3	37	786
40–47	Transporation	—	—	14	—	26	17	—	57
48–49	Communication and utilities	1	—	5	2	2	—	—	10
50	Wholesale trade	61	71	45	109	1	2	—	289
52–59	Retail trade	199	76	149	197	31	7	25	684
60–67	Finance, Insurance and Real Estate	3	2	4	—	6	2	—	17
70–89	Services	30	112	52	73	8	—	41	316
	Other	4	2	46	15	22	4	—	93
	Total	448	565	536	711	113	37	111	2,521

* Data not available.
Source: Compiled by the authors.

TABLE 4.14

Returns from Direct and Indirect Taxes on
Nonlabor Expenditures of 50 Projects
(dollars and percent of returns on expenditures)

Project Type	Nonlabor Expenditures	Direct Taxes (Effective Rate)	Indirect Taxes (Effective Rate)	Total Taxes (Effective Rate)
Public-works	$447,445	$16,222	$54,736	$70,958
construction		3.6	12.2	15.9
Civil-works	565,027	21,971	42,597	64,568
construction		3.0	7.5	11.4
Forestry,	536,281	17,661	49,728	67,389
recreation		3.3	9.3	12.6
Rehabilitation,	710,776	21,845	69,991	91,836
repair		3.1	9.8	12.9
Service	113,608	3,965	12,388	16,353
		3.5	10.9	14.4
Training	37,302	1,117	3,783	4,900
		3.0	10.1	13.1
Other	111,330	3,469	7,307	10,776
		3.1	6.6	9.7
Total	2,521,769	86,250	240,530	326,780
		3.4	9.5	13.0

Source: Compiled by the authors.

TABLE 4.15

Returns from Nonlabor Costs as a Proportion
of Total Expenditures: 50 Projects

Project Type	Total Expenditures	Total Taxes on Nonlabor Expenditures	Return Rate
Public-works construction	$1,146,108	$70,958	6.2
Civil-works construction	1,043,235	64,568	6.2
Forestry, recreation	2,697,520	67,389	2.5
Rehabilitation, repair	3,434,962	91,836	2.7
Service	1,830,984	16,353	0.9
Training	1,256,229	4,900	0.4
Other	334,460	10,776	3.2
Total	$11,743,498	$326,780	2.8

Source: Compiled by the authors.

The nonlabor expenditures of the 50 projects are detailed, by industry, in Table 4.13. As can be seen from the table, durable goods (concrete, steel, pipes, tools, other construction materials) and the retail trades account for the largest proportions of nonlabor purchases. Together, these two categories account for over 58 percent of labor expenditures by the sample of 50 projects. The relatively high level of expenditures for services largely reflects projects' tendencies to lease or rent equipment, rather than to purchase it outright.

For each type of project, direct and indirect taxes are calculated by applying tax rates to expenditures in each industry category. These rates, presented in Appendix C, are derived from aforementioned data in the *Survey of Current Business*. Direct- and indirect-tax returns from the nonlabor expenditures of each type of project are presented in Table 4.14.

The estimated total tax return to government from the nonlabor expenditures of 50 projects is $326,780, or 13 percent of the total nonlabor expenditures. Almost three-quarters (73.6 percent) of returns are from indirect taxes (sales, excise, property). Tax returns vary somewhat by type of project, but the variation is not great. Tax returns on nonlabor costs, as a proportion of total project costs, however, differ considerably by project type, as shown in Table 4.15.

Taxes on nonlabor expenditures of construction projects return 6.2 cents for every dollar of funds granted to such projects. This rate of return is more than twice as great as the rates for forestry projects (2.5 percent) and rehabilitation projects (2.7 percent). Returns from nonlabor expenditures of service and

TABLE 4.16

Federal and State/Local Shares of Tax Returns on Nonlabor Expenditures: 50 Projects

Project Type	Federal Government			State/Local Governments		
	Direct Taxes	Indirect Taxes	Total	Direct Taxes	Indirect Taxes	Total
Public-works construction	$13,789	$5,214	$19,003	$2,433	$49,522	$51,955
Civil-works construction	18,675	7,824	26,499	3,296	34,773	38,069
Forestry, recreation	15,012	4,846	19,858	2,649	44,882	47,531
Rehabilitation, repair	18,568	8,161	26,729	3,277	61,830	65,107
Service	3,370	1,967	5,337	595	10,421	11,016
Training	949	704	1,653	168	3,079	3,247
Other	3,949	856	3,805	520	6,451	6,971
Total	73,312	29,572	102,884	12,938	210,958	223,896
Percent	85.0	12.3	31.5	15.0	87.7	68.5

Source: Compiled by the authors.

training projects are almost negligible. Overall, every Title X dollar has returned 2.8 cents in taxes on the nonlabor expenditures of the 50 sampled projects.

The distribution of returns to the federal government or state/local governments vary greatly with the type of tax. In general, most of the direct taxes bring returns to the federal government, while most of the indirect taxes accrue to state and local treasuries. Unpublished BEA data provide a basis for estimating the distribution of indirect returns, while projections from time-series data in the *Statistical Abstract of the United States* yield a distribution of direct returns. The estimated distribution of direct and indirect tax returns to the federal government and state/local governments appears in Table 4.16.

Most of the direct taxes (85 percent) go to the federal government, an expected finding in light of federal tax rates on corporate profits. Most of the indirect taxes (87.7 percent) go to state and local treasuries; these are sales, property, excise, and other taxes that are most often levied by nonfederal governments. Overall, 68.5 percent of total taxes on nonlabor expenditures accrue to state and local governments. It should be noted that, in proportion to their Title X investments, state and local governments benefit (relative to the federal government) from tax returns on nonlabor expenditures. For the 50 sampled projects, the federal share of estimated cost is about 85 percent. Yet, state and local governments get almost 70 percent of the tax benefit from nonlabor expenditures. Expressed another way, the tax return on nonlabor purchases is about 28 percent of total project dollars. The return on investment to the federal government is only 1.0 percent; the return on investment to state and local governments is 13.2 percent.

These findings from a sample of 50 projects cannot be regarded as precisely generalizable for the entire Job Opportunities Program. The sample includes only 2.2 percent of Title X projects and 1.6 percent of total project funds. However, rough estimates of the returns to government from nonlabor expenditures of Title X money may be calculated by weighting the sample to the universe in a similar manner to that employed for labor returns. Table 4.17 gives estimates of tax returns from nonlabor expenditures for the Job Opportunities Program.

Overall, direct and indirect taxes return about $32 million to governments, from almost $237 million in Title X nonlabor expenditures. This represents a return of 13.5 cents for each dollar of nonlabor spending. Indirect taxes account for a majority of the returns (74.8 percent). Public-works construction projects, which received 13.1 percent of total Title X funds, are the source of 27.2 percent of tax returns on nonlabor expenditures. Public- and civil-works construction projects provide 39.8 percent of tax returns on nonlabor costs, even though they receive only 21.3 percent of Title X dollars. In contrast, service and training projects (receiving 32.9 percent of Title X funds) provide only 19.9 percent of returns on nonlabor costs.

The distribution of returns to the federal government or to state/local governments from taxes on nonlabor expenditures is presented in Table 4.18.

TABLE 4.17

Returns from Direct and Indirect Taxes on Nonlabor Expenditures: Job Opportunities Program
(thousands of dollars)

Project Type	Nonlabor Expenditures	Direct Taxes	Indirect Taxes	Total Tax Returns
Public-works con- struction	55,094	1,997	6,740	8,737
Civil-works con- struction	35,233	1,370	2,656	4,026
Forestry, recreation	27,820	916	2,580	3,496
Rehabilitation, repair	71,493	2,197	7,040	9,237
Service	36,940	1,289	4,028	5,317
Training	7,292	219	739	958
Other	2,785	87	183	270
Total	236,657	8,075	23,966	32,041

Source: Compiled by the authors.

TABLE 4.18

Federal and State/Local Shares of Tax Returns from Nonlabor Expenditures: The Job Opportunities Program
(thousands of dollars)

Project Type	Federal Share	State/Local Share
Public-works construction	2,339	6,398
Civil-works construction	1,653	2,373
Forestry, recreation	1,030	2,466
Rehabilitation, repair	1,688	6,549
Service	1,736	3,581
Training	324	634
Other	95	175
Total	9,865	22,176
Percent	30.8	69.2

Source: Compiled by the authors.

NET COST OF TITLE X

State and local governments received more than $22 million in taxes from the $237 million spent on nonlabor items in the Job Opportunities Program. This represents 69.2 percent of the total taxes on nonlabor expenditures. The federal government receives almost $10 million, or 30.8 percent of indirect taxes on nonlabor spending.

THE NET COST OF THE
JOB OPPORTUNITIES PROGRAM

The estimates of primary returns from the labor and nonlabor investments of Title X can be combined to arrive at a total estimate of the net cost of the Job Opportunities Program, prior to indirect and induced effects of expenditures. Table 4.19 presents estimates of both the unadjusted and the adjusted cost, the latter accounting for probable employment in the absence of the program.

Of the $758 million that will have been spent on the Job Opportunities Program by the federal government and by state and local governments, almost $188 million returns directly to government coffers via increased taxes and

TABLE 4.19

Net Cost of the Job Opportunities Program:
Unadjusted and Adjusted

Measure	Unadjusted Cost		Adjusted Cost	
	Amount (thousands of dollars)	Percent	Amount (thousands of dollars)	Percent
Gross program expenditures	757,924	100.0	757,924	100.0
Tax returns from labor costs	110,211	14.5	77,649	10.3
Transfer savings from labor costs	45,099	6.0	44,555	5.9
Tax returns from nonlabor costs	32,041	4.2	32,041	4.2
Total primary returns	187,351	24.7	154,245	20.4
Net program cost	570,573	75.3	603,679	79.6

Source: Compiled by the authors.

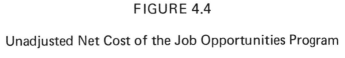

FIGURE 4.4

Unadjusted Net Cost of the Job Opportunities Program

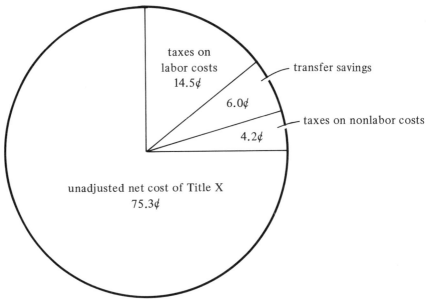

Source: Constructed by the authors.

reduced transfer payments. The net unadjusted program cost of Title X is about $570 million, 75.3 percent of gross outlays. (See Figure 4.4.) A majority of returns, 53.8 percent, are increased taxes generated by labor expenditures. Transfer savings account for about 24.1 percent of returns. Taxes from nonlabor expenditures encompass 17.1 percent of returns, even though nonlabor costs are 31.2 percent of total Title X costs.

When the probable employment of Title X participants in the absence of the program is controlled for, the estimate of the net cost of the Job Opportunities Program increases to almost $604 million. Direct returns to government are 20.4 percent of gross outlays. Discounts for expected employment in the absence of Title X primarily affect tax returns on labor costs, which drop to 10.3 cents per gross dollar of outlay (as shown in Figure 4.5), or 50.3 percent of total returns. Transfer savings drop only marginally, to 5.9 percent of gross program costs, and taxes on nonlabor expenditures remain constant. Thus, the adjusted net cost of the Job Opportunities Program is 79.6 percent of gross program expenditures.

FIGURE 4.5

Adjusted Net Cost of the Job Opportunities Program

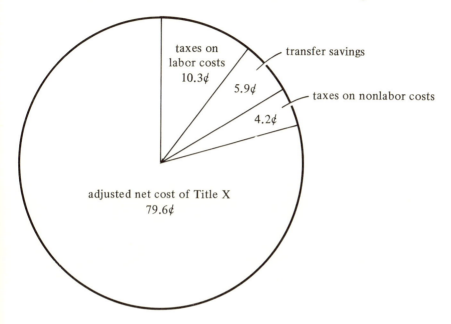

Source: Constructed by the authors.

The dynamics of program investments and returns bring about a redistribution of funds from the federal government to the state/local governments, a phenomenon which should be of interest to policy makers. The flow of funds is shown in Figure 4.6.

Total federal funds for the Job Opportunities Program (Title X plus other federal funds) are about $620 million, or 81.9 percent of total funds. Returns to the federal government are slightly over $121 million, or 19.6 percent of federal funds granted to the program. Thus, the net federal cost is about $499 million, or 87.4 percent of net program costs. In contrast, returns to state and local governments are almost $66 million, which is fully 55.9 percent of state and local investments in the program. The net program cost to state and local governments is only about $52 million, or 9.1 percent of net Title X costs. In other words, for every dollar the federal government grants to Title X, it gets back 19.5 cents. States and localities receive back 55.9 cents for every dollar granted to the program.

FIGURE 4.6

Flow of Funds (Unadjusted) among the Federal and State/Local Governments

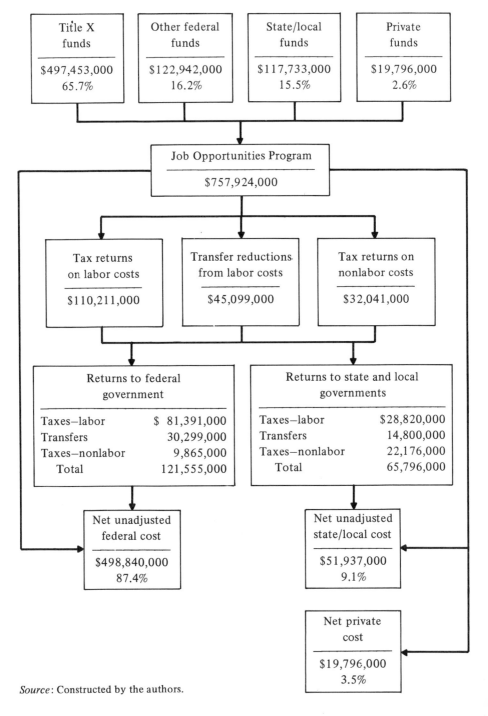

Source: Constructed by the authors.

TABLE 4.20

Adjusted Flow of Funds among the Federal and the State/Local Governments

Measure	Federal (thousands of dollars)	State/Local (thousands of dollars)	Private (thousands of dollars)
Gross program outlays	620,395	117,733	19,796
Tax returns on labor costs	57,366	20,283	—[a]
Transfer savings on labor costs	26,418	18,137	—
Tax returns on nonlabor costs	9,865	22,176	—
Total returns	93,649	60,596	—
Percent of gross outlays	15.1	51.5	0
Net program cost	526,746	57,137	19,796
Percent of gross outlays	84.9	48.5	100
Percent of net cost	87.2	9.5	3.3

[a] Data not available.
Source: Compiled by the authors.

Another way of looking at this shift in returns is to project the net unadjusted costs that would be borne by the federal and the state/local governments if returns were proportional to investments. This provides an estimate of the dollars shifted from the federal government to state and local governments as a result of Title X's pattern of program expenditures. Such a calculation shows that proportional returns to the federal government would be about $158 million, in comparison to actual returns of about $121 million. This means that Title X expenditures have resulted in a shift of about $37 million in returns from the federal treasury to state and local budgets. Such a shift is entirely consistent with the goals of the Job Opportunities Program, which is intended to provide a countercyclical stimulus to local areas with high unemployment and lagging economies.

The preceding analysis deals with unadjusted returns and net costs, since these represent the actual flow of dollars resulting from Title X investments. However, the employment-opportunity costs to workers (and resultant discounts, in returns) represent real costs to governments, since tax returns from projected earnings in the absence of Title X would, indeed, have been received by governments. Thus, the adjusted returns and net costs are a more accurate indicator of the impact of the Job Opportunities Program on different levels of government. These costs and returns are summarized in Table 4.20.

As seen in Table 4.20, the federal government receives only 60.7 percent of adjusted returns, even though it supplies 81.9 percent of the Title X investment. The net cost to the federal government is fully 84.9 percent of gross outlays, in comparison with only 48.5 percent for state and local governments. The true distributional impact of adjusted returns to different levels of government is an effective shift of almost $36 million in revenues from federal to state and local treasuries, prior to the multiplier effects of spending. This shift amounts to fully 30 percent of the state and local contribution to the program, and 23 percent of total adjusted returns to the program. Clearly, the Job Opportunities Program provides an economic stimulus to state and local governments, even when the employment-opportunity cost to workers (employment in the absence of Title X) is considered.

Another series of findings that would interest policy makers addresses the question of relative net costs of different types of programs. If net cost is an important factor in funding decisions, then certain types of programs appear somewhat more appealing than others, as shown in Table 4.21.

TABLE 4.21

Adjusted Returns and Net Cost by Project Type

Project Type	Total Expenditures (thousands of dollars)	Total Adjusted Returns (thousands of dollars)	Net Adjusted Cost (thousands of dollars	Percent of Gross Cost
Public works	99,391	16,513	82,878	83.4
Civil works	62,071	8,918	53,153	85.6
Forestry/recreation	123,624	25,914	97,710	79.0
Rehabilitation/repair	211,797	36,894	174,903	82.6
Service	208,955	54,810	154,145	73.8
Training	40,425	8,947	31,478	77.9
Other	11,661	2,249	9,412	80.7
Total	757,924	154,245	603,679	79.6

Source: Compiled by the authors.

Net costs as a proportion of gross costs are somewhat higher for construction projects than for other types funded under Title X. This phenomenon is a function of two factors. First, construction projects spend more than other projects on nonlabor items, which, on the average, bring lower returns to government than labor expenditures (13.5 percent versus 23.4 percent). Second,

TABLE 4.22

Gross and Adjusted Costs per Person-Year by Project Type

Project Type	Labor Cost per Person-Year		Total Cost per Person-Year		Person-Years of Employment per $1 Billion in Net Expenditures
	Gross	Net	Gross	Net	
Public works	$10,100	$8,400	$22,700	$19,060	52,600
Civil works	10,900	8,900	25,300	21,700	46,100
Forestry/recreation	8,800	6,700	11,300	9,000	111,100
Rehabilitation/repair	9,300	7,500	14,000	11,600	86,200
Service	10,900	7,800	13,200	9,800	102,000
Training	6,400	4,800	7,800	6,000	166,700
Other	10,400	8,100	13,700	11,100	90,100
Total	$ 9,500	$7,300	$13,900	$11,100	90,100

Source: Compiled by the authors.

employees on Title X construction projects are less likely to have been receiving transfer payments (including unemployment compensation) prior to Title X than is the average Title X employee.

Service projects are the best investment from a direct-net-cost point of view alone, returning, directly to governments, 26.2 cents per dollar of project expenditures. Such returns are more than 50 percent greater than those generated by public- and civil-works construction projects (16.6 cents and 14.4 cents per dollar, respectively). Training-project expenditures also stimulate relatively high direct returns, with net adjusted returns representing 22.1 percent of gross costs.

The relative net costs of different project types should also be examined for their effects upon person-year costs, as we do in Table 4.22. Adjusted returns reduce the labor cost per person-year of Title X employment from a gross cost of $9,500 to a net of $7,300. The net total cost per employment-year of the Job Opportunities Program is $11,100, down from a gross cost of $13,900. Overall, $1 billion in net direct expenditures on Title X would support about 90,100 positions for a full year.

Net costs per person-year are much lower for training projects than for any other project type. This would be expected from their high labor intensity and relatively low wages. Forestry projects also show net labor and net total costs that are lower than average. Even though service projects return more per dollar to governments, their net labor costs per person-year are slightly higher than the average. However, because they are quite labor intensive, service projects have a relatively low total net cost per person-year, $9,800. The net person-year costs for public- and civil-works construction projects are substantially higher than those for other project types. Construction projects average $8,600 in net labor costs and $19,900 in net total costs per person-year, compared with only $7,100 and $9,800 for nonconstruction projects. A $1 billion net direct investment in Title X construction projects would create about 50,200 person-years of employment, less than half the employment (102,200 person-years) that would be created by the same investment in nonconstruction Title X projects.

SUMMARY

The net-cost analysis of the Job Opportunities Program shows that the adjusted direct program cost to government is 79.6 cents for each dollar expended. Returns to government are substantially higher for labor expenditures (23.4 percent) than for nonlabor expenditures (13.5 percent), meaning that projects which are highly labor intensive cost governments less per dollar than projects which are not labor intensive. Thus, Title X training projects cost less than any other project type, with net costs for construction projects far exceeding those of other project types.

Taxes account for almost three-quarters of the adjusted direct returns to government from labor and nonlabor expenditures of Title X. About one-eighth of returns come from savings in unemployment compensation; reductions in means-tested transfers also account for one-eighth of returns. The dynamics of Title X expenditures and consequent returns favor state and local governments over the federal government. State and local governments receive a much higher proportion of direct returns (39.3 percent) as compared to their share of gross costs (15.5 percent), the result being an effective shift of about $36 million from federal to state and local treasuries. Since a high proportion of indirect and induced effects of Title X expenditures are also local, the dynamics of returns from the Job Opportunities Program provide an extra stimulus to local and state economies.

NOTES

1. See Congressional Budget Office, *Temporary Measures To Stimulate Employment: An Evaluation of Some Alternatives* (Washington, D.C.: Government Printing Office, 1975).

2. Ibid., summary table 1.

3. See, for example, George Johnson and James Tomola, "The Efficacy of Public Service Employment Programs," *Technical Analysis Paper 17A* (Washington, D.C.: Department of Labor, Assistant Secretary for Policy, Evaluation and Research (ASPER), 1975); National Planning Association, *An Evaluation of the Economic Impact Project of the Public Employment Program* (Washington, D.C.: National Planning Association, May 1974); Michael Wiseman, "Public Employment as Fiscal Policy," *Brookings Papers on Economic Activity*, vol. 1 (Washington, D.C.: Brookings Institution, 1976), pp. 67–114. Furthermore, a study recently funded by the Department of Labor will examine the costs and feasibility of several large-scale countercyclical public job-creation options.

4. See Appendix B for a detailed discussion of the discounting methodology and model. See also Ralph E. Smith, "A Simulation Model of the Demographic Composition of Employment, Unemployment and Labor Force Participation," Urban Institute Working Paper (Washington, D.C., June 1976), to be published in *Research in Labor Economics*, ed. Ronald Ehrenberg, vol. 1 (forthcoming), 1979.

5. Bureau of Labor Statistics, *Consumer Expenditure Survey Series: Interview Survey, 1972 and 1973* (Washington, D.C.: Government Printing Office, March 1976).

5

ESTIMATION OF
THE INDIRECT AND
INDUCED IMPACTS OF
TITLE X

Congressional debate prior to the passage of Title X centered on the issue of how many jobs could be created (and at what speed) with a given expenditure of public money. Comparisons were made among programs, based on expected wages, timing, need, and other political-economic factors. The debate never turned to the issue of the number of indirect and induced jobs that would be created by a given government expenditure. Efforts were concentrated on estimating only the direct job-creation impact of federal programs.[1]

Everyone knows, however, that a dollar of expenditure has a greater impact than the dollar itself. These secondary effects increase, then diminish, and eventually die out over time. The often-used analogy of a stone being thrown into a pond is useful here. The stone creates a big splash and ripples, which fade away with time and with distance from the impact site. The rippling or multiplier effects mean that a dollar of new expenditure creates more than a dollar of new income. Similarly, the total number of jobs created is larger than that created directly by the new expenditure. In this chapter, the multiplier effects of the Title X program are estimated.

Multipliers include both indirect and induced effects. At the simplest level, the indirect effect of additional government spending is measured by the additional puchases of goods and services by those firms (or government units) whose own outputs are being purchased with that extra spending.* For

---

*Given the nature and purpose of the Title X program, we are assuming that all federal spending on the program is new, that is, debt financed. Thus, we will not address the issue of the opportunity costs of Title X vis-a-vis other programs or private-sector alternatives.

142

example, HUD approves the construction of several units of public housing, and the construction contractors, in turn, purchase additional building materials. (However, this stimulus to the building-materials industry may require the latter to demand additional construction activity. Indirect multiplier effects do take such feedbacks into account.) When consumers (households) then respond to the associated changes in gross earnings (and net income) as well—that is, when the additional income generated by the expansion of production affects consumers' demands for additional goods and services—the multipler effects become even larger. The additional consumption effect is called the induced effect of the original increase in government spending.

THE INCOME MULTIPLIER

The ratio between the total amount of direct, indirect, and induced new income generated and the original direct new expenditure is called the income multiplier. Income multipliers will vary for different areas, depending not only upon the production functions (technologies) for industries in different regions, but upon income leakages. For example, multiplier effects will be dampened by any leakage of income from the flow of respending. At the national level (in the United States, at least), leakages in the form of purchases of imports are still a small-enough proportion of GNP to have little dampening effect on the multiplier. This is not so, however, for subareas (regions) within the United States. For any given degree of intraregional, interindustry linkage, the size of any regional or local multiplier depends on the degree to which the economy under study is self-sufficient. The more self-sufficient the local or regional economy, the relatively fewer goods and services it buys from outside the area, and, hence, the higher will be its multiplier. But, since there are always leakages to other regions or locales, regional or local multipliers are, without exception, smaller than the corresponding national multiplier.

Unfortunately, there are very few econometric estimates of subnational-level multipliers. Moreover, though it is known that the production functions of different regions vary, most regional or state models ultimately assume that regional economies are the same as the national economy. Thus, one must rely upon national multpliers for the estimation of indirect and induced effects of Title X.

There are many national econometric estimates of income multipliers, and all cannot be discussed here. Among the most accessible and, in our estimation, most valid are those published by Michael Evans, now the president of Chase Econometric Associates, Inc. Evans has simulated the income multipliers for a variety of changes in government spending and taxation policies using the Wharton econometric model.[2] His simulations not only provide an estimate of the multiplier appropriate to the Title X program, but also offer a comparison of the

FIGURE 5.1

Income Multipliers from Nondefense Expenditures and Personal Income Tax Cuts

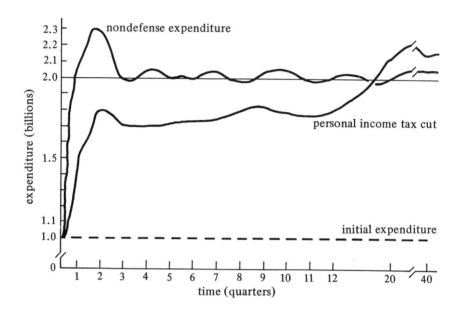

Source: Constructed by the authors.

timing of the impact of various programs. For example, the multiplier effect of a cut in personal income taxes is eventually about the same as that for an equivalent federal nondefense expenditure. However, the nondefense multiplier reaches its maximum after only one quarter, while it takes the decrease in personal income taxes almost 20 quarters to reach the same level.[3] Graphically, this can be illustrated as shown in Figure 5.1. The multiplier for nondefense expenditures reaches a peak of 2.35 by the end of the second quarter (based on a $1 billion stimulation), and levels out to 2.13 by the twentieth quarter. For the cut in personal taxes, the multiplier is at 1.19 in the first quarter and peaks at 2.61 after 40 quarters. We have chosen to round out these findings, and use an income multiplier of 2. Actually, this is a somewhat conservative estimate in light of· Evans's work, but it is both consistent with the conservative approach adopted throughout this study and generally accepted as a rule of thumb within the economics profession.*

Indirect- and induced-employment impacts may also be estimated. Determination of an employment multiplier, however, presents serious problems to the researcher, in that many assumptions about the structure of the demand for labor have to be made in order to estimate employment generation. The most common technique is to assume some simple average labor productivity (for example, $10,000 per job), and divide this into total program expenditures multiplied by the econometrically estimated income multiplier. A less simplistic technique would utilize an econometric equation (or set of equations) relating month-to-month employment changes, by industry, to changes in income.[4]

The most systematic derivation of employment multipliers has been undertaken by MIT Professor Karen Polenske, through simulations using her multiregional input-output (MRIO) model of the U.S. economy.[5] Using 1963 technical (that is, input-to-output) coefficients and industry output and employment data by region, Polenske has studied the national employment (as well as the income) effects produced by $1 billion in new final demand for various goods and services (products of agriculture and mining, of construction and manufacturing, business services, sales to households) produced in three major U.S. regions. For example, Polenske estimates the additional outputs required from all industries in the country to realize a $1 billion increase in demand for, say, the goods of the New England construction and manufacturing industries. She multiplies this estimated direct-, indirect-, and induced-output forecast by an industry sector-weighted estimate of the average productivity of labor, that is, average output per worker. The result is a transformation of the output forecast into an employment forecast. For instance, it might cost $20,000 to directly create a new job. However, by the time the new final demand works its way through the economy, an additional job may have been created, in which case the net final demand (social cost) per job is only $10,000.

For the four major industry groups and three regions, the model therefore generates 12 estimates of the amount of new final demand in that region and industry needed to create one new job in the country as a whole (taking into account interregional trade flows).† Rather than simply taking an average of the 12 estimates from Polenske's model, an effort has been made in our study to tailor her estimates to the Job Opportunities Program. The agriculture-and-

---

*Some macro economists have reestimated their rule-of-thumb multiplier to about 1.5. But the consensus still holds the rule at about 2.

†Like all existing closed input-output models, Polenske's is only partially closed; that is, household consumption is endogenous to the multiplier process, but private investment is not. The result is to bias Polenske's income and employment multipliers downward—again, in the conservative direction.

mining industry group, for example, has little direct relevance to Title X and is ignored in this analysis. The distribution of project types suggests that about 70 percent of Title X activity is in construction or related industries (repair, rehabilitation, forest improvement). About 30 percent involves service delivery (including training) of one kind or another.

On this basis, we computed a weighted average of the appropriate (but as yet unpublished) industry-related estimates from the MRIO model. Polenske's unweighted interregional average for the construction/manufacturing sector is $6,359 in new final demand per job created (in 1963 prices). For business services and sales to households, it is $6,455. Thus, the weighted average relevant to Title X is, .7 × $6,359 + .3 × $6,455, or $6,388 in new final demand per job. Using the GNP deflator to inflate this 1963 estimate to 1976 prices, one arrives at an average social cost, per new job, of $10,300 (1.612 × $6,388).

Suppose, for example, Title X had injected $1 billion in new direct spending into the economy, directly creating 75,000 new direct full-time equivalent jobs. Using the MRIO-derived employment figure, one would infer that Title X was responsible for 97,087 direct jobs ($1 billion ÷ $10,300), plus indirect and induced new jobs in the economy. This implies an employment multiplier of 1.29 (97,087 ÷ 75,000).

In applying the income multiplier of 2, and the employment-estimation technique based on the MRIO-derived figure of $10,300 per job, two additional factors—government respending of returns and budget-substitution effects—must be considered. First, if governments respend the additional taxes and transfer savings that accrue from Title X, multiplier effects are not affected. However, if they do not respend returns, the multiplier effect will be dampened. First-round returns ($154,245,000 in the case of Title X) essentially become leakages from the economy. Since we do not know the spending behavior of governments, we will sequentially consider each extreme, 100 percent respending in one case, zero respending in the other.

Second, multiplier effects depend upon the degree of budget substitution that occurs. If a portion of program funds would have been spent anyway in the absence of the program, then the income effects attributable to the program are reduced. In the case of the Job Opportunities Program, at least the Title X allocations ($497,453,000) must be considered as new expenditures. Since Title X funds are directly invested in projects, rather than being distributed as grants to state and local governments, the Title X funds are not subject to the kind of local substitution of federally funded job slots for previously locally funded job slots that allegedly has been widespread with public-service employment programs.

The same assumption, however, cannot be made for other funds that have been applied to Title X projects. Funds from other federal sources ($122,942,000) might or might not have been spent in the absence of the program. Similarly, state and local funds ($117,733,000) and private contributions ($19,796,000) may or may not represent new expenditures. These expenditures may have been debt financed in order to facilitate the administration of the program, or they may have come out of operating funds that would have been spent without the program. Again, data are unavailable. Therefore, we will treat budget substitution parametrically, first assuming zero substitution, and then 100 percent substitution, occurring out of the other federal, state, local, and private funds (a total of $260,471,000).[6] Thus, four sets of calculations for indirect and induced effects are made, corresponding to the four sets of assumptions shown in Table 5.1.

TABLE 5.1

Four Alternative Cases for Multiplier Calculations

Budget Substitution	Subsequent-Round Government Respending of Tax and Transfer Returns from Round One	
	100 percent	0 percent
0 percent	Case 1	Case 2
100 percent	Case 3	Case 4

Source: Constructed by the authors.

The multiplier effects of the Job Opportunities Program are summarized in Table 5.2, for each of the four cases defined above. Together, they provide a range for the estimated total impact of Title X upon income and employment.

Case 1—full government respending of tax and transfer returns, and no substitution—produces the highest estimate of new national income. The income multiplier of 2 is applied to total Title X program expenditures of $757,924,000, resulting in an aggregate direct-, indirect-, and induced-income impact of $1,515,848,000 in new national income.

The returns to government from Title X program expenditures are $154,245,000, resulting in a direct net cost to government of $603,679,000. Assuming that the returns from the succeeding rounds of spending are of the same relative scale as first-round returns,* the long-run net cost of Title X is,

---

*This assumption is necessary, since there are no data to support an alternative assumption. If anything, the assumption is probably a conservative one. On the one hand, Title X employees are more benefit prone than most populations, meaning that Title X returns in transfer savings are probably higher than should be incorporated into subsequent-round returns. On the other hand, Title X employees also report extremely low income,

TABLE 5.2

Multiplier Effects of the Job Opportunities Program

Evaluation Criteria	Case 1 (no budget substitution; full government respending of returns)	Case 2 (no budget substitution; zero government respending of returns)	Case 3 (100 percent budget substitution; full government respending of returns)	Case 4 (100 percent budget substitution; zero government respending of returns)
Initial new expenditure (millions of dollars)	758	758	497.5	497.5
New national income created (millions of dollars)*	1,516	1,362	995	894
Effective income multiplier (2 ÷ 1)	2.0	1.8	2.0	1.8
Net cost (millions of dollars)	449	481	449	481
Benefit-cost ratio (2 ÷ 4)	3.4	2.8	2.2	1.9
Direct new jobs created	54,601	54,601	35,837	35,837
Total new jobs created	73,585	66,096	48,296	43,381
Implicit employment multiplier (7 ÷ 6)	1.35	1.21	1.35	1.21

*Based upon an income multiplier of 2.
Source: Constructed by the authors.

$603,679,000 minus another $154,245,000, or $449,434,000. Thus, it costs governments about $449 million to produce new income of $1.51 billion, a benefit-cost ratio of about 3.4.

Title X new program expenditures of $757,924,000 have provided 655,211 person-months, or 54,601 person-years, of direct employment. Since Polenske's MRIO data are annual, defining a job as a person-year of employment, we can say, for purposes of this estimation, that Title X created 54,601 direct jobs. With no income substitution, these are all new jobs. The total number of direct, indirect, and induced new jobs is calculated by dividing Polenske's new direct income per job ($10,300, after being adjusted for inflation) into the direct new program expenditure of $757,924,000. This produces an estimate of 73,585 total new jobs. The implicit employment multiplier is, therefore, 1.35 (73,585 ÷ 54,601).

Case 2 assumes no substitution and no government respending of tax and transfer returns. As in case 1, total Title X program expenditures are $757,924,000. However, the effective income multiplier is no longer 2, since respending is constrained by the fact that governments do not respend the first-round returns of $154,245,000. Essentially, this is a leakage from the economy. Only $603,679,000 is subject to the multiplier of 2. Thus, the total new income created is $757,924,000 in the first round, plus $603,679,000 in subsequent rounds, or $1,361,603,000. The effective income multiplier is 1.8 ($1.36 billion ÷ $758 million).

Initial returns to government are the same as in case 1, but subsequent returns are not. Instead of being based upon subsequent new income of $758 million, they are based upon subsequent-round income of $603,679,000. Assuming the same rate of return to government as in case 1 ($154 million ÷ $758 million, or .204), the first-round returns to governments are only $123,151,000 ($603,679,000 × .204). Thus, the overall net cost of Title X is, $603,679,000 minus $123,151,000, or $480,528,000. The benefit-cost ratio is, therefore, about 2.8 ($1,361,603,000 ÷ 480,528,000).

As in case 1, the number of direct new jobs created by Title X is 54,601. However, the total number of new jobs created is less than in case 1, because the income multiplier is constrained in case 2 by the fact that governments do not respend returns. Estimation of the total job-creation impact is difficult, since Polenske's simulations (from which the direct new income per job is derived) assume an unconstrained (no leakage) income multiplier. Moreover, there is no

---

meaning that direct-tax returns for Title X are calculated at rates lower than would be the case in subsequent rounds of returns. Taxes account for a majority of returns and are quite sensitive to the tax rate chosen. Thus, the overestimate of transfer savings in subsequent-round returns is probably more than compensated for by the underestimate of increased taxes.

literature upon which to base a different estimate. The only recourse in this study is to adjust the direct new income per job of $10,300, by assuming that there is an inverse linear relationship between total new income and direct new income per job.* In other words, the job-creation estimate is based upon the following average direct new income per job:

$$\$10,300 \times (\$1,515,848,000/\$1,361,603,000) = \$11,467$$

Applying this figure, the total number of new jobs created by Title X is 66,096 ($757,924,000 ÷ $11,467). The implicit employment multiplier becomes 1.21.

Case 3 assumes full government respending of tax and transfer returns, but also assumes 100 budget substitution for all but the EDA Title X grant funds. Thus, total new first-round expenditures are only $497,453,000, this being the Title X allocation. With a multiplier of 2, new national income is $994,906,000.

Net cost is the same as in case 1, since net cost is not affected by substitution effects. The first-round net cost is $603,679,000. Subtracting returns to government, $154,245,000, generated by succeeding rounds of spending, the long-run net cost in case 3 is $449,434,000, and the benefit-cost ratio is 2.2.

Unlike the previous cases, not all of the 54,601 direct jobs are new jobs. Only those resulting from new direct expenditures are, in fact, new jobs. Since the estimated cost per job for Title X is $13,881, the number of direct new jobs created in case 3 is 35,837 ($497,453,000 ÷ $13,881). The total number of direct, indirect, and induced jobs is 48,296 ($497,453,000 ÷ $10,300). Thus, the implicit employment multiplier, as in case 1, is 1.41.

Case 4 assumes zero government respending of returns and 100 percent budget substitution. As in case 3, new first-round expenditures are $497,453,000. However, indirect and induced income is not an additional $497,453,000, because the government does not respend returns, of $154,245,000. About 65.6 percent of these returns, or $101,237,000, are attributable to new first-round expenditures. If these returns are not respent by government, the additional income impact is, $497,453,000 minus $101,237,000, or $396,216,000. Thus, total new income is only $893,669,000. As in case 2, the effective income multiplier is 1.8.

Net cost, affected by the government's lack of respending, but not by substitution, is identical to that for case 2, $480,528,000. As a consequence, the benefit-cost ratio for case 4 is only about 1.9, the lowest among the four scenarios.

---

*Clearly, when new income is lower, the number of new jobs created will be lower, all other things being equal. Thus, if the direct new income in case 2 is the same as the direct new income in case 1, the average direct new income per job will be higher. A reasonable assumption is that the cost per job is inversely proportional to total new income. On this basis, the direct new income per job estimate is adjusted upward for case 2 and case 4.

Direct new job creation, as in case 3, amounts to 35,837 jobs, since only $497,453,000 of the direct Title X expenditure represents new spending. The total number of direct, indirect, and induced jobs, however, is reduced by lack of government respending, as in case 2. Making the same assumption as in case 2, the total number of new jobs created is 43,381 ($497,453,000 ÷ $11,456). Thus, the implicit employment multiplier is about 1.21.

The four cases presented above and in Table 5.2—incorporating opposite assumptions about budget substitution and government respending of returns— provide a broad range of the possible direct, indirect, and induced impacts of the Job Opportunities Program. The true impact of Title X lies somewhere between the two extremes, probably closer to the high limit than to the low limit. In 1976-77, with the economy still recovering from the 1974-75 recession, the federal government was still running large deficits and was surely respending most, if not all, of the tax and transfer returns. It is also likely that at least some portion of the local share would not have been spent in the absence of Title X.

The dynamics of indirect and induced effects illustrated by the four cases are of both policy and research interest. For example, if governments do not respend returns from initial expenditures, new income is reduced and net cost is increased. If budget substitution occurs, new income is further reduced, but net cost is unaffected. Considering the extremes of the four cases, the total gross expenditure of $757,924,000 results in a final net-cost range of only $449,434,000 to $480,528,000—only 59-63 percent of the gross outlay. And each dollar of new Title X expenditure generates an additional $0.90-$2.40 in new national income, depending upon substitution and government respending.

Of particular policy interest are the job-creation effects. The final net cost per new job created ranges from $6,108 in case 1 to $11,077 in case 4. Moreover, full budget substitution affects job creation more than government nonrespending of returns. Budget substitution reduces the number of new jobs by 22,715-25,289, or by 34.4 percent. The impact on the net cost per new job is an increase of $2,907-$3,200 per job. In contrast, if returns are not respent, new job creation is reduced by only 4,915-7,489 jobs (10.2 percent), and net cost per job increases by $1,162-$1,769. However, if a certain level of budget substitution is expected, governments can significantly increase job-creation impact by respending the tax and transfer returns from the initial program expenditure.

It should be noted that the implicit employment multipliers for Title X are quite low, 1.21-1.35,[7] about 67.5 percent of the income multiplier in each of the four cases. Employment multipliers will always be lower than income multipliers, as long as the direct investment is fairly labor intensive. In general, the employment multiplier will vary inversely (though not necessarily in a linear manner) with the labor intensity of the original investment. Thus, CETA public-service employment programs, which are more labor intensive, and have a lower direct cost per job, than Title X, should have an even smaller employment multiplier than Title X. Conversely, a program of direct government purchases will have a high employment multiplier.

The employment multiplier is sometimes referred to as an indicator of the total job-creation impact of an investment. As Table 5.2 shows, however, it is a deceptive indicator. Estimates of total jobs created under Title X are not directly related to the size of the employment multiplier. Indeed, for any investment in which budget substitution may occur, the employment multiplier will be an inaccurate proxy for total job-creation impact. The greater the budget substitution, the larger the employment multiplier must be to create the same number of jobs.

As a summary, it is useful to present the findings of this analysis in a $1 billion scenario. If $1 billion were expended on the Job Opportunities Program, it would generate new national income of $1.18-$2.0 billion at a net cost of only $593-$634 million. Fully 72,040 direct jobs would be created, but, depending upon budget substitution, new direct job creation could be as low as 47,283 jobs. Concurrently, total new job creation would range from 97,087 jobs down to 57,237, with the net cost per job as low as $6,108 or as high as $11,077.

NOTES

1. For example, see Bureau of Labor Statistics, *Factbook For Estimating the Manpower Needs of Federal Programs*, B.L.S. Bulletin #1832 (Washington, D.C.: Department of Labor, 1975). In this volume, the BLS estimates the amount of employment, by industry and occupation, that is generated by $1 billion in outlays. This is done through the use of an interindustry-employment model coupled with an industry-occupation model. The interindustry-employment model traces the purchase of goods and services through each sector of the economy, determining the employment needed in each industry to support these purchases. The industry-occupation model maps total employment in each industry for 160 different occupational categories. Thus, for example, the models, taken together, can give an estimate of the number of additional tool and die makers in the machine-tool industry who would be employed as a result of an additional $1 billion in nondefense expenditures.

2. Michael K. Evans, *Macroeconomic Activity: Theory, Forecasting and Control* (New York: Harper and Row, 1969), especially chaps. 19-20.

3. Ibid., pp. 567-74.

4. This latter technique was used in Georges Vernez et al., *Regional Cycles and Employment Effects of Public Works Investment* (Santa Monica: Rand Corp., January 1977).

5. See, particularly, Karen R. Polenske and Denise DiPasquale, "Output, Income and Employment Input-Output Multipliers" (Paper presented at a Workshop in the Methodology of Economic Impact Analysis, Hueston Woods State Park, Ohio, April 14, 1977). By systematic we mean that the method produces employment and income multipliers that are fully consistent with one another, having been generated by the same model.

6. We have decided to beg one other set of questions having to do with multiplier effects, spelled out in Martin Bailey and James Tobin, "Direct Job Creation, Inflation, and Unemployment" (Paper presented at the Brookings Conference on Direct Job Creation, Washington, D.C., April 7–8, 1977), pp. 9–15. They observe that the multiplier effect of any "direct job-creation" program like Title X will be larger if the "marginal propensity to consume" is higher and the tax bracket (and therefore the tax leakage) of the program's enrollees is lower. We assume that Title X enrollees do not differ from the population at large in either respect, to a sufficient degree, to warrant undertaking the expensive research project that would be needed to find out. In fact, given the low-income profile of Title X employees, this assumption probably results in an understatement of the multiplier effects we calculate here.

7. In contrast, the aforementioned Rand study of public works estimates three off-site jobs created for each on-site public-works job, implying a multiplier of 4. See Vernez et al., op. cit., especially chap. 6.

6

COUNTERCYCLICAL EMPLOYMENT
UNDER TITLE X

INTRODUCTION

In debates over the advantages and disadvantages of various kinds of countercyclical tools, one argument in favor of job-creation programs is that they can have immediate and discernible impact upon high-unemployment areas. Although it would take a massive program to significantly affect the national unemployment rate in the short run, it is nonetheless true that, unlike other countercyclical measures, job-creation programs have the principal objective of providing new employment opportunities, with wages from new jobs being the primary vehicle for stimulating demand and the economy. It has been shown, however, that public-employment programs have displacement effects, federal funds being used to support some positions that would have been supported by other sources in the absence of the programs.[1] Moreover, a not infrequent criticism of job programs is that many of the jobs created are, at best, only obliquely related to the prior employment experience and career paths of the employees. At worst, they are seen as subsidized make-work jobs requiring skills far below the capabilities of the employees.

Since the jobs themselves are a major distinguishing feature of countercyclical employment programs, the question of whether they are real opportunities or merely a wage alternative to unemployment compensation and other transfers is significant to policy makers. This question was examined as a secondary objective of the Title X study and is the focal point of this chapter. Our analysis of Title X occupations is based primarily upon responses from the 1969 Title X employees with whom personal interviews were conducted. The employees selected represent the distribution of occupations and wages reported for all employees at their respective projects. The 195 projects selected for interviews are representative of the universe of Title X projects, in both project type and region. Since analysis of ED-110X payroll data shows a high correlation between project type and occupation (see Chapter 3), most findings presented here are broadly representative of the entire Job Opportunities Program.

Several distinguishing features of the occupational analysis should be noted. First, much of it is conducted in a comparative context. Title X jobs are compared with the employees' prior jobs and usual occupations, to explore the relative quality and value of the Title X employment. By placing the subsidized job within the analytic context of other jobs held by the employee, measures of relative job quality and, in some cases, career movement are possible. Second, most of the data are reported directly by employees, not by the projects or secondary data systems. Thus, employees' perceptions of the strengths and weaknesses of Title X jobs in relation to other jobs can be explored. The pros and cons of employee reports versus project records, vis-a-vis bias and errors, can be argued, and areas of possible bias are discussed in this chapter. In Title X, however, the choice of method is moot, since local projects were not required to keep employee data, and the content, form, and completeness of local records vary sharply.

Third, there is only a partial post-Title X dimension to the analysis. This is a necessary limitation of the study. Limited resources and the short duration of the study precluded extensive followup. Moreover, because of Privacy Act interpretations given by the Department of Commerce during the design and initial implementation stages of the methodology, the employee survey could include only those reported on ED-110X payroll reports as currently working on a Title X project. Under a subsequent reinterpretation, a limited followup of terminees was conducted and a second substudy of a small sample of terminees initiated. Thus, there are data on employment status and occupation subsequent to Title X, but only on a relatively small subset of employees.

The occupational analysis is presented in Chapters 6 and 7. Chapter 6 is devoted to the comparative analysis of Title X employment in relation to other jobs held by the full sample of employees. First, Title X jobs and the employees' prior jobs are compared by occupational category, wage/salary level, and average weekly earnings. In addition, employees' perceptions of the relative work quality and skills required in the two jobs are examined. Second, a parallel analysis is conducted on Title X jobs and the employees' usual occupations, the types of work the employees say that they usually do to earn a living. Third, interrelationships among a variety of independent and dependent variables are tested, using cross-tabular and multivariate analysis.

Chapter 7 discusses the labor market experiences of terminees after they have left the Title X program. Because this is based upon a small number of observations, Chapter 7 findings must be regarded as tentative and suggestive, not generalizable for the Title X program as a whole. In the analysis, Title X jobs and subsequent jobs are compared for those employees who have gotten work following Title X employment. In addition, general data reported on the labor market experience of terminees are presented. Finally, prior jobs, usual jobs, Title X jobs, and subsequent jobs are examined to identify any discernible career sequences of which Title X may be a part.

COMPARISONS WITH PRIOR JOB

Occupational Categories

In assessing the quality of employment provided under Title X, the principal comparison is with the employee's job prior to Title X. Comparative analysis of the types of jobs provided, wages and weekly earnings, and employees' perceptions of jobs generates the principal indicators of relative job quality. It should be understood that, since less than 20 percent of Title X employees were working immediately before Title X hire, the prior job experience has, in most cases, been followed by a period of unemployment. Given the long period of unemployment of many Title X employees, the prior job had often terminated three months, six months, a year, and, in some cases, several years before Title X hire.

A preliminary comparison of prior and Title X occupations is presented in Table 6.1. When occupational categories are examined, considerable differences between prior and Title X jobs are evident. For example, there have been fewer

TABLE 6.1

Prior versus Title X Jobs
(percent of total)

Occupational Category	Prior Jobs	Title X Jobs
Manager/administrator	3.4	2.2
Professional/technical	6.0	4.4
Supervisor/foreman	3.9	10.6
Construction trades	16.3	17.0
Construction laborer	5.7	12.3
Miscellaneous laborer	5.3	10.1
Operative/technician	12.3	1.7
Forestry, parks, recreation	3.4	13.1
Government/social service	1.3	2.9
Service	22.0	16.9
Clerical	12.0	8.6
Other	8.4	0.2

Source: Compiled by the authors.

managerial and professional jobs under Title X than among the prior jobs of participants. In contrast, Title X has supported a higher number of supervisory positions, more than balancing the lower number of managerial and professional jobs. Fully 17.2 percent of Title X jobs are supervisory, professional or administrative jobs, in contrast with 13.3 percent of the employees' prior jobs.

Naturally, many of the Title X supervisory jobs are construction related, and the occupational comparison underscores the Title X emphasis on construction-related and forestry/recreation jobs. Laborers and forestry/recreation jobs account for 35.5 percent of Title X jobs, but only for 14.4 percent of prior jobs. Jobs likely to require outdoor and/or physical work comprise 64.8 percent of the Title X jobs and only 46.9 percent of prior jobs. Note, however, that construction-trade positions are virtually the same proportion of Title X and prior jobs. This suggests, subject to further analysis, that there has been a relative stability between prior and Title X work in the construction trades.

In addition to the overall movement toward construction and forestry/ recreation types of positions, there are patterns of movement away from certain prior occupational categories. For example, 12.3 percent of Title X employees were previously in operative/technician jobs, but only 1.7 percent of Title X jobs are in these categories. Fully 23.3 percent formerly held government or service (including personal service) jobs, which, under Title X, account for 19.8 percent of positions. There are also fewer clerical positions under Title X. Finally, a substantial number of Title X employees (8.4 percent) were previously in other types of jobs or situations, almost all of which (for example, farmer, student, housewife, self-employed) were not part of the occupational array under Title X.

Since the study applied a common occupational-code structure to all jobs held by participants, it is possible to trace and analyze the movement of each employee from one job to the next. One aspect of the job transition—and part of the overall assessment of the meaningfulness of Title X positions—is the extent to which the Title X job is similar to, or different from, the other (in this case, the prior) job. If a number of Title X jobs are similar to employees' prior jobs, then Title X has at least offered some degree of general occupational continuity. Similarity of jobs is also preliminary evidence—subject to analysis of other comparative indicators—that Title X has provided employment of a quality comparable with the employees' prior jobs.

Analysis of the occupational codes reveals that 29.8 percent of Title X employees had moved from a prior job of the same occupational category. If one eliminates employees in situations not comparable to Title X (farmer, housewife, self-employed), the proportion increases to 32.2 percent. Thus, for virtually one-third of Title X employees, the Title X job was the same basic job (broadly speaking) as their prior job. This finding is confirmed by employees' answers to a question asking them to compare their prior and Title X jobs: 8.1 percent report that in both jobs they performed the "identical

TABLE 6.2

Occupational Matches between Title X and Prior Jobs

Prior Job	Percent of Employees with Same Title X Job
Manager/administrator	21.5
Professional/technical	22.4
Supervisor/foreman	54.5
Construction trades	45.9
Construction laborer	37.6
Miscellaneous laborer	41.2
Operative/technician	3.8
Forestry/parks/recreation	28.8
Government/social service	46.2
Service	33.1
Clerical	36.8
Total	32.2

Source: Compiled by the authors.

type of work," and another 35.7 percent describe the jobs as "similar or related types of work."

The proportion of occupational matches varies considerably across different occupational categories. Table 6.2 presents these differences, showing the proportion of employees whose Title X job has been similar or identical to their prior job. In four occupational categories, a large proportion of employees found Title X work very similar to their prior work. Over 50 percent of prior foremen or supervisors were hired for Title X positions of the same type. Close to 50 percent of construction-trade workers and government/social-service employees also found similar jobs under Title X. In addition, over 40 percent of miscellaneous laborers took jobs of a comparable type on Title X projects. Matches of Title X jobs with prior jobs were less likely for managers and professionals, and extremely rare for operatives/technicians. In all three cases, particularly the last, the infrequency of matches is a function of the relative scarcity of the same kinds of jobs under Title X.

One would expect that the occupational matches in Table 6.2 should be related to whether there are more or fewer jobs available in the various occupational categories under Title X as compared with prior employment (shown in Table 6.1). In other words, if there are more jobs, in a certain occupational category, available under Title X, there is a better chance that people whose prior job was in that category would find a similar job under Title X. In fact, this is not quite the case. Of the five occupational categories showing the highest proportion of matches, two (construction trades and clerical) are cases where there are the same or fewer Title X jobs available in that category than were held as prior jobs. In three categories (supervisor, miscellaneous laborer, and government/social service) the high proportion of matches is related to the greater number of jobs in those categories that have been available under Title X.

The figures presented in Table 6.2 are appealing, because they assume that the local labor force and the prior experience of candidates for a Title X job are given factors that the project has to work with. The figures, thus, could reflect upon the care with which a project was designed to meet the labor-force needs of the area, and the degree to which prior employment guided Title X hiring. However, as explained above, the matching figures are subject to distortion (and, thus, misinterpretation) by the relative representation of each occupational category in the Title X work force. Thus, another way to express matching, which controls for this possible distortion, is to calculate the matching percentage as the number of matches in a category divided by the number of prior jobs in the category, or by the number of Title X jobs in the category, whichever is lower. The lower number sets a maximum on the number of matches that are possible, given the prior jobs of Title X employees and the spectrum of available Title X jobs.* Such percentages are presented in Table 6.3.

The revised approach to prior-job/Title X job matches shows that Title X provided supervisors/foremen and clerical workers with similar jobs in over 50 percent of the possible cases. Matching was also considerably above average for government/social-service workers, the construction trades, and employees in service jobs. Matches were much less frequent for former operatives and technicians, forestry-related workers, professionals, and managers. Across all occupational categories, the 44.5 percent of matches further strengthens the generalization that Title X has provided employment which may, in many cases, utilize the individual skills of participants.

Job similarity does not, of course, mean that Title X offered jobs which were better than, or even of the same quality as, prior jobs held by employees. Job quality is discussed later, using several partial but objective measures (wages, hours, weekly earnings), and a subjective but more encompassing measure

---

*For example, say 2,000 Title X employees held prior jobs in category A, and 2,000, in category B. Analysis shows that there are 500 matches of prior jobs with Title X jobs in each category. In Table 6.2, the matching percentage for each would be 25 percent (500/2,000). However, in category A there are 2,500 Title X jobs and in category B only 1,500 jobs. Under the Table 6.3 procedure, the maximum matching percentage in category A is 100 percent, but for category B it is only 75 percent. The procedure adopted in Table 6.3 controls for this distortion. Applying it, the matching percentage in category A would be 25 percent (500 ÷ 2,000). For category B, it would be 33.3 percent (500 ÷ 1,500).

TABLE 6.3

Occupational Matches—A Second Look

Occupational Category	Percent of Matches
Manager/administrator	35.0
Professional/technician	33.3
Supervisor/foreman	54.5
Construction trades	48.0
Construction laborer	37.6
Miscellaneous laborer	41.2
Operative/technician	26.5
Forestry/parks/recreation	28.8
Government/social services	46.2
Service	45.9
Clerical	55.5
Total	44.5

Source: Compiled by the authors.

(employees' assessments of jobs). However, the occupational codes can be utilized to develop another measure of job quality.

For all job comparisons, an arbitrary but intuitively appealing hierarchy of occupational categories was created and applied. The basic occupational categories were divided into four ranks, as follows:

Rank	Category
1	Manager/administrator
	Professional/technical
	Supervisor/foreman
2	Construction trades
	Operatives/technicians
	Government/social services
3	Construction laborer
	Other laborer
	Bus or truck driver
	Service
	Forestry related
	Clerical

Rank	Category
4	Farmer, farmworker
	Student
	Housewife

Movement from a lower rank to a higher rank was regarded as an upward job change. Movement within the same rank was considered a lateral job change. Movement from a higher rank to a lower rank was judged to be a downward job transition. While the accuracy of the hierarchy can be debated, particularly on the premise that movement within a rank could easily be positive or negative, the hierarchy nevertheless provides a broad framework appropriate to Title X, and within which the quality of job changes can be analyzed.

Applying the hierarchy to the transition from prior jobs to Title X jobs brings the findings shown in Table 6.4.

TABLE 6.4

Occupational Movement Represented by the Transition from Prior to Title X Jobs

Movement	Percent of Employees
Upward	24.4
Lateral	54.5
Downward	21.1

Source: Compiled by the authors.

As would be expected, a majority of job transitions are lateral. However, almost 25 percent of the Title X employees are working in Title X jobs that, as defined under the hierarchy, represented an upward movement from their prior jobs. About an equal number (21.1 percent) moved from a higher prior rank to a lower Title X rank. Thus, using the rough tool of occupational ranks, Title X appears to provide employment at a level comparable to that of employees' prior jobs.*

---

*There is a small degree of implicit bias in the application of the ranking categories, since Title X offers no jobs classified in rank 4. Thus, an employee can move upward from rank 4 but not downward into rank 4. For housewives and students, this is clearly defensible,

Wages, Hours, and Weekly Earnings

When wages, hours, and weekly earnings are examined, Title X jobs are again comparable to employees' prior jobs. As shown in Table 6.5, there are no significant differences between prior and Title X jobs on these variables. Mean hours worked per week are virtually the same, and the medians are identical. The effective hourly wage on the Title X job is slightly above the prior-job hourly wage, but only by about 2 percent.* The median hourly wage for the Title X job is about 6 percent higher than that for the prior job. Average weekly earnings are marginally higher on the prior job, but by an insignificant 1.7 percent. Median weekly earnings are, in fact, higher on Title X jobs by about 3 percent. The similarity in wages and weekly earnings of prior and Title X jobs lends further support to the hypothesis that Title X has provided meaningful job opportunities.

TABLE 6.5

Wages, Hours, and Earnings: Prior and Title X Jobs

Measure	Prior Job	Title X Job
Mean hours per week	39.6	38.6
Median hours per week	40.0	40.0
Mean hourly wage	$3.46	$3.54
Median hourly wage	2.95	3.14
Mean weekly earnings	$137.80	$135.60
Median weekly earnings	119.00	123.00

Source: Compiled by the authors.

---

since a move into the labor force is a positive employment move. For farmers and farmworkers, the rank 4 classification may appear more arbitrary. However, survey data show a substantially lower prior weekly wage for this group than for other prior jobs. It should be noted that if farmers and farmworkers were classified in rank 3, the percentage of upward changes in Table 6.4 would decrease to 21.3 percent; lateral changes would increase to 57.6 percent.

*Some jobs pay weekly, bitweekly, or monthly salaries. For purposes of this analysis, they were converted to an hourly rate, by dividing salaries by the actual number of hours reported by each employee.

TABLE 6.6

Distribution of Weekly Earnings: Prior and Title X Jobs

| Weekly Earnings | Percent of Employees | |
	Prior Job	Title X Job
$0–100	39.4	28.0
101–125	16.1	23.6
126–150	12.4	19.9
151–175	8.6	14.0
176–200	7.5	7.0
201–250	6.4	2.4
251–300	3.3	2.3
Over 300	6.3	2.9

Source: Compiled by the authors.

Carrying the analysis a step further, Table 6.6 presents the distribution of weekly earnings from prior and Title X jobs. The table indicates that there are different earnings distributions for prior and Title X jobs. Weekly earnings from the prior job are spread more toward the high and low extremes, while Title X earnings are more frequently in the middle ranges. For example, more Title X employees previously held jobs which paid less than $100 per week (39.4 percent) than held jobs paying $101–$175 per week (37.1 percent). Fully 16 percent earned more than $200 per week from prior jobs. In contrast, weekly earnings from the Title X jobs are more concentrated in the middle ranges, with 57.5 percent earning $101–$175 per week. Only 7.6 percent earn more than $200 per week from their Title X jobs.

The differences in weekly earnings distributions suggest that Title X does not have a broad comparative-earnings impact upon employees, because of the simple fact that the mean weekly earnings of the two jobs are virtually identical. Rather, it is likely that, for a substantial group of people, weekly earnings from Title X jobs are considerably higher than those from their previous jobs. For another group, Title X has provided substantially lower weekly earnings than did the prior job. This likelihood is strengthened by the fact that 23.0 percent of employees earned less than $2.25 per hour on their prior jobs, while 13.5 percent earned more than $5.00 per hour. In contrast, only 3.9 percent received Title X wages of less than $2.25 per hour and only 8.4 percent received more than $5.00 per hour.

The hypothesis is confirmed in Table 6.7, which presents the increase or decrease in weekly earnings reported for the Title X job in comparison to the prior job.

TABLE 6.7

Change in Weekly Earnings: Title X Job as Compared with Prior Job

Change in Weekly Earnings	Percent of Employees		
	Title X Earnings Higher	Title X Earnings Lower	Earnings the Same
$0	_a	—	8.9
1-50	34.8	23.3	—
51-100	12.0	9.2	—
101-150	2.8	4.0	—
Over 150	1.4	3.8	—
Total	50.9	40.2	8.9

aData not available.
Source. Compiled by the authors.

Title X represents an increase in weekly earnings over the prior job for 50.9 percent of employees. Only 40.2 percent of employees had higher weekly earnings from their prior jobs. Thus, measured by the change in weekly earnings from the prior job to the Title X job, Title X provides a better job to over one-half of its employees, a worse job to about four in every ten. Note, however, that increases in weekly earnings are, on the average, smaller than decreases. More than 68 percent of the increases are $50 per week or less, in comparison with 58 percent of the decreases. Only 8.2 percent of the increases, but 19.4 percent of the decreases, were over $100 per week.

The preceding discussion suggests another question worthy of examination: In comparison with prior jobs, what kinds of people have received earnings benefits from Title X? In Chapter 3, it was shown that average weekly earnings on Title X jobs differ substantially by demographic characteristics. It is possible, however, that the differences were even greater on prior jobs. In other words, Title X may have had differential-earnings impacts, improving the relative earnings of groups less fortunate on their prior jobs. Table 6.8 addresses this possibility, displaying the mean weekly earnings from prior jobs and Title X jobs for different demographic groups.

Title X jobs have had a strong effect in balancing the weekly earnings of different demographic groups, as is reflected in Table 6.8. Every major demographic group whose prior weekly earnings were below the mean weekly earnings for prior jobs has earned more per week under Title X; every group who was above the mean prior weekly earnings has earned less than before under Title X. Whereas the weekly income gap between men and women on prior jobs was

TABLE 6.8

Average Weekly Earnings: Employees on Prior and Title X Jobs

	Weekly Earnings		
Category	Prior Job	Title X Job	Change
Age			
15–19	93.74	110.01	+16.27
20–24	121.35	129.30	+ 7.95
25–34	147.88	144.57	– 3.31
35–44	159.88	146.47	–13.41
45–59	162.88	146.17	–16.71
60 and over	112.90	152.61	+39.71
Sex			
Male	151.53	147.84	– 3.69
Female	93.49	108.53	+15.04
Race			
White	152.16	141.81	–20.35
Total black and			
other races	120.47	128.34	+ 7.87
Black	114.91	113.65	– 1.26
American Indian	126.58	153.35	+26.77
Other	137.53	150.55	+13.02
All employees	137.80	135.60	– 2.20

Source: Compiled by the authors.

$58.04, under Title X it is $39.31. The differences in weekly prior-job income between whites and nonwhites was $31.69. Under Title X, it is $13.47. Thus, Title X employment has resulted in a substantial relative increase in the weekly earnings of groups who were earning less in their prior jobs (and who traditionally have earned less in the labor market). Since the burden of recession tends to fall most heavily upon such groups, the distribution equity implied by these earnings patterns is consistent with the general objectives of countercyclical programs.

Employees' Job Comparisons

Another source of information on the relative quality of Title X jobs is a series of ratings made by employees. Employees were asked to compare their Title X jobs with their prior jobs, with regard to the similarity of work (identical, similar, or dissimilar), skills required (more skills on the Title X job, the same number, or fewer) and overall job quality (better, the same, or worse). The employee ratings are perception based. Their validity as definitive measures of Title X job quality may be questioned, since the rating may be subject to employee or situational biases that have little to do with the substance of the job. However, taken for what they are, measures of employees' opinions about their Title X jobs, they add an important and extremely relevant dimension to the research.

Employees' comparisons of prior and Title X jobs are summarized in Table 6.9. A majority of Title X employees (56.1 percent) judge their Title X jobs to be dissimilar and unrelated to their prior employment. However, a substantial number of employees (38.3 percent) feel that the Title X job requires more skills than their previous job. In contrast, less than one in four (23 percent) perceive their jobs to demand fewer skills than their previous jobs. Most impressive is the fact that more than six in ten (61.8 percent) rate their Title X jobs as better than their previous jobs, and less than one in ten (9.9 percent) judge them to be worse. This is a strong endorsement of the quality of employment provided by Title X.

The consistency of employees' job comparisons with other measures adds to their possible validity. For example, job-similarity ratings are consistent with occupational matches. Those persons whose prior jobs were as supervisors or as government/social-service workers most often rated prior and Title X jobs as identical or similar. Fully 71 percent of the former and 78.3 percent of the latter gave such ratings. These are also the two occupational categories in which the highest proportion of matching between prior and Title X jobs is found. Conversely, operatives and technicians, who found very few matched jobs under Title X, also rated their prior and Title X jobs as most dissimilar (83.1 percent). Overall, 71.2 percent of the employees whose prior and Title X occupational

TABLE 6.9

Employees' Comparisons of Prior and Title X Jobs

Items of Comparison	Response (percent of employees)
Similarity of work	
Identical	8.1
Similar or related	35.8
Dissimilar, Unrelated	56.1
Skills required	
More on Title X job	38.3
About the same	38.7
Fewer on Title X job	23.0
Job quality	
Title X job is better	61.6
Jobs are about the same	28.6
Title X Job is worse	9.9

Source: Compiled by the authors.

categories match also rated the jobs as identical or similar. Only 2.6 percent of those with unmatched occupational categories considered their prior and usual jobs to be identical; a majority (69.4 percent) called them dissimilar and unrelated.

Employees' ratings of skills required are also consistent with the analysis of matched jobs and upward and downward movements in rank. For example, better than one-half (53 percent) of employees whose prior and Title X jobs are in the same occupational category rate the skills required by the two jobs as being "about the same." Less than one-third (32.5 percent) of the employees whose jobs are not in the same category rate their jobs as requiring the same number of skills. Similarly, more than one-half (53.8 percent) of those who, by their pattern of occupational movement, may have moved upward in rank, also perceive the skills required on their Title X jobs to be greater than those on their previous jobs. In contrast, only one-quarter (26.6 percent) of those who have moved downward in rank rate the Title X job as requiring more skills, while 43.2 percent of them rate the Title X job as requiring fewer skills. This finding provides support for the arbitrary occupational-ranking procedure introduced earlier in this chapter.

The occupational ranking is further supported by employees' ratings of overall job quality. One would expect employees who have moved upward to rate the Title X job more favorably than those who have moved to a job of

TABLE 6.10

Title X Job Quality as Compared with Prior Job: A Multivariate Analysis

Independent Variables	Maximum-Likelihood Estimate	Standard Error	T-Statistic	Beta Coefficient
Demographic characteristics				
White	-.063	.068	.923	-.046
Male	-.203*	.087	2.307	-.129
Age	-.020	.015	1.350	-.395
Age squared	.0002	.0001	1.382	.321
Prior job				
Quit job	.234*	.082	2.827	.152
Job subsidized	-2.93*	.096	3.053	-.157
Employed full time	-.034	.136	.248	-.015
Employed part time	-.161	.117	1.375	-.061
Title X job characteristics				
Weeks worked	.007*	.002	2.967	.142
Wage differential	.004*	.0005	8.036	.427
Skills—more than on prior job	.804*	.085	9.449	.580
Skills—fewer than on prior job	.393*	.083	4.734	-.247
Upward occupational change	.195*	.090	2.171	.120
Downwad occupational change	.025	.085	.293	.015
Training	-.147	.122	1.211	-.067
Constant term	1.692	.319	5.298	—

*Statistically significant at the 1-percent level or better.
Note: -2 times log-likelihood ratio = 394.5; N = 1,462.
Source: Compiled by the authors.

lower rank. This, in fact, is the case, and the correlation between movement in rank and the overall Title X job-quality rating is statistically significant at .001 level. Overall job-quality ratings are also consistent with other measures. For example, females, nonwhites, and younger workers—the very groups whose weekly earnings increased under Title X—tend more often to rate their Title X jobs as better than their prior jobs. Fully 70.3 percent of women (compared with 58.6 percent of men) judge the Title X job to be better. The same rating is given by 64 percent of nonwhites (versus 59 percent of whites) and by 67.5 percent of workers under 25 (versus 58.4 percent of older employees). Moreover, there is a significant correlation across the entire sample between job-quality ratings and increases in weekly earnings, and between job-quality and job-skill ratings. These factors tend to lend considerable weight to the employees' job comparisons.

The preceding discussion must be qualified by the understanding that employees' ratings of comparative job quality are likely to be affected by a variety of factors. Thus, it is appropriate to investigate the underlying determinants of the job-quality ratings in a multivariate context. In this analysis, three groups of independent variables are used: socioeconomic characteristics of employees, characteristics of prior employment, and attributes of the Title X job. The dependent variable is the employees' overall job-quality rating. The three categories of job quality (better, the same, or worse) imply an underlying continuous variable. However, since the variable is categorical, multiple-regression analysis is not the appropriate statistical technique.[2] An alternative model, not subject to the statistical deficiencies of linear regression, is probit analysis.[3]

The results of the multivariate probit analysis are presented in Table 6.10. As can be seen, age and race do not exert a statistically significant influence upon a person's job-quality rating of Title X. However, sex does; male workers are more likely to have a lower opinion of their Title X jobs, in comparison to their former jobs, than are female employees. Wage differentials, comparative-skill ratings, change in occupational ranking, and other factors are controlled for, so that the relationship of job quality to sex is independent of these factors.

The strongest indicators of an employee's opinion of relative Title X job quality are the perceived skills of the Title X job in relation to the prior job, and the wage differential between the two jobs. This finding is expectable, suggesting that employees' attitudes toward their Title X employment are directly related to the skills provided and the wages received. An upward change in occupational rank is also correlated with the job-quality ratings. However, the provision of training does not appear to be significantly related to employees' perceptions of job quality.

Summary

The comparative analysis of Title X and prior jobs shows that Title X has provided a similar type of work (compared to prior jobs) for one-third of its employees, and an upward occupational change for another one-quarter of employees. Mean wages and weekly earnings from Title X are about the same as from prior jobs, and more than one-half of employees have experienced an increase in weekly earnings under Title X. Moreover, Title X wages have tended to reduce the weekly earnings differential between males and females, and between whites and nonwhites, which is apparent on prior jobs. Finally, employees rate their Title X jobs highly in relation to their prior work. A majority judge their Title X jobs to be of higher quality than their prior jobs, and more feel that the Title X job requires more skills. Overall, a positive picture of Title X jobs emerges, a picture which is further confirmed in the next section.

COMPARISONS WITH USUAL JOB

Occupational Categories

Another reference point for analyzing the quality of Title X jobs is the Title X employees' usual job. Each employee was asked about "the work which you usually do to earn a living," with questions paralleling those asked about prior and Title X jobs. The latitude for respondents to designate their usual line of work is intended to provide a general career perspective, encompassing more than the prior job, a perspective within which Title X jobs can be evaluated. The simplicity of the usual-job concept may, in fact, make it more useful for evaluation than an extensive job history. Because the frame of reference is less specific, however, it was hypothesized that some responses might be subject to bias. The most likely source of bias was expected to be overstatement of the quality of the usual job. The analyses presented in this section, however, do not give evidence of such a bias, nor do other studies of the data. In fact, 4 percent of respondents specifically identified their Title X job as the last instance of work in their usual occupational category, and another 7 percent identified their usual jobs as being so close to the Title X job; in category, wage, and weekly earnings, that it could be argued that they were referring to the same jobs.[4]

The comparisons between usual and Title X jobs parallel those made between prior and Title X jobs in the previous section. First, Table 6.11 presents usual and Title X jobs by occupational category.

In the aggregate, the patterns of movement from usual jobs to Title X jobs differ very little from those already seen for prior jobs. Title X has provided fewer managerial, professional, clerical, and operative/technician jobs than Title X employees have usually held. More Title X positions are in the supervisory,

TABLE 6.11

Usual versus Title X Jobs

Occupational Category	Usual Jobs	Title X Jobs
Manager/administrator	2.8	2.2
Professional/technical	6.9	4.4
Supervisor/foreman	3.3	10.6
Construction trades	18.1	17.0
Construction laborer	7.4	12.3
Miscellaneous laborer	6.9	10.1
Operative/technician	10.0	1.7
Forestry, parks, recreation	2.6	13.1
Government/social service	1.9	2.9
Service	17.1	16.9
Clerical	11.7	8.6
Other	11.3	0.2

Source: Compiled by the authors.

laborer, and forestry categories, and are construction related. About one in every nine employees cites the "other" category in referring to his or her usual occupation. Most of them are farmers or farmworkers (7 percent), students (2.5 percent), or housewives (1.1 percent). The relatively high incidence of "other" usual occupations—higher in fact than the incidence of "other" prior jobs (8.4 percent)—is of some interest. Title X appears to have attracted noticeable numbers of farmers and farmworkers—most of whom had rather low weekly earnings—despite the fact that much of Title X work in round-two projects spanned the planting-growing-harvest seasons.

The extent to which Title X has provided work in an occupation of the same category as the employees' usual work is shown in Table 6.12. The table includes the percentage of such matches calculated by both methods presented earlier to analyze prior jobs, after "other" jobs are eliminated. For 37.5 percent of employees, Title X has provided work in the same general category as that of their usual work. If one adjusts to control for differences in occupational distribution, the proportion of possible matches increases to 48.8 percent. The fact that three of every eight Title X employees hold jobs similar to their usual jobs, and that, given the distribution of the work forces, virtually one-half of the possible matches have been made, is partial evidence that Title X has provided jobs which offer occupational continuity to participating employees.

Examining the distribution of matches across occupational categories, one finds the same pattern noted for prior jobs. Close to 60 percent of employees who are usually supervisors/foremen found similar jobs under Title X. Higher-

TABLE 6.12

Occupational Matches between Title X and Usual Jobs

Usual Occupational Category	Percent with Same Title X Occupation	Percent of Possible Matches
Manager/administrator	20.4	28.9
Professional/technical	27.1	48.0
Supervisor/foreman	58.5	58.5
Construction trades	47.3	55.7
Construction/laborers	38.0	38.0
Miscellaneous/laborer	36.4	36.4
Operative/technician	4.19	18.8
Forestry/parks/recreation	40.8	40.8
Government/social service	44.7	44.7
Service	42.2	47.6
Clerical	46.5	68.2
Total	37.5	48.8

Source: Compiled by the author.

than-average percentages of matches are also evident for persons who usually hold jobs in the construction trades, and in the clerical, government/social-service, and service categories. Matches are rarer for managers and professionals, and virtually nonexistent for persons usually employed as operatives or technicians. A high proportion of possible matches is observed for clerical workers, the construction trades, and supervisors or foremen.

The proportion of matches with usual occupations is somewhat higher than the proportion of Title X matches with prior jobs, regardless of which method of analyzing matches is used. However, the differences (37.5 percent versus 32.2 percent; 48.8 percent versus 44.5 percent) are almost entirely due to the fact that 4 percent of employees considered their Title X job to represent their usual occupation.

Lateral, upward, or downward occupational movement can be examined by applying the same hierarchy of occupational ranks that was applied to prior jobs. As shown in Table 6.13, better than one in every four job transitions is an upward occupational movement from usual work to Title X work. One in every five appears to be a transition to an occupation of lower rank. These proportions closely parallel those observed in the transition from the prior job to the Title X job. Clearly, regardless of the occupation being compared, Title X appears to have achieved the goal of providing employment that, for a large number of employees, may have called for previously acquired skills or enhanced skills.

TABLE 6.13

Occupational Movement Represented by the Transition from Usual Title X Jobs

Movement	Percent of Employees
Upward	25.8
Lateral	53.9
Downward	20.3

Note: If farmers are classified as rank 3, the percentage of upward occupational changes reduces to 21.3 percent; lateral moves increase to 58.4 percent.

Source: Compiled by the authors.

Wages, Hours, and Weekly Earnings

Wages, hours, and weekly earnings on usual and Title X jobs are comparable, as shown in Table 6.14; no significant differences between the two jobs are found on these measures. On the average, both usual and Title X jobs are full-time positions, with the mean hours per week worked on the usual job being slightly higher than the mean for Title X. The slight difference in means, however, disguises a substantial difference in the distributions of hours worked per week. Fully 12 percent of Title X employees reported they worked less than 35 hours per week on their usual jobs, and 22 percent worked more than 40 hours per week. In contrast, Title X jobs more often (89 percent of the time) require 35-40 hours per week, rarely (3 percent) involve overtime, and less often (8 percent) are part time.

TABLE 6.14

Wages, Hours, and Earnings: Usual and Title X Jobs

Measure	Usual Job	Title X Job
Mean hours per week	40.4	38.6
Median hours per week	40.0	40.0
Mean hourly wage	$3.53	$3.54
Median hourly wage	3.00	3.14
Mean weekly earnings	$141.50	$135.57
Median weekly earnings	120.00	123.00

Source: Compiled by the authors.

TABLE 6.15

Distribution of Weekly Earnings:
Usual and Title X Jobs

Weekly Earnings	Percent of Employees	
	Usual Job	Title X Job
$0–100	38.8	28.0
101–125	16.0	23.6
126–150	12.6	19.9
151–175	9.0	14.0
176–200	6.9	7.0
201–250	6.7	2.4
251–300	3.9	2.3
Over 300	6.0	2.9

Source: Compiled by the authors.

The mean effective hourly wages of usual and Title X jobs are virtually identical, though the median wage for Title X jobs is almost 5 percent higher. The median weekly earnings for Title X jobs are also insignificantly higher, but because of overtime pay, mean weekly earnings are 4 percent higher for usual jobs than for Title X jobs. The distribution of weekly earnings for usual jobs, like the earnings distribution for prior jobs, is somewhat different from the earnings distribution under Title X, as shown in Table 6.15.

Weekly earnings from the usual job are more likely to be very low or very high. Fully 38.8 percent of Title X employees earned $100 per week or less from their usual jobs, while 16.6 percent earned over $200 per week. In contrast, 28 percent of employees earn $100 per week or less on Title X jobs and only 7.6 percent earn over $200 per week. The differing distribution of weekly earnings parallels the differing distribution of hours worked per week. Moreover, it suggests that, in comparison with usual work (as well as with prior jobs), Title X provided substantially higher or substantially lower weekly earnings to a large proportion of people. This generalization is confirmed in Table 6.16.

Fully 84.6 percent of Title X employees have experienced a change in weekly earnings, as compared to their usual jobs, by working under Title X. Better than three in every ten have Title X earnings that vary by more than $50 per week (higher or lower) from their usual weekly earnings. Title X represents an increase in weekly earnings for 44.5 percent, a decrease for 40.1 percent. Thus about the same number of people appear to have benefited from Title X than have lost weekly earnings, vis-a-vis usual jobs. For a temporary job-creation program, which is intended to help the unemployed, but is not explicitly aimed

TITLE 6.16

Change in Weekly Earnings: Title X Job as Compared with Usual Job

Change in Weekly Earnings	Percent of Employees		
	Title X Earnings Higher	Title X Earnings Lower	Earnings the Same
$0	_a	—	15.4
$1–50	29.9	23.3	
51–100	10.5	8.9	
101–150	2.7	3.6	
Over 150	1.4	4.4	
Total	44.5	40.1	15.4

a Data not available.

Source: Compiled by the authors.

to provide jobs which are as good as, or better than, employees' usual jobs, this is a positive finding. One should note, however, that the size of weekly earnings increases is smaller than the size of decreases. Fully 67 percent of increases, but only 58 percent of decreases, are $50 per week or less. Almost 20 percent of decreases are more than $100 per week, while only 9 percent of weekly earnings increases are this large.

The positive effect of Title X jobs in balancing earnings, which was evident in comparing them to prior jobs, is also noticeable in comparing them to usual jobs. Table 6.17 shows that those demographic groups most poorly paid in their usual jobs have been paid more under Title X. Every group who had less than the mean weekly earnings for the usual job has increased its weekly earnings under Title X. The one exception is black employees, who receive disproportionately low weekly earnings on both jobs. Conversely, all groups with higher-than-average usual weekly earnings have earned less per week under Title X. Although there are still noticeable differences in the Title X weekly earnings for different demographic groups, the Job Opportunities Program has acted to some degree as an earnings equalizer.

Employees' Job Comparisons

Employees' comparisons of usual and Title X jobs further support the perceived value of Title X. As shown in Table 6.18, better than 50 percent judge the work required by Title X to be similar or identical to that of their usual jobs.

TABLE 6.17

Average Weekly Earnings: Employees on Usual and Title X Jobs

| Category | Weekly Earnings | | |
	Usual Job	Title X Job	Change
Age			
15–19	$ 98.32	$110.01	+11.69
20–24	122.26	129.30	+ 7.04
25–34	153.20	144.57	− 8.63
35–44	162.69	146.47	−16.22
45–59	164.23	146.17	−18.06
60 and over	120.98	152.61	+31.63
Sex			
Male	155.17	147.84	−$7.31
Female	96.97	108.53	+11.56
Race			
White	154.59	141.81	−$12.78
Total black and other	123.50	128.34	+ 4.84
Black	119.00	113.65	− 5.35
American Indian	126.64	153.35	+26.71
Other	146.73	150.55	+13.82
All employees	141.50	135.60	−$5.90

Source: Compiled by the authors.

TABLE 6.18

Employees' Comparisons of Usual and Title X Jobs

Item of Comparison	Percent of Employees
Type of work	
Identical	10.5
Similar or related	40.7
Dissimilar, unrelated	48.8
Skills required	
More skills on Title X	31.8
Same number of skills	41.5
Fewer skills on Title X	26.7
Overall Job Quality	
Title X job better	52.6
Jobs about the same	35.1
Title X job worse	12.3

Source: Compiled by the authors.

This is consistent with the findings on occupational matches presented earlier. When employees are asked to rate the skills required, Title X holds its own with employees' usual occupations. Better than 40 percent judge the skills required by the two jobs to be the same number, and more than three of every ten employees (31.8 percent) report that their Title X jobs require more skills than their usual jobs. Only about one in four (26.7 percent) feel that fewer skills are needed on their Title X jobs.

Overall, more than one-half of employees (52.6 percent) regard their Title X jobs to be better than their usual work. Only about one in eight (12.3 percent) judge the overall quality of the Title X job to be worse. Moreover, Title X gets higher ratings from the demographic groups who earned the least in their usual jobs, those same groups for which Title X meant an increase in weekly income. Fully 65 percent of females, compared to 48.7 percent of males, judge their Title X jobs to be better than their usual work. A higher quality rating is given by 56 percent of nonwhites, in contrast to 49.8 percent of whites. Moreover, 57.5 percent of employees under 25 or over 59 years of age, but only 49.2 percent of the 25–59 age group, judge Title X as superior.

A multivariate analysis confirms these findings, as shown in Table 6.19. More women and younger workers perceive Title X jobs to be better than do men and older workers. Increased skills, higher wages, longer job duration under Title X, and upward changes in occupational rank are all positively correlated with the job-quality rating. There are no significant relationships between race, prior employment status, or Title X training and the ratings of overall job quality.

TABLE 6.19

Title X Job Quality as Compared with Usual Job: A Multivariate Analysis

Independent Variables	Maximum-Likelihood Estimate	Standard Error	T-Statistic	Beta Coefficient
Demographic characteristics				
White	-.023	.063	0.365	-.016
Male	-.302*	.080	3.755	-.179
Age	-.052*	.014	3.688	-.976
Age squared	.0006*	.0001	3.640	.915
Title X job characteristics				
Training	.079	.090	0.880	.039
Weeks worked	.010*	.002	4.720	.201
Wage differential	.003*	.0004	7.374	.323
Skills–more than on usual job	.499*	.079	6.311	.328
Skills–fewer than on usual job	-.421*	.075	5.641	-.268
Upward occupation change	.260*	.084	3.065	.148
Downward occupation change	-.089	.080	1.119	-.049
Employed part time on prior job	-.043	.126	.343	-.015
Employed full time on prior job	.0002	.107	.002	.001
Constant term	1.973*	.281	7.011	—

*Statistically significant at the 1 percent level or better.
Note: -2 times log-likelihood ratio = 350.7; N = 1,534.
Source: Compiled by the authors.

Thus, in comparison with employees' usual work, Title X emerges as having provided meaningful employment. As in the examination of prior jobs, comparative analyses of occupations, earnings, and employees' perceptions of usual and Title X jobs offer a generally positive picture of the quality of employment provided under Title X.

SUMMARY

Whether one's point of reference is prior jobs or usual work, Title X jobs are roughly comparable. Hourly wages, hours worked per week, and average weekly earnings on Title X jobs are roughly the same as those on either prior or usual jobs. Perhaps more important for policy makers is that more people have experienced an increase in weekly earnings than have experienced a decrease. Moreover, most of the earnings improvements have accrued to those demographic groups who generally earn less in the U.S. labor market, whether on usual jobs, on prior jobs, or on Title X jobs. Youthful and older workers, women, and minorities have experienced the principal increases in weekly earnings and hourly wages under Title X. Even though they still earn less under Title X than other groups, Title X has clearly had a short-term positive impact on their weekly earnings relative to other groups.

Generally speaking, between 32 and 45 percent of employees have had Title X jobs similar to their prior jobs. Between 38 and 49 percent have had Title X jobs similar to their usual work. A quick-startup, countercyclical jobs program that shows this degree of occupational continuity may, in fact, have provided jobs which utilize or build upon the skills of employees. Indeed, occupational rankings developed in this chapter suggest that more employees have moved up in their jobs under Title X than have moved down. And a large majority of employees (about 75 percent) report that their Title X jobs require more skills than, or the same number as, their prior or usual jobs. For every two employees who feel that Title X requires fewer skills, about three employees say that the Title X job demands more skills.

Finally, employees compare their Title X jobs favorably to prior or usual jobs. Regardless of the comparison, a majority of employees feel that their Title X jobs are of a better overall quality as compared with their other (usual or prior) work. Only about one in nine ratings reflect employee opinions that their Title X jobs are of lower quality. No major demographic group rates their Title X jobs negatively. The most positive ratings come from those selected segments with particular disadvantages in the general labor market—women, minorities, the young, and the old.

In sum, the occupational results of Title X are tentatively positive. They are positive in that there have been clear redistributive effects; the jobs receive high marks from employees; and employment under the program is comparable to prior or usual work on whatever other measure is observable. They are tentative because the nature, resources, and timing of the study preclude a full examination of postprogram employment experience, an examination which could confirm or contradict the direction of the findings presented here. Postprogram findings based upon limited observations are presented in Chapter 7, findings which, though not generalizable, are nonetheless consistent with the positive picture of Title X jobs seen in this chapter.

NOTES

1. See Michael Wiseman, "Public Employment as Fiscal Policy," *Brookings Papers on Economic Activity*, vol. 1 (Washington, D.C.: Brookings Institution, 1976), pp. 67–114; George E. Johnson and James Tomola, "The Efficacy of Public Service Employment Programs," *Technical Analysis Paper 17A* (Washington, D.C.: Department of Labor, ASPER, 1975); and National Planning Association, *Evaluation of the Economic Impact Project* (Washington, D.C.: National Planning Association, May 1974).

2. The statistical problems of regression analysis applied to a categorical dependent variable are discussed in Robert S. Pindyek and Daniel L. Rubinfield, *Econometric Models and Economic Forecasts* (New York: McGraw-Hill, 1976), pp. 237–64.

3. Binary probit analysis has been extended to handle more than two categories on the dependent variable, in William Zavonia and Richard McKelvey, "A Statistical Model for the Analysis of Legislative Voting Behavior" (Paper presented at the annual meetings of the American Political Science Association, New York, 1969). The basic assumption of probit analysis is that the data fit a linear-regression model with the usual assumptions, but only a discrete number of responses (in our case, three) on the underlying scale for the dependent variable are observed. A maximum-likelihood iterative procedure is utilized in probit to estimate the coefficients in the multivariate model. Interpretation of probit is most easily understood by relating it to traditional multiple-regression analysis. The variation in the dependent variable that is explained in a regression model is measured by the coefficient of determination, R^2. The probit technique constrains the predicted values to an interval and does not investigate the underlying continuous dependent variable. Thus, no measure that analyzes the total variation in the dependent variable exists with probit. The overall statistical significance of probit is measured by the likelihood-ratio test. This corresponds to the F-test of the regression model. With respect to the maximum-likelihood estimates of probit, they are not partial effects. This results because of the noncontinuous nature of the dependent variable. Moreover, due to the fact that more than two categories exist on the dependent variable, the coefficients cannot be interpreted as conditional-probability estimates. Interpretation of the probit maximum-likelihood coefficients is limited to direction of influence and statistical significance. Since maximum-likelihood estimates are in different units (dollars, for estimating wage differentials, and time, for weeks worked), they cannot be compared directly. To overcome this, the coefficients are converted into units of standard deviation. The results of these calculations, the beta coefficients, are reported in Table 6.10. The procedure for converting regression coefficients into units of standard deviation is discussed in Taro Yarmane, *Statistics: An Introductory Analysis*, 2d ed. (New York: Harper and Row, 1967), pp. 761–63.

4. On the surface, this suggests the possibility of substantial local substitution, of the sort explored in George Johnson and James Tomola, "The Efficacy of Public Service Employment Programs," *Technical Analysis Paper 17A* (Washington, D.C.: Department of

Labor, ASPER, 1975). The data base is not constructed in a way which allows for conclusive examination of this issue. However, it should be noted that the survey questionnaire asks for the last instance of work in the usual occupational category, allowing a respondent to name the Title X job even if he or she has not otherwise had work in the usual occupational category for a considerable period of time. Moreover, those for whom Title X represents their first job will also cite it as their usual job. Thus, it is unlikely that the finding cited above is, itself, evidence of substantial substitution.

7

POST-TITLE X
EMPLOYMENT

For a number of reasons, the postprogram experiences of Title X employees could not be documented fully in this study. First, no system of collecting data on participants was imposed upon Title X projects, except for a payroll report completed by a sample of projects. Thus, there are no routinely collected data on participants' characteristics, prior work experience, project work experience, or postprogram labor-market experience. Second, the timing of this study required that primary data be collected at one point in time, while the short-term projects were still in operation; thus, most employees were still working on their Title X jobs. Third, limitations of both timing and resources ruled out a longitudinal study.

Despite these limitations, a significant effort was made to establish a partial postprogram dimension, since it is critical to any assessment of employment effects. Three sources of data were utilized. First, at 52 projects visited to study potential long-term project impacts, Abt staff searched records, where they existed, to try to discover the employment status of terminees. Second, about 10 percent of the major employee sample had terminated employment prior to being interviewed; data on their employment immediately after termination were collected. Third, a special small sample of terminees, independent of the major sample, was taken for study. Twenty-one projects that had completed work 2-6 months prior to sampling were selected. Small cohorts of former project employees were tracked and interviewed, thus providing a small data base on their postprogram experience several months after the completion of Title X work. Because of the size and nature of the data bases, it would be misleading to use them to generalize about the entire Title X program. The data, however, do provide a partial and suggestive picture of the likely short-term employment impacts of Title X.

PERCENT EMPLOYED

An initial impression is given by data collected from the 52 projects studied for long-term impact. Information—sometimes partial, sometimes complete—was available on terminees from 45 of the projects and is shown in Table 7.1.

A total of 2,288 persons had terminated employment at the 45 projects at the time of site visits. Of these, employment information was available on 1,585. No information was available on 703 terminees, from either project records or project staff. Thus, two sets of calculations are presented in Table 7.1. If one assumes that all the terminees of unknown status were unemployed (an overly conservative assumption), then 32.9 percent of terminees were employed after Title X termination. If one limits attention to the terminees of known employment status, postprogram employment increases to 47.4 percent. The latter figure is probably more accurate.* Regardless of the overall employment percentage, the data in Table 7.1 are encouraging. First, recalling that over 80 percent of Title X employees were unemployed prior to the program, even the conservative postprogram employment estimate of 32.9 percent is an improvement. Second, a majority of employed terminees (55 percent) had found work in the private sector. Third, very few had moved on to another subsidized job; only about 4 percent of employed terminees had switched from Title X to another subsidized program

The data from 45 projects are only the grossest indication of employment status after Title X termination. Samples from two surveys provide complete data, though based in each case upon a small number of employees.

Sample A includes 198 persons from Abt's large-study sample who terminated from their Title X jobs between the time of project selection and the time of the interviews. About 40 percent terminated because the project or their job on the project was ending. Almost 19 percent quit to take another job. The rest quit without taking another job or left for other reasons (including being fired). Sample A illustrates the employment status of terminees very shortly after Title X termination, with the mean time between termination and the interview

---

*In the absence of other information, a case could be made that those terminees of unknown status are more likely to be unemployed than those of known status, having dropped out of contact with local institutional information sources and possibly out of the labor force. A counterargument is also possible, based upon the hypothesis that a number of unknown terminees may have moved to another job, found a job outside the local area, or, because of full-time employment, become less visible to local institutional information sources.

TABLE 7.1

Employment Status of Terminees

Employment Status	Number of Terminees	Percent of Terminees	Percent of Known Terminees
Hired by Title X agency or employer	219	9.6	13.8
Other private-sector (unsubsidized) job	414	18.1	26.1
Other public/nonprofit (unsubsidized) job	87	3.8	5.5
Subsidized job	31	1.4	2.0
Other (school, institutionalized, armed forces)	111	4.9	7.0
Unemployed	723	31.6	45.6
Unknown	703	30.7	—
Total	2,288	100.0	100.0

Source: Compiled by the authors.

being 3.5 weeks. Because the sample is a subsample of Abt's large statistical Title X sample, results may be considered generalizable within the limitations of sample size.

Sample B includes 122 terminees from 21 projects selected specifically for followup on terminees. Fully 86 percent terminated because the project or their job on the project was ending. Only 1.7 percent quit to take another job, and the remainder either quit without taking another job or terminated for other reasons. Unlike sample A, sample B cannot be considered statistically representative of Title X, since the 21 projects could not be chosen in a representative manner.* Samples A and B differ in one other respect: In sample B, the mean time lapse between termination and the date of interviewing is 18.6 weeks. Thus, sample B illustrates the employment status of Title X terminees about 4.5 months after termination.

Table 7.2 shows that 39 percent of sample A terminees were employed approximately 3.5 weeks after termination; 45 percent were unemployed and

---

*Sample B consisted of four public-works construction projects, four civil-works construction projects, four forestry/recreation projects, four rehabilitation and repair projects, four service projects, and one training project. As a result, construction-related occupations are overrepresented, service and government occupations underrepresented.

TABLE 7.2

Employment Status of Terminees

Employment Status	Sample A (n = 198)	Sample B (n = 122)
Employed	39%	58%
Full time	34	51
Part time	5	7
Unemployed	61	42
Looking for work	45	33
Not in labor force	16	9

Source: Compiled by the authors.

looking for work, while 16 percent were technically no longer in the labor force. Within 18.6 weeks of termination, 58 percent of sample B were employed, with 33 percent looking for work; only 9 percent were not actively seeking a job. Because of the differences in the samples, these percentages cannot be relied upon with certitude to establish a postprogram employment trend. They are, however, in the same ballpark as the findings available from the 45 out of 52 projects studied for long-term impact, and, even considered separately, represent higher levels of employment than are observed for the period prior to Title X employment. Moreover, as in the 45 projects, the private sector accounts for a majority of jobs found by persons in both sample A (55 percent) and sample B (51 percent). However, more terminees from each sample report that their new job is subsidized (14 percent and 27 percent, respectively).*

TERMINEES VERSUS REMAINING EMPLOYEES

Before continuing our examination of the jobs obtained by Title X employees after termination, two questions should be addressed. First, are the terminees from the Title X program substantially different from other employees who were still working under Title X when the survey was conducted? If there are systematic differences between terminees and nonterminees, it could suggest that

---

*This relatively high degree of subsidized postprogram employment should be examined more closely. It suggests the desirability of a more systematic and large-scale followup than has been possible in this study.

TABLE 7.3

Demographic Characteristics:
Title X Terminees and Remaining Employees

Characteristic	Remaining Employees	Terminees (sample A)*
Male	76%	82%
Female	24	18
White	56	65
Total black and others	44	35
Age		
15–19	9	15
20–24	27	30
25–34	29	25
35–44	14	16
45–59	15	11
60 and over	6	3
Income		
$0–$4,000	28	35
4–6,000	32	20
6–8,000	16	15
8–10,000	11	9
10–15,000	8	11
15–20,000	3	8
Over 20,000	2	2

*The remainder of this chapter focuses upon sample A, those persons in the original sample who had terminated their Title X employment at the time of the survey. Sample B data confirm the direction of most of the findings from sample A. However, because the employees in sample B are quite different from those in sample A—having been chosen from a nonrepresentative group of projects—data on them are not presented here.

Source: Compiled by the authors.

TABLE 7.4

Prior Employment Status: Remaining
Title X Employees and Terminees

Prior Employment Status	Remaining Employees	Terminees (sample A)
Employed full time	11.3%	9.0%
Employed part time	7.1	6.3
Unemployed	81.7	84.7
Duration of unemployment		
Mean duration	28.8 weeks	28.9 weeks
1–4 weeks	17.7%	19.5%
5–13 weeks	24.3	18.9
14–26 weeks	21.3	26.8
27–52 weeks	20.0	17.6
Over 52 weeks	16.7	17.1
Mean weekly earnings from prior job	$137.49	$140.59

Source: Compiled by the authors.

certain types of enrollees, or enrollees with certain types of labor-market or program experiences, are more likely to terminate employment in a program such as Title X. Moreover, it could imply that the labor-market experiences of nonterminees are likely to differ somewhat from those observed among terminees.

The question may be addressed, first, by examining the demographic characteristics of Title X terminees and remaining employees in the main Abt sample (see Table 7.3).

Men and whites are more represented among Title X terminees than among remaining employees. Given national labor-market statistics, these proportions would tend to favor terminees over remaining employees in the labor market after Title X employment. This possibility is balanced by the fact that terminees are somewhat younger than remaining employees and, as such, more likely to be unemployed. Total family income is slightly, but not substantially, higher for terminees than for remaining employees. On balance, there are differences among terminees and remaining employees, but not of the scale to warrant a conclusion that the experience of remaining employees in the labor market after Title X job termination is likely to be greatly different from that of terminees.

Prior employment status or labor-market experience might also be related to the likelihood of termination or to postprogram labor-market experience. This hypothesis is tested in Table 7.4.

As seen in Table 7.4, there are no notable distinctions between Title X terminees and remaining employees. Terminees appear slightly less likely to have been employed prior to Title X, but the difference is not significant. Mean duration of unemployment is almost identical for the two subsamples, and the distribution of weeks unemployed varies only slightly among terminees and remaining employees. Average weekly earnings on prior jobs might be another expected difference between remaining employees and terminees. The differences, however, are very slight. Remaining employees earned an average of $137.49 per week on their prior jobs, while terminees earned $140.59 per week.

A third possible difference between remaining employees and terminees could be their employment experience under Title X, an experience which could affect both the likelihood of termination and the chances of finding a job after leaving the program. Available measures are presented in Table 7.5.

Clearly, there are no notable differences between the Title X hours, wages, or weekly earnings of terminees and nonterminees. This is evidence that the Title X employment experience may not be related to termination. The only objective measure upon which terminees and remaining employees differ substantially is mean weeks worked under Title X, a figure which, almost by definition, will be lower for terminees.

Differences do, however, appear on some of the subjective measures. For example, Title X jobs of terminees were of a slightly lower rank (in applying the

TABLE 7.5

Measures of Title X Jobs of Terminees and Nonterminees

Measure	Nonterminees	Terminees
Mean hours per week	38.5	39.2
Median hours per week	40	40
Mean hourly wage	$3.55	$3.48
Median hourly wage	$3.13	$3.20
Mean weekly earnings	$135.50	$136.60
Median weekly earnings	$120.00	$124.00
Matches with prior job	33.3%	22.5%
Matches with usual job	37.8	31.9
Rank of Title X Job*		
1	17.5	14.9
2	21.9	19.7
3	60.6	65.4
Weeks worked under Title X	36.6	22.5

*The occupational ranking presented here was described in Chapter 6.
Source: Compiled by the authors.

occupational ranking introduced earlier) than the jobs of nonterminees. Similarly, the extent to which Title X jobs match with either the prior or the usual jobs of terminees is lower than for remaining employees. Moreover, the ratings given by terminees comparing their usual jobs with their Title X jobs are more negative than those given by nonterminees. Only 21.4 percent of terminees (compared with 33.0 percent of nonterminees) reported that their Title X jobs required more skills than their usual jobs. Fully 40.1 percent (compared with 25.3 percent for nonterminees) said they required fewer skills. Job-quality ratings were also consistently lower, with 35.7 percent of terminees saying their Title X job was better than their usual job, and 21.4 percent rating it worse. In contrast, 54.6 percent of nonterminees judged their Title X job to be better, and only 11.1 percent considered it worse.

Overall, the differences between terminees and nonterminees are slight, not sufficient to support hypotheses regarding likelihood of termination or likely differences in postprogram experience. The employment status and recent labor-market experience of each group are comparable, as are the wages, hours, and weekly earnings under Title X. There are slight demographic differences, but not of a sort to warrant any tentative thoughts about termination or postprogram employment probabilities. Only the differences in occupational matches and job-quality ratings are sufficiently large and consistent to justify tentative hypotheses on the likelihood of terminating. First, it may be argued that persons whose Title X jobs are different from their prior and/or usual jobs are more likely to terminate than those for whom a match is achieved. Second, a rather self-evident finding is that those who are less happy with their jobs are more likely to terminate than those who are not. Otherwise, the analysis shows no notable differences between terminees and nonterminees.

EMPLOYED TERMINEES VERSUS UNEMPLOYED TERMINEES

A second major question concerns differences between employed terminees and nonemployed terminees. Are there differences in demographics, prior labor-force status, or Title X experience that are related to the ability to find a job after Title X job termination? In fact, this question cannot be addressed with certainty, since the number of terminees interviewed is too small to support conclusions. However, as suggestive and tentative information, the data on terminees from the major Abt sample are worthy of examination.

Demographic characteristics of terminees are presented in Table 7.6. Working terminees are somewhat more likely to be female, and are slightly younger, than terminees who are not working. Considering these attributes alone, one would expect, from general labor-force data, that they would have greater difficulties finding a job. There is no difference in the ethnic composition

TABLE 7.6

Demographic Characteristics:
Employed and Not Employed Title X Terminees

Characteristic	Terminees	
	Employed	Not employed
Male	78%	85%
Female	22	15
White	65	65
Total black and other	35	35
Age		
15–19	14	16
20–24	35	26
25–34	27	23
35–44	20	13
45–59	4	16
60 and over	0	5
Income		
$0–4,000	31	37
4–6,000	18	22
6–8,000	20	13
8–10,000	9	8
10–15,000	16	8
15–20,000	5	10
Over 20,000	1	2

Source: Compiled by the authors.

TABLE 7.7

Prior Employment Status:
Employed and Non-Employed Terminees

Prior Employment Status	Employed Terminees	Non-employed Terminees
Employed	22%	11%
Unemployed	73	76
Not in labor force	5	13
Duration of unemployment		
Mean duration	22 weeks	34 weeks
1–4 weeks	31%	12%
5–14 weeks	24	16
15–26 weeks	25	28
27–52 weeks	9	23
Over 52 weeks	11	21
Prior job		
Mean weekly earnings	$153.20	$133.25

Source: Compiled by the authors.

of employed and not employed terminees. The employed have a slightly higher family income than the unemployed, but the difference is not very striking. Overall, demographic differences between the employed and unemployed are not extreme and, in comparison with labor-market data, not associated with the likelihood of employment.*

Distinctions in prior employment status, however, are more noticeable, as shown in Table 7.7. Twice the proportion of employed as not employed terminees had been employed at the time of hire under Title X, and fewer had been out of the labor force. Moreover, the duration of prior unemployment for the previously unemployed averages substantially less for working terminees. Finally, the average prior weekly earnings of employed terminees has been 15 percent greater than prior weekly earnings of not employed terminees. Clearly, the employment experience prior to Title X has been more positive for those who

---

*The special sample of terminees shows a similar pattern. More working terminees are female (25 percent versus 15 percent), younger, and have a higher family income. Ethnic differences are marginal.

TABLE 7.8

Measures of Title X Jobs of Working and Nonworking Terminees

Measure	Employed Terminees	Unemployed Terminees
Mean hours per week	39.1	39.3
Median hours per week	40.0	40.0
Mean hourly wages	$3.38	$3.51
Median hourly wages	$2.92	$3.26
Mean weekly earnings	$133.47	$139.47
Median weekly earnings	$111.65	$130.41
Matches with prior job	15.3%	27.7%
Matches with usual job	27.8	34.5
Rank of Title X job		
1	18.7	11.5
2	24.0	16.8
3	57.3	71.7
Weeks worked under Title X	18	24

Source: Compiled by the authors.

have found jobs after Title X employment, though the number of terminees observed is too small to draw strong conclusions.*

Finally, measures of Title X work experience are shown in Table 7.8.

Indicators of the Title X experience of employed and non-employed terminees are very mixed. Both groups had full-time work under Title X, and the rank of Title X jobs held by employed terminees was somewhat higher than that held by terminees who are not employed. However, on the other measures, non-employed terminees seem to have fared better under Title X. Their mean hourly wages and weekly earnings are somewhat higher, and the medians are substantially higher, indicating the fact that a few of the employed terminees received very high wages under Title X while others received lower amounts.

The wage and weekly earnings figures are surprising, given the superior prior wages and labor-force status of employed terminees. Moreover, non-employed terminees stayed longer on their Title X jobs, and a higher proportion

---

*Results from the special sample of terminees parallel those presented above. Prior employment was 42 percent among employed terminees and only 26 percent among unemployed terminees. Mean duration of unemployment was also lower for employed terminees (11 weeks versus 21 weeks). Average weekly earnings, however, were virtually identical for both subgroups.

received Title X jobs that were similar to their prior and/or usual jobs. Clearly, in this small sample of terminees the Title X work experience is not positively related to postprogram employment status. If anything, it appears to be negatively related. Part of the answer could lie in the fact that only 26 percent of employed terminees left a project because the project or job was ending, compared with almost 49 percent of unemployed terminees. It is reasonable to hypothesize that many employed terminees—because they had lower wages and Title X jobs that did not match their prior and/or usual jobs—were more motivated to look for and accept subsequent employment. Unemployed terminees, on the other hand, might have been more satisfied with their Title X employment, particularly in relation to other labor-market opportunities. They tended to remain on a project until it ended, without lining up a subsequent job.

Overall, postprogram employment status is related only to preprogram labor-force experience. Working terminees are more likely to have been in the labor force and to have been working prior to their Title X jobs. They experienced a shorter duration of employment than nonworking terminees and earned more on their prior jobs. However, the demographic differences between the two groups are not great, and Title X employment experience seems to be entirely unrelated to employment status after the program.

Occupational Comparison

Postprogram jobs of terminees may be compared with Title X jobs in the same manner as that of comparing Title X jobs with prior and usual jobs. However, because the number of respondents with subsequent jobs is very small, the comparative findings are only suggestive and not generalizable. Moreover,

TABLE 7.9

Ranking of Title X and Subsequent Jobs

Occupational Rank	All Title X Jobs	Title X Jobs of Employed Terminees	Subsequent Jobs
1	17.2%	18.7%	17.3%
2	21.6	24.0	33.3
3	61.2	57.3	45.3
4	—[a]	—	4.0

[a] Data not available.
Source: Compiled by the authors.

certain types of comparisons cannot be made. For example, the distribution of subsequent jobs by occupational category produces cell sizes too small to be worthy of examination. It should be noted, however, that 37.5 percent of employed terminees found jobs which were of the same occupational category as that of their Title X jobs. This incidence of occupational matching is somewhat higher than the 32.2 percent incidence of matching noted between Title X and prior jobs, and identical to the 37.5 percent matching observed with usual jobs.

In Table 7.9 the distribution of Title X and subsequent jobs by rank is summarized. One can observe that subsequent jobs are, in general, of a slightly higher rank than either the Title X jobs held by employed terminees or the overall distribution of Title X jobs. However, the differences are only slight. Moreover, in moving from Title X to other work, exactly the same proportion of employed terminees (20 percent) moved up in rank as moved down in rank. Overall, the Title X and subsequent jobs of employed terminees appear comparable.

A slightly different picture emerges from a comparison of wages and weekly earnings. As shown in Table 7.10, subsequent jobs—like Title X jobs—are usually full-time positions. However, subsequent jobs pay more. An employed terminee receives 27 cents per hour more than the typical Title X employee, a difference of 7.6 percent. Average weekly earnings from subsequent jobs are $18.10 greater than from the average Title X job, an increase of 13.3 percent. Even greater differences are noted when subsequent jobs are compared with Title X jobs of employed terminees. The average individual who leaves the

TABLE 7.10

Wages, Hours, and Weekly Earnings: Title X and Subsequent Jobs

Measure	All Title X Jobs	Title X Jobs of Employed Terminees	Subsequent Jobs
Mean hours per week	38.6	39.2	39.6
Median hours per week	40.0	40.0	40.0
Mean hourly wage	$3.54	$3.38	$3.81
Median hourly wage	$3.14	$2.92	$3.16
Mean weekly earnings	$135.60	$133.47	$153.70
Median weekly earnings	$123.00	$111.65	$125.00

Source: Compiled by the authors.

TABLE 7.11

Distribution of Weekly Earnings:
Title X and Subsequent Jobs

Weekly Earnings	Title X Jobs of Employed Terminees	Subsequent Jobs
$0–100	31.4%	31.4%
101–125	34.3	20.0
126–150	14.3	18.6
151–175	7.1	2.9
176–200	5.7	8.6
201–300	1.4	10.0
Over 300	5.7	8.6

Source: Compiled by the authors.

Title X program and finds another job receives an hourly wage increase of 12.7 percent, or 43 cents an hour. Average weekly earnings increase by 15.2 percent. In other words, persons who have terminated their Title X jobs and found other work experience an average increase in earnings of $20.23 per week. The weekly earnings distribution for employed terminees, for their Title X and subsequent jobs, further illustrates the earnings differences (see Table 7.11).

At the low end of the weekly-earnings spectrum, the same proportion of employed terminees (31.4 percent) earned $100 per week or less from both Title X jobs and subsequent jobs. However, a substantially larger proportion of subsequent jobs than of Title X jobs pay a reasonably high weekly wage. Fully 18.6 percent of employed terminees earned over $200 per week from their subsequent jobs, in contrast to only 7.1 percent earning over $200 for their Title X jobs. Thus, one would expect that a high percentage of employed terminees received increased weekly earnings from their subsequent jobs. This, in fact, is the case; more than twice as many employed terminees (58.6 percent) experienced an increase in weekly earnings as experienced a decrease (28.6 percent). Fully 11.4 percent have earnings increases of more than $100 per week over their Title X jobs, as shown in Table 7.12.

The positive earnings experience of employed terminees on their post-program jobs is consistent with their favorable comparisons of subsequent jobs with their Title X jobs. As has been the case in comparisons of Title X jobs with prior and usual jobs, a majority of respondents consider the two jobs to involve dissimilar types of work. However, unlike the other jobs, the subsequent job is compared favorably with the Title X job on both skills required and overall job

TABLE 7.12

Change in Weekly Earnings Experienced by Employed Terminees in Going from Title X Job to Subsequent Job

Change in Weekly Earnings	Title X Earnings Higher	Title X Earnings Lower	Earnings the Same
$0	_a	–	12.8%
1–50	20.0%	30.0%	–
51–100	8.5	17.1	–
101–150	–	5.7	–
Over 150	–	5.7	–
Total	28.6	58.6	12.8

a Data not available.
Source: Compiled by the authors.

quality. A plurality of employed terminees rate their subsequent jobs as requiring more skills than their Title X jobs. Fully four times as many judge their new jobs to be better, overall, than their Title X jobs as judge them to be worse. Thus, though analysis of occupational-rank changes does not reveal much differ-

TABLE 7.13

Employees' Comparisons of Title X and Subsequent Jobs

Item of Comparison	Response
Type of work	
Identical	10.3%
Similar or related	28.2
Dissimilar or unrelated	61.5
Skills required	
More on Title X	11.7
About the same	40.3
Fewer on Title X	48.1
Job quality	
Title X job is better	11.7
Jobs are about the same	41.6
Title X job is worse	46.8

Source: Compiled by the authors.

ence between Title X jobs and subsequent jobs, both wages and employee ratings favor the subsequent jobs. Recalling that Title X jobs have been shown to be comparable to, or better than, prior and usual jobs on most measures, the favorable data on subsequent jobs suggest the possibility that Title X may have had positive effects on the short-term career movements of employees. This possibility is explored in the following section.

SHORT-TERM CAREER PATHS

Occupational Change

The number of persons in our sample who have terminated their Title X jobs and found other work is quite small. However, questions regarding the effects of Title X upon career paths of employees are important enough to warrant tentative investigation. The small size of the subsample does not allow the results of this investigation to be generalizable. They are, nevertheless, of sufficient interest to deserve presentation.

Examination of career paths is based upon the hypothesis that Title X may have had some effect on the short-term career movements of employees. In other words, the occupational movements of employees from prior jobs to Title X jobs to subsequent jobs may represent a positive or negative path that could possibly have been affected by Title X. Once this possibility is admitted, the analysis can be conducted by following the movements of Title X employees from usual and/or prior jobs to Title X jobs to subsequent jobs. Since the usual job is a general reference point for occupational analysis, and not confined to a particular period of employment, it is used only as a frame of reference in this analysis. The analysis focuses on the holding of prior, Title X, and subsequent jobs in consecutive order. First, an overview of usual, prior, Title X, and subsequent jobs held by all Title X employees is presented in Table 7.14.

In general, Title X employees have tended to move out of professional/ technical, operative/technician, clerical, and "other" occupational categories, in going into Title X, and then have moved back to prior categories. In contrast, construction-related jobs are much more frequent under Title X than among usual, prior, or subsequent jobs of Title X employees.* This movement toward construction-related work under Title X, and out of it in subsequent work, is the major trend to be observed. However, there are a number of other interesting trends that should be noted. First, professional/technical jobs show a decline in

---

*This generalization does not apply to construction-trades occupations, which are relatively evenly represented among usual, prior, Title X, and subsequent jobs.

TABLE 7.14

Usual, Prior, Title X, and Subsequent Jobs, by Occupational Category

Occupational Category	Usual Job	Prior Job	Title X Job	Subsequent Job
Manager/administrator	2.8%	3.4%	2.2%	1.3%
Professional/technical	6.9	6.0	4.4	10.4
Supervisor/foreman	3.3	3.9	10.6	6.5
Construction trades	18.1	16.3	17.0	14.3
Construction laborer	7.4	5.7	12.3	3.9
Other laborer	6.9	5.3	10.1	7.8
Forestry, recreation	2.6	3.4	13.1	3.9
Operative/technician	10.0	12.3	1.7	14.3
Government/social service	1.9	1.3	2.9	3.9
Service	17.1	22.0	16.9	16.9
Clerical	11.7	12.0	8.6	11.7
Other	11.3	8.4	0.2	5.2

Source: Compiled by the authors.

TABLE 7.15

Changes in Occupational Category Experienced by Employed Terminees in Going from Prior to Title X to Subsequent Jobs

	Employed Terminees	
Change	Number	Percent
No change—all three jobs are the same	8	11
Title X and subsequent jobs are the same	20	27
Title X and prior jobs are the same	3	4
Prior and subsequent jobs are the same	17	23
All jobs are different	27	36
Total	75	100

Source: Compiled by the authors.

TABLE 7.16

Ranking of Prior, Title X, and Subsequent Jobs Held by Employed Terminees

Rank	Prior Jobs	Title X Jobs	Subsequent Jobs
1	11	14	13
2	22	18	25
3	33	43	34
4	9	—	3

Source: Compiled by the authors.

the movement from prior or usual jobs to Title X jobs, but then are a higher proportion of subsequent jobs than under any prior circumstance. The proportion of managerial jobs is lower after Title X work, but the total proportion of managerial and professional jobs is higher in subsequent work than at any other point. Second, the proportion of positions in the construction trades is relatively stable across usual, prior, Title X, and subsequent jobs.

Given this overview, the analysis then focuses upon a longitudinal examination of the prior, Title X, and subsequent jobs held by the 75 terminees in our sample who were working after Title X employment. First, changes in occupational category are presented in Table 7.15

In most cases, there have been changes in occupational category in the movement from prior jobs to Title X jobs to subsequent jobs. For 89 percent of employed terminees, an occupational change has occurred. In many instances (36 percent), all three jobs are different. For a substantial number (27 percent), Title X and subsequent jobs are of the same type, but different from the prior job. In contrast, only three persons had prior and Title X jobs of a similar type but now hold a different subsequent job. About one-quarter (23 percent) of the working terminees have subsequent jobs similar to their prior jobs, but different from Title X jobs. Thus, there has been considerable occupational movement, and it is possible that Title X has had an effect on short-term career movement. This question can be partially tested by applying the hierarchy of occupational ranks introduced in Chapter 6 to prior, Title X, and subsequent jobs. The ranking of these jobs held by employed terminees is shown in Table 7.16.

For each employed terminee, changes in rank experienced in the movement from prior jobs to Title X jobs to subsequent jobs can be examined, with patterns of movement providing tentative support for various hypotheses on the role of Title X employment in the short-term career paths of employees. Such hypotheses, based upon patterns of job movement, are presented below, accompanied by diagrams portraying the job movement. (In all diagrams, P = prior job, T = Title X job, and S = subsequent job; the diagrams provide a picture of upward, lateral, or downward movement in rank from one job to the next.)

1. If the subsequent job is of a higher rank than the prior job, and the Title X job is not of a lower rank than the prior job, then Title X may have provided an opportunity for positive career transition.

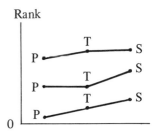

2. If the Title X job is of a higher rank than either the prior or subsequent job, Title X has provided a relatively high-quality interim employment opportunity.

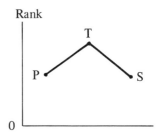

3. If all three jobs are of the same rank, then Title X has probably filled the role of providing useful interim employment to persons unemployed between jobs.

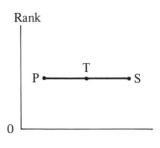

4. If the rank of the Title X job is lower than both the prior- and subsequent-job ranks, Title X has probably provided lower-quality stopgap employment, but without affecting the short-term career level of the employee.

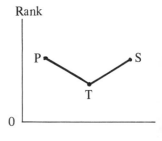

5. If the rank of the prior job is higher than the ranks of both the Title X and subsequent jobs, then Title X might have been part of a downward career transition.

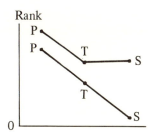

6. If the ranks of the prior and Title X jobs are the same, but are higher than the subsequent-job rank, it is hard to conclude anything about short-term career influence of Title X.

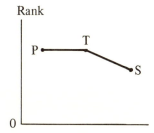

Of the six hypotheses, the first three suggest positive effects of Title X. The fourth indicates a minimal Title X role in short-term career movement, while the fifth suggests that Title X may have a negative role. In the sixth case, it is

TABLE 7.17

Occupational Sequences: Prior Job to Title X Job to Subsequent Job

Occupational Sequence: Effect of Title X	Employed Terminees	
	Number	Percent
Positive		
Sequence 1	19	25
Sequence 2	10	13
Sequence 3	27	36
Minimal		
Sequence 4	9	12
Negative		
Sequence 5	7	9
Indeterminate		
Sequence 6	3	4

Source: Compiled by the authors.

hard to conclude anything about a Title X role. The number of employed termi-nees whose job movement fits into each of the six occupational sequences is shown in Table 7.17.

Based upon changes in job rank, it is apparent that most (75 percent) of the employed terminees experienced positive occupational changes. In fully 39 percent of the cases, there was an upward movement in job rank, or Title X was of a rank superior to that of other jobs. Only 9 percent experienced consistent downward movement (13 percent if the indeterminate sequences are included). Thus, if Title X has had an impact upon short-term career movement, that impact is positive. One must remember, however, that this finding is based on only 75 cases and on data representing short-term occupational movements that may not be related to longer-term career changes.

Wages, Hours, and Earnings

The generally positive findings of the preceding discussion are further confirmed by an examination of hours, wages, and weekly earnings. First, an overview of these measures for all Title X employees is presented in Table 7.18.

All jobs are, on the average, close to full-time positions. Wages and weekly earnings are also relatively similar for all jobs, but with the subsequent job pay-ing somewhat more per hour and per week. These statistics, however, include all Title X employees. A more germane comparison can be made by limiting atten-tion to the prior, Title X, and subsequent jobs of the employed terminees only.

When one examines the wages and earnings of employed terminees only, the impression alters: Hourly wages and weekly earnings from Title X jobs are

TABLE 7.18

Wages, Hours, and Weekly Earnings for All Title X Employees: Subsequent Job and Other Jobs

Measure	Usual Jobs	Prior Jobs	Title X Jobs	Subsequent Jobs
Mean hours per week	40.4	39.6	38.6	39.6
Median hours per week	40.0	40.0	40.0	40.0
Mean hourly wage	$3.53	$3.46	$3.54	$3.81
Median hourly wage	$3.00	$2.95	$3.14	$3.16
Mean weekly earnings	$141.50	$137.80	$135.60	$153.70
Median weekly earnings	$120.00	$119.00	$123.00	$125.00

Source: Compiled by the authors.

TABLE 7.19

Wages, Hours, and Weekly Earnings of Employed Terminees:
Prior, Title X, and Subsequent Jobs

Measure	Prior Jobs	Title X Jobs	Subsequent Jobs
Mean hours per week	40.6	39.2	39.6
Median hours per week	40.0	40.0	40.0
Mean hourly wage	$3.50	$3.38	$3.81
Median hourly wage	$2.91	$2.92	$3.16
Mean weekly earnings	$150.48	$133.47	$153.70
Median weekly earnings	$120.00	$111.65	$125.00

Source: Compiled by the authors.

lower than from either prior or subsequent jobs. Moreover, weekly earnings from subsequent jobs are only $3.22 more than the earnings which employed terminees received from their prior jobs. By either measure, it appears that for this group, Title X is a less remunerative hiatus between prior and subsequent jobs.

One can take this analysis a step further by looking at the patterns of increase and decrease in weekly earnings covering the three jobs, in a manner similar to that employed above with occupational ranks in Table 7.17. If one applies the same hypotheses and patterns to average weekly wage as were applied to occupational ranking, the result is the distribution of employed terminees displayed in Table 7.20.

Fully 59 percent of employed terminees have experienced a positive sequence of weekly earnings in moving from prior jobs to Title X jobs to subsequent jobs. Either their subsequent earnings are higher than their prior earnings (without Title X earnings being lower than both), or Title X earnings have been higher than those from both prior and subsequent jobs, or earnings from all jobs have been the same. For 25 percent, the Title X job has yielded lower earnings than either of the other jobs, but earnings from the subsequent job have been roughly comparable to earnings from the prior job. In other words, the Title X job has appeared to perform a minimal maintenance role between jobs. For 15 percent of employed terminees, the weekly earnings trend has been consistently downward, suggesting that Title X may have been a step in a movement toward work earning less per week. Overall, however, a majority of employed terminees appear to have benefited from the job movement from prior jobs to Title X jobs to subsequent jobs.

TABLE 7.20

Weekly Earnings Changes Experienced by Employed Terminees in Going from Prior Jobs to Title X Jobs to Subsequent Jobs

	Employed Terminees	
Weekly Earnings Change	Number	Percent
Positive		
Sequence 1	24	32
Sequence 2	14	19
Sequence 3	6	8
Minimal		
Sequence 4	19	25
Negative		
Sequence 5	11	15
Indeterminate		
Sequence 6	1	1

Source: Compiled by the authors.

This finding is confirmed by a comparison of average weekly earnings from prior jobs and subsequent jobs. Weekly earnings increases have been experienced by 39 (or 52 percent) of employed terminees. Only 36 percent have experienced earnings decreases, while 12 percent report identical earnings from prior and subsequent jobs.

A final set of suggestive indicators of the possible effects of Title X on short-term occupational movement is generated by employee job ratings. Earlier in this chapter, it was noted that employed terminees generally considered their subsequent jobs to require more skills and be of better overall quality than their Title X jobs. These same employees also compared their Title X jobs with their usual jobs. A comparison of the two sets of ratings is of some interest. First, it should be noted that employed terminees compared their Title X jobs less favorably with their usual jobs than did the entire sample of Title X employees, as shown in Table 7.21.

As one can observe, employed terminees found that, in comparison with their usual jobs, their Title X jobs were dissimilar, requiring fewer skills, and of less overall quality than did the sample as a whole. This pattern is similar to that already observed for terminees in comparing prior and Title X jobs and may be a subjective indicator related to termination. More interesting, however, is a comparison of each employed terminee's assessment of the Title X job in relation to two different jobs (usual and subsequent). Again, a way to view these assessments is to think of them as sequences, in the same manner employed for

TABLE 7.21

Employees' Job Comparisons: Usual and Title X Jobs

Item of Comparison	All Title X Employees	Employed Terminees Only
Type of work		
Identical	10.5%	6.6%
Similar or related	40.7	36.8
Dissimilar, unrelated	48.8	56.6
Skills required		
More skills on Title X job	31.8	28.0
Same skills	41.5	36.0
Fewer skills on Title X job	26.7	36.0
Overall job quality		
Title X job better	52.6	32.0
Jobs about the same	35.1	42.7
Title X job worse	12.3	25.3

Source: Compiled by the authors.

Tables 7.17 and 7.20. If the six sequence patterns are applied to job-quality and skills ratings for Title X jobs in relation to usual and subsequent jobs, they form the distribution shown in Table 7.22.

TABLE 7.22

Job-Quality and Skills Assessments: Title X Jobs in Relation to Usual and Subsequent Jobs

Sequence	Job Quality		Skills Required	
	Number	Percent	Number	Percent
Positive				
Sequence 1	31	41	29	39
Sequence 2	4	5	3	4
Sequence 3	16	21	14	19
Minimal				
Sequence 4	15	20	19	25
Negative				
Sequence 5	4	5	8	11
Indeterminate				
Sequence 6	5	7	2	3

Source: Compiled by the authors.

Employees' assessments of overall job quality show Title X in a positive light in Table 7.22. Almost one-half of employed terminees either assess their Title X job to be the best job (5 percent) or judge their subsequent job to be the best—with the Title X job not being the worst (41 percent). The assessments of more than two-thirds show a positive pattern, while only 5 percent are clearly negative. For one in five, Title X is considered to have been minimal stopgap employment. The same pattern is seen in assessments of skills required for the three jobs, but the contrasts are less pronounced. About six of every ten assessments of skills follow a positive sequence, with a minimal Title X role suggested by one-quarter of the ratings. Only 11 percent of the ratings are clearly negative.

SUMMARY

Data on the small sample of terminees, and on the smaller group of working terminees, suggest a number of findings worthy of further examination. First, almost four in ten terminees were employed very shortly after leaving Title X. The proportion appears to increase over time (almost 60 percent were employed after four-and-a-half months). Since only about two of every ten Title X employees were employed prior to the program, Title X may very well have assisted in moving people out of unemployment and into unsubsidized employment. While improvements in local economies may have something to do with this pattern, the pre/post-program differences are great enough to warrant attention.

In general, persons who have found employment after terminating their Title X jobs have moved to more lucrative positions. While occupational analysis suggests a consistently lateral movement from Title X jobs to subsequent jobs, hourly wages and weekly earnings increase by 12.7 percent, respectively. Almost six in ten employed terminees earn more after Title X employment than during it, with only about one in four earning less. About one-half consider their subsequent jobs to require more skills than their Title X jobs. Almost as many regard the overall quality of subsequent jobs to be better than that of Title X work. In contrast, only about one in nine consider their Title X jobs to require more skills or to be of higher overall quality. These findings, considered in light of the general comparability of Title X jobs with prior and usual jobs, suggest that the Job Opportunities Program may have had positive effects on the short-term career movement of employees.

This hypothesis gains support from longitudinal data on the job movement of employed terminees. Changes in job rank suggest that Title X may have played a positive role for 75 percent of employed terminees. Moreover, weekly earnings of about 60 percent have been maintained or enhanced, either because Title X jobs paid more than prior and subsequent jobs or because subsequent weekly earnings increased over earnings from prior employment. The same pattern is noted in employees' assessments of overall job quality and skills required of usual, Title X, and subsequent jobs.

In the absence of comprehensive data on postprogram labor-market experience, these small-sample findings are, at the very least, suggestive. On every count—percent employed, comparative measures of Title X and subsequent jobs, and possible Title X effects upon short-term occupational movement—the findings are positive. While one cannot conclude that Title X has had such impacts, the positive hypotheses are at least strengthened by the findings.

8

LONG-TERM IMPACTS
OF TITLE X—
A SUMMARY

INTRODUCTION

Title X was funded primarily to provide a short-term countercyclical stimulus to local economies. Long-term impacts were not intended to be the focus of the program, and neither the Emergency Jobs and Unemployment Assistance Act (1974) nor its official regulations explicitly state long-term goals. General descriptions of possible long-range effects were requested as part of the application process, but they were not key elements in funding decisions. Consequently, long-term impact was not a major objective of most projects.

Nevertheless, there is an interest in the potential long-term impacts that Title X projects may have upon local areas, since these represent extra benefits that may not accrue from other types of countercyclical employment programs. Thus, 52 Title X projects were visited by field personnel, in January 1977, who conducted discussions with project administrators; local, state, or regional planners; and other relevant individuals or groups (councils of government, chambers of commerce, employment-service staff, mayors, local bankers, newspaper editors, and representatives of community and economic-development groups).

The perspective, information, and educated projections of these persons were combined with secondary data on local economic growth and social trends to construct a profile of each project and its potential long-term effects within its local context. Given the timing and duration of site visits, estimates of potential long-term impact also rely heavily upon the experience and judgment of Abt's professional staff. Fifty-two case studies were prepared, and this chapter represents a summary of the findings.

The initial study design focused upon evidence of long-term economic impact, which was defined to include direct improvements in, or enhancement of, the prospects for job and income growth in a community or local project area. Such impacts also included permanent improvements in the quality or quantity of a public service provided without commensurable reduction in disposable income. As the design progressed, it became clear that EDA was interested in a broader variety of project effects, including both economic and quasi-economic benefits of both a long-term and an immediate nature. The focus of this impact assessment was consequently broadened. Moreover, since projects were to be assessed either while still in operation or shortly after their termination, it became important to develop a series of proxy measures and interim indicators that would either show immediate impact or suggest the likelihood of long-term impact. As a result, a checklist of indicators was developed as a guide to field work and analysis. The indicators used are:

1. demand for project output;
2. the use of project output;
3. the relationship of a project to area plans;
4. the influence of the project on particular locational or developmental decisions;   .
5. impact on a critical development blockage;
6. the use of leveraging of current or subsequent funds;
7. influence on the overall economic-development process;
8. human-capital development;
9. short-term employee impact;
10. quality-of-life impact;
11. community satisfaction/acceptance.

It should be noted that the 52 projects were selected purposively and, thus, are not a statistically representative sample of the universe of 2,255 Title X projects. The sample was limited to those projects participating in the ED-110X payroll-reporting process of the Title X program. Moreover, selection was controlled so that the 52 projects were located in 15 geographic clusters of two to six projects each. This clustering permitted greater efficiency in data collection and allowed the development of a broader perspective on particular project areas.

Despite these practical limitations, the sample for measuring long-term impact represents a broad range of project types, project sizes, and labor-market areas. The distribution by project type is roughly proportional to the distribution of the universe. Activities of the sample projects run the gamut, from building the country's first solar-heated health facility to clearing rubbish out of drainage bayous. They ranged in funding size from $10,000 to $937,912 and employed from two to 410 workers. Thirty-four projects represent new ventures; 12 projects augment existing programs, and six projects combine new and previous activities. The projects are geographically distributed among 16 states, with 50 percent located in urban areas and 50 percent in rural communities.

Thus, while no pretense is made that the sample is representative of the universe, the sample does encompass a very broad spectrum of projects. As such, the findings in the next section and in the subsequent case studies warrant careful attention.

GENERAL FINDINGS

Almost by definition, all 52 projects have had some immediate impact, if only in that they have had positive earnings effects on those persons employed under the project. On the other hand, clear evidence of major long-term economic impact is rare. Only two projects have demonstrated conclusive evidence of significant economic impact, while six others are judged as being likely to yield long-term economic returns to their areas. At the opposite extreme, 24 projects are extremely unlikely to have any impacts of a long-term economic nature. For the remaining 20 projects, long-term economic impact might or might not occur, but impact depends upon events and developments that have not yet occurred and are beyond the control of persons directly associated with the projects.

The fact that very few projects are likely to have significant economic impact is understandable. Most projects are quite small, representing an insubstantial proportion of the local economy or of public and private investment in economic growth. Thus, long-term economic impacts are difficult to isolate, and more difficult to quantify. Moreover, they are often dependent upon other decisions or development work outside the project, decisions or work that had often not taken place at the time of site visits.

Consistent with this finding, the strongest proxy indicators of long-term economic impact are rarely in evidence at the sample projects. For example, not a single project has influenced a particular industry locational decision. Likewise, no project has directly removed a critical blockage to future development. Five projects, however, have conducted work that could very well encourage further development, if other decisions and complementary investments are made in the future.

Of interest is the fact that a number of projects (15 out of 52, or 29 percent) are likely to have long-term impacts of a preventive nature, impacts which in some cases could considerably reduce future expenditures. Preventive or conservational types of impact might be expected to occur frequently, because a large number of projects (59 percent of the universe; 52 percent of the project sample) had objectives of repair/renovation or improvement of conservation/forestry facilities. Eight of the 15 sample projects are drainage-clearance or flood-control (dam-repair) activities that could prevent, or reduce the likelihood of, disasters which could cost a community many millions of dollars in damages. In addition to drainage projects, three energy-conservation projects should reduce the costs of fuel for the individuals or community served. Two home-winterization projects and the construction of a solar-heated building should bring energy economies of a preventive nature. Finally, four repair and maintenance projects are likely to have modest preventive impacts.

The effects of Title X projects on an area's development and planning process, and their relationships to local development plans, or OEDPs, were explored during site visits. In general, it was found that the extremely short time frame allowed for the submission of Title X applications encouraged activities which responded to immediately perceived needs, and which could be implemented with little or no new planning. Projects whose plans were already on the shelf were usually promoted. If these happened to fit within an OEDP, or another long-term plan for service or development, then the projects were considered to be related to plans. Sixteen of the projects (31 percent) were indeed directly related to prior plans, eight other projects were indirectly or inadvertently consistent with larger plans. However, the quick-startup, short-term nature of the projects is probably responsible for the fact that there is little evidence of any project influencing the overall development or planning process of a local area.

Most Title X projects planned to use Title X funds as leverage to obtain concurrent funds from other sources, in support of project activities. Funded activities of the 2,255 Title X projects suggest a Title X/other-funds ratio of about two to one, with approximately $250 million in other funds being joined with about $500 million under Title X.

It is encouraging that 39 (75 percent) of the sample projects did in fact supplement Title X grants with other funds from state, local, private, or other federal sources. In total, a bit more than $10 million in Title X funds was distributed to the sample projects. More than $2.5 million was received from other sources, about half of it coming from local governments. This latter figure is probably understated, since in-kind contributions were not uniformly reported by projects. Whether these other funds would have been spent in the absence of the Title X grant is problematic. Thirty-two projects report that the work would not have been done at a particular time if they had not received the grant. However, there is insufficient evidence to ascertain whether or not the non-Title X funds would have been spent for other purposes.

It should be noted that two of the 52 sample projects have continued to use leverage to gain other funds, to carry on their work after the Title X grant expires. Three more projects have applied for other funds to continue the project work.

Clearly, the extent of initial leveraging is one indication of the demand for the project and the local need for its output. Local interviews suggest further that demand was high for one-half of the projects. Either the project pursued an activity that was clearly felt to be needed, or its output was desired and used, or the demand had been expressed by the activity's inclusion in a local development plan. Demand for 12 projects was judged to be moderate, with little evidence of demand being found for 14 projects.

Despite the lack of major evidence of long-term economic impact, it is felt that over 80 percent (42 of 52) of the projects will have residual impacts that will last at least one year after the conclusion of the project. In a majority of these instances, the impacts will be minor, probably not great enough to justify the EDA investment on this criterion alone. However, the nature of the Title X program itself created a situation in which projects were more likely to have impacts which are not strictly describable in traditional economic terms. Title X funding was, by definition, a short-term infusion of dollars into a community, requiring immediate application, quick project startup, and short duration. The program's employment-generating goal meant that most projects were highly labor intensive, limiting the degree to which large-scale improvements of physical infrastructure were pursued. While not many projects are likely to have solid long-term economic impacts, all are affecting their communities in other ways, as suggested by the following indicators: quality-of-life impact, community satisfaction/acceptance, human-capital development, and short-term employee impact.

Every project was judged to have provided some degree of immediate or long-term improvement in the local quality of life. Thirty-nine projects (75 percent) were considered to have had significant long-term impact on the quality of life. In 19 cases, the improvement affected only a specific audience, as when elderly citizens received transportation or nurse's-aide services, or when school-yards and playgrounds in minority neighborhoods were drained and landscaped. In 20 others, involving, for example, the construction of a health facility, or the paving of sidewalks throughout a town, the improvements affected the entire community.

When there was general awareness of the project, community acceptance and satisfaction were high. In no case was active resistance, or a significant expression of skepticism, toward the project noted. However, identification of the project with the Title X program was quite limited; as a program with an identity, Title X was relatively invisible. In 13 project communities, even those aware of the project did not associate it with Title X. In fact, many assumed that the project was funded under CETA.

Significant human-capital improvements were noted at a few projects. Of the three training projects examined for long-term impacts, one was not judged to have imparted significant new skills that were in demand in the local area. However, several projects that did not have training as their principal objective do, in fact, appear to have provided employees with new marketable skills. The fact that relatively few projects had significant human-capital impacts is attributable largely to the principal purpose of Title X, which was to provide immediate countercyclical employment opportunities. Major training and skills upgrading, on the job, were subordinated to the primary employment goal.

As discussed in other portions of this study, impact in regard to postprogram employment was high. At the 52 projects, fully 48 percent of identified project terminees had found other jobs, with only 2 percent of them being subsidized employment. Noteworthy is the fact that 26 percent had jobs with private employers, and another 14 percent had been hired by the Title X project employer or agency. In addition, most projects focused on instilling good work habits and attitudes that would help employees to maintain their Title X jobs and to obtain reemployment. Most project coordinators were aware of the different problems that hard-to-employ persons experience. Project responses to this situation included job counseling, and assistance through seminars on workers' compensation, unemployment insurance, and health and safety issues. Some projects simply explained the rules of employment to each worker (the number of absences and late arrivals permitted, and the level of productivity expected), and, if individuals did not abide by the rules, they were fired. Others maintained very flexible rules and were willing to give the Title X workers more leeway than they gave regular employees.

Finally, despite the relative scarcity of projects that clearly will have long-term impacts, the nature and administration of Title X have resulted in certain advantages that should not be ignored. First, the flexibility in using and accounting for Title X funds has permitted the funding of a wider range of projects than would be expected under most federal programs. In fact, many projects completed work which they believed could not have been funded under other federal assistance programs. Projects were generally designed to address immediate needs, and there is little doubt that almost every project was needed. Similarly, projects were often organized on the local level through separate work forces, not through temporary or federally supported jobs on the local payroll. Several project administrators believe that this separateness avoided the implicit stigma of a subsidized job and fostered the development of workers' pride, leadership, and greater productivity.

FACTORS AFFECTING LONG-TERM IMPACT

In the process of analyzing the 52 case studies, several project variables were examined to identify relationships between variables that had the likelihood of long-term impact. Project type, urban/rural location, funding size, and whether the project was a new or ongoing venture, were compared with the nature of a project's impact, the likelihood of long-term economic impact, effects on the quality of life, and the demand for a project's output. No significant relationships emerged from this analysis.

The only trend of importance becomes clear when one separates projects into two groups: construction, rehabilitation, and forestry projects versus service and training projects. This collapsing of six project types into two categories is intrinsically appealing, since most policy and program people assume that service and training projects will have impacts distinctly different from those of construction and repair projects. And, the labor intensity of service and training projects funded under Title X is significantly higher than that of other projects.

Study of the 52 projects shows that service and training projects are less likely to have residual impacts lasting over one year than are construction, rehabilitation, and forestry projects. Only six of the 12 training or service projects (50 percent) have prospects for long-term impact of any kind, in comparison with 36 of the 39 construction, rehabilitation, or forestry projects (92 percent). This finding is hardly unexpected, since the latter projects usually built or improved a structure that had lasting value to the community. In contrast, the former projects provided services which often could not be continued in the absence of project funds.

A related finding is that service and training projects were often perceived as having a high impact on the quality of life of a community or specific group. Eleven of 12 projects (92 percent) were so judged, in contrast to 27 of the 39 construction, rehabilitation, or forestry projects (69 percent). This, too, is not surprising, since the former projects had goals which were more explicitly related to quality of life.

Clearly, 52 projects represent a small sample and, by virtue of the selection procedure, these findings cannot be used to generalize about all Title X projects. However, the absence of strong relationships between long-term impact and such factors as urban/rural location, project size, and project type is, in our opinion, noteworthy. At least within the sample of projects measured for impact, there is little evidence to support funding decisions that attempt to maximize long-term impact by relying on these factors to determine distribution of funds.

The factors which do appear to affect a Title X project's likelihood of long-term impact, whether social or economic, are, in our opinion, more related to the timing and the process of project funding, the status of local planning, local leadership and administration, labor-intensity requirements, and the short duration of projects.

Beginning at the federal level and continuing down to the local level, Title X operated under a mandate to allocate funds and start projects quickly. The speed with which local agencies had to react bore directly on the types of projects that were proposed and, ultimately, on their outputs and impacts. Several projects indicated that they had only two to three days to prepare and submit their grant applications. Many projects were not quite so rushed, but turnaround time of less than two weeks was common. Understandably haste made it difficult to prepare a carefully considered proposal or to develop the linkages between the proposed project and area development plans that might promote a more effective local project. Time constraints meant that many projects were conceived to address an immediate local need or whatever issue happened to be crossing the desks of local officials.

Local response was further complicated by the fact that 43 sponsoring agencies and regional commissions participated in the funding process. The lines of communication from the Department of Commerce, through the many sponsoring agencies, to the local level sometimes resulted in incomplete, confusing, or erroneous information at the local level that made it harder to prepare already-rushed grant applications.

Another factor important to the ultimate impact of a project was the involvement of knowledgeable local planning units. Where there was an active local planning agency, this unit's participation enhanced the likelihood of project impact. Planning units such as tribal councils, councils of government, or state planning departments, if they were involved in the process, helped to ensure that project objectives were integrated with a recent and relevant planning document or local development initiatives. In several areas, planning units provided ongoing assistance and administrative support. One example is the South Carolina council of government (COG), which assisted all program grantees in the seven-county South Carolina Appalachian region. The COG helped with grant applications and then implemented internal program-management procedures for each project, under which planned goals were established for each quarter. One individual from the COG served as Title X coordinator for all projects, thereby eliminating confusion or duplication of effort among grant recipients and contractors.

Long-term impact was also enhanced by the presence of creative and enthusiastic local leadership. This generalization may seem like a truism, but it applies to Title X as much as to any other program. Projects like the solar-heated medical facility in Bladenboro, North Carolina, or the Absentee Shawnee tribe's construction work in Oklahoma, or the Job Re-Entry project in Valdosta, Georgia benefited greatly from capable and enthusiastic local administrators and community support. Continuity of leadership is also important. In several cases where those responsible for preparing the grant application were not involved in the implementation of the project, initial work foundered, project objectives were not well understood, and the project's impact was undermined.

Another factor affecting long-term impact was the labor-intensity constraint of Title X. Although official regulations do not clearly set a minimum level of labor intensity, EDA administratively emphasized the fact that 75 percent of Title X funds should be spent on wages and fringe benefits.[1] This guideline was understood by most applicants, and very few projects were funded with lower levels of planned labor intensity.

The labor-intensity constraint is perfectly consistent with the major goal of Title X: to provide a large number of short-term, countercyclical jobs. It is also consistent with the program's focus on employing the long-term unemployed. However, the high level of labor intensity meant that Title X projects rarely attempted work which required major materials costs or capital investments.

Furthermore, the easiest and most frequent course was to propose projects which required mainly unskilled labor. These two tendencies eliminated from consideration certain types of capital-intensive projects requiring large inputs of skilled labor, projects which might be expected to produce output of a long-term value. Indeed, the 75 percent labor requirement meant that long-term impacts from Title X funds were more likely to result from human-resource investments than from capital investments. One would expect greater impact from human-resource investments that provided substantive training in addition to employment, and that stressed the transition of employees from the project to other work. Less return would be expected from projects focusing on low-skilled employment, without the provision of training, particularly in a one-shot program. More Title X projects tended to provide the latter type of experience than the former, and this was in keeping with Title X goals.

One should note, however, that there were exceptions to this pattern. Several projects, such as the Kiamichi Vocational-Technical School in McAlester, Oklahoma, or the Horticultural Gardens project in Clemson, South Carolina, took unskilled workers and created meaningful job-training situations that are likely to benefit both the employees and the community. Others recognized that the 75 percent labor restraint applied only to Title X funds, and supplemented the grant with substantial funds from other sources. These funds were often spent on materials and equipment, not labor.

A final factor affecting impact was the program's selection of projects which could be started quickly and largely completed within one year. Like the labor-intensity requirement, this discouraged the proposing of projects which required major construction or large-scale capital assets.

In summary, Title X has not been a program which intended to have major long-term impacts. Consequently, long-term impact was not a major objective of the majority of the projects. Only two projects of the 52 visited have demonstrated conclusive evidence of significant economic impact, and another six projects are likely to yield long-term economic returns to their communities. However, long-term impacts of a noneconomic nature are discernible in a majority of cases studied. The nature of the program, and the requirements for rapid project planning and startup minimized the chances that long-term economic impacts would be achieved. In the light of this, the degree of likely long-term impact that has been discovered in the sample projects is encouraging and represents an extra benefit from a program which was intended to achieve other objectives.

PROJECT HIGHLIGHTS

Several of the projects visited in this study deserve individual mention, either because they are likely to have substantial long-term impacts, or because they represent particularly interesting uses of Title X to respond to local needs. The projects highlighted here are not all likely to contribute economic returns to their communities. In fact, only the Agrirama project in Tifton, Georgia, and a series of projects in Cherokee County, North Carolina have already conclusively demonstrated economic impact. Valdosta, Georgia; Shawnee, Oklahoma; Lumberton, North Carolina; Bladenboro, North Carolina; and Fall River, Massachusetts have projects which may eventually show economic returns. These projects and five others were chosen for discussion here because they illustrate one of the following characteristics: actual or potential economic returns; successful linkage of the project with other work, funds, or planning efforts; unique project output; a unique audience for projects; impacts typical of several other projects.

Agrirama Project

The Agrirama project in Tifton is noteworthy because the infusion of Title X funds in this case accelerated the project's impact. Agrirama utilized Title X funds to augment state funding and, in so doing, was able to complete an ongoing effort to recreate a 70-acre Georgia farmstead as it existed before 1900. Agrirama had been scheduled to open in July 1976, but work had seriously lagged behind schedule in the summer of 1975. The missing component was funds that could be directly used for restoring the nineteenth century buildings that had been acquired. The availability of Title X funds that could be used for this type of labor-intensive work matched Agrirama's need and allowed most of the work to be completed on schedule. Without the Title X funds, the project director estimated that the project would have opened in July with only three structures; Title X funds meant that 15 more buildings were completed for the public opening.

State and local planning for the Agrirama project took place during a span of six years, from 1970 to 1976. The state of Georgia had committed $1.3 million to Agrirama before Title X funds became available. Because of the commitment by the state to establish this rural, agricultural village, the need for the project must be considered a priority of the state rather than of Tifton or the county. Yet the economic benefits and impacts will ultimately contribute more to the Tifton area than to the entire state. From July through December 1976, Agrirama generated revenues of $68,000 from admissions and store sales; 20,000 tourists visited the farmstead. Therefore, an estimated total of $128,000 was added to the local economy in 1976.* The jobs created by Agrirama (20 full-time

---

*Revenues for 1976 were estimated based on admissions and store sales of $68,000, plus $3.00 per person for tourist-related expenditures. Revenues for 1977 were estimated based on 100,000 visitors for the year, each spending $5.00 ($2.00 for entry and $3.00 for tourist-related expenditures).

and 38 part-time positions); the locally contracted services; the tourist expenditures for food, automotive products, and accommodations; and the materials purchased by the project added approximately $500,000 to the Tifton economy in 1977. Estimates of further returns on the investment are $750,000 in 1978, $1 million in 1980, and $2 million in 1984, depending on the physical expansion of Agrirama and the increasing rate of Agrirama visitors each year. Not all of these economic impacts can be directly attributed to Title X, but, in the words of the project director: "Without the funds provided by Title X we would have opened Agrirama in July 1976 with a country store, a barn and an information center. Instead, we opened with 15 restored buildings and a beautifully landscaped physical setting that tells the story of rural Georgia the way we had hoped to present it to the public."

By allowing Agrirama to open on schedule with a full complement of facilities, Title X accelerated the project's immediate impacts and will contribute to increasing the long-term impacts at a faster rate than if the Title X funds had not been available. While it is difficult to isolate the long-term direct economic impact attributable to Title X, one could estimate it in proportion to its share of the entire investment. Title X provided 9.6 percent of the funds; approximately $852,000 of the $8.88 million in 1976–84 expected revenues could reasonably be attributed to Title X funding.

Job Re-Entry Project

The Valdosta Job Re-Entry project is another project which creatively utilized Title X funds to increase income for area residents; the direct economic impacts of the project could be considerable. This Title X project, conceived and administered by the Coastal Plain Area Economic Opportunity Authority (CPAEOA), initiated an ambitious job reentry program for placing unemployed persons directly in positions in private industry. Unlike many public-work projects, the Title X employees did not work for a city, state, or federal agency; instead, they went to work for a private company and immediately became accountable to the private employer. Potential employers in the ten-county area served by the project were contacted by a representative from the CPAEOA about the possibility of hiring a new employee; payment of the employee's wages would be apportioned between the project agency (62 percent) and the private employer (38 percent), with the stipulation that the employer could not fire an existing employee to make room for the new employee. In other words, the job had to be a new, incremental position with the firm.

The employer's incentive to hire was primarily an economic one since payment of the wages of the new employee was apportioned; instead of paying the minimum wage of $2.20 per hour, the employer paid $0.84 per hour, with the project agency paying the remaining $1.36. Subsidization continued for up to nine months, depending on the terms of the original agreement, the productivity of the new employee, and the economic health of the employer. The positions created were basically unskilled, often in sales, general labor, or assembly work. A particularly attractive feature of this project was the fact that employees went to work directly for a private-sector firm and felt a sense of security and future employment that employees in public-work projects often do not feel.

Although not completed at the time of the site visit, the Job Re-Entry project had created and filled over 50 new positions in the private sector. Federal funds of $113,315 under Title X, and $25,000 from other sources were originally planned to be supplemented by $42,380 from private-sector firms for employee salaries. The success of the program, however, will have increased the private share to about $77,000 when the program ends.

At the time of the site visit, 73 persons had completed their work on the project. Fully 29 were now working on private jobs, but no longer with a Title X subsidy. Another two had found other subsidized public work or nonprofit work, and three had been institutionalized. Thirty-six people had not stayed in their jobs long enough to be made permanent employees, but were receiving job-placement services. The rate of placement in permanent unsubsidized jobs, 42 percent (31 ÷ 73), is impressive. In addition, 40 other employees were currently working on jobs developed through the project, with 62 percent of the wage being paid with Title X funds. The project director estimated that about 20 would become permanent unsubsidized employees.

The direct economic impacts of the Job Re-Entry project could be considerable. For example, the $77,000 private contribution, though part of the funds contributed to the project, could also be considered as a new income stream for the community. Beyond the life of the project, new wages in the private sector will be greater. Assuming minimum wage, the annualized income of the 31 permanently placed employees would be more than $142,000. If an additional 20 are permanently placed, the total new annual wage bill will be almost $235,000. If course, there is likely to be some attrition, which would reduce these numbers. Finally, the project is reported to have rescued four small retail businesses from bankruptcy by providing labor at a price the businesses could afford.

Absentee Shawnee Project

The Absentee Shawnee tribe's Title X project is particularly interesting because of the way it was integrated with other tribal projects. The Absentee Shawnee utilized $600,000 of Title X funds to restore and renovate six major tribal buildings on the tribe's 33 acres of land south of Shawnee, Oklahoma. The buildings house the offices of the Shawnee tribe, the Indian Health Service, the

Absentee Shawnee Housing Authority, and the United Tribes of Western Oklahoma and Kansas. The buildings are more than 40 years old, and were badly in need of repair and interior remodeling. Several had been vacant during recent years.

The tribe hired unemployed, unskilled workers from the Shawnee area, many of them members of the tribe, which was reporting a 47 percent unemployment rate in December 1975. Workers were given on-the-job training in construction skills, provided by experienced foremen, and were encouraged to participate in several crews to learn different skills. At the time of the site visit, 160 persons had worked on the project. Of the 99 persons no longer on the project, 67 had found other jobs, only nine of which were federally subsidized.

The Absentee Shawnee tribe integrated Title X funds with funding for other tribal projects, through several sources. The tribe has secured $17,000 from the Home Improvement Program of the Bureau of Indian Affairs (BIA), $100,000 in HUD community development funds, and has applied for $100,000 from the Campaign for Human Development. A total of 39 homes can be renovated with these funds. In addition, the nearby city of Norman will receive a large Community Development Block Grant, much of which will be used for housing rehabilitation. A portion of the HUD funding is being used to specially train three of the best Title X employees to become independent construction contractors, able to bid on construction and rehabilitation work available in the entire area. Each of these three has agreed to hire and train two more Title X workers. In addition, the Title X project provided an experienced work force of over 100 people to assist the contractors or pursue some of the housing-rehabilitation work.

The fortuitous linkage of the Title X project with other work, encouraged by the tribe's OEDP, shows promise in creating new small construction businesses and in providing a more stable wage and income stream for tribal members. In addition, the renovations funded under Title X have resulted in a permanent capital improvement that also contributes to the quality of life of this small tribe.

Bladenboro Project

In Bladenboro, North Carolina, the local Community Development Corporation combined $72,558 in EDA funds with $55,000 in state aid and $25,000 in private contributions to construct the nation's first solar-heated health facility. The building is approximately 40 percent solar heated, with collecting panels, holding tanks, and a circulating system representing the current state of the art. Aside from its unique cost-saving energy system, the medical facility is significant because Bladenboro previously had neither a resident physician nor a medical facility. The nearest doctor is still 20 miles away. The town is currently seeking a permanent physician, and, if one is secured, the impact of the project upon the quality and cost of local medical care could be substantial. The imaginative and ambitious project was enthusiastically supported by local residents, a fact attested to by the high level of private local contributions.

The medical building is integral to the town's economic-development goals. Bladenboro has recently embarked upon an aggressive program of facilities improvements, including a new fire station, a new sewage-treatment facility, new rescue-squad building, and a large-scale drainage project. Such activities improve both the local quality of life and community infrastructure, thereby making the community a more desirable location for industry. Five large parcels of land are now being marketed by the Bladen Development Corporation, the town's nonprofit industrial-development organization.

Clemson Projects

In Clemson, South Carolina, Title X funds were used to support a unique horticulture-therapy project that provided significant skills training for 14 handicapped persons. The Appalachian Regional Commission received $75,000 in Title X funds to support a horticultural-therapy project directed by Clemson University's Horticultural Department. The 14 project workers were mentally and physically impaired; they included retarded and blind individuals, ex-offenders, and substance abusers. They were trained in horticultural techniques, carpentry, masonry, propagation, garden development, and greenhouse construction. The project was unique in that it represented the first time in which persons with mental and emotional disorders were combined with persons with physical handicaps in a horticultural-therapy project. The purpose of horticultural therapy, like that of music or art therapy, is to provide a handicapped individual with both skills training and a therapeutic environment for emotional reinforcement and improved mental health. Because of the psychologically debilitating effects of their various handicaps, few would have been able to perform in a regular employment situation prior to entry into the program. Skills learned by the participants in the Title X project make the workers suitable for employment with florists, contract landscapers, nurseries, and small truck farms. Their high productivity and relative lack of absenteeism during the project make them excellent candidates for employment after termination from their Title X work.

Another South Carolina project provided facilities which will be used by physically and mentally handicapped individuals from the entire state. In this project, Clemson University's Department of Physical Plant was granted $102,152 under Title X to expand the physical facilities of a camp site for the physically and mentally handicapped, located on a wooded lake front approximately seven miles from the university campus. Construction work on Camp Hope was first initiated in 1975. The camp, when fully completed, will consist of two subcamps, each of which will have ten cabins and a capacity for 30 residents. Camp Hope is the only facility of its kind in the state of South Carolina. It provides a camp experience for persons confined to wheelchairs, in an environment which has been totally designed for such persons. The primary users of the camp are handicapped children, to whom most of the programs are offered for free; the camp has also been used for groups of senior citizens. Thus, two special populations of the state are beneficiaries of the outputs of the project.

Lumberton Project

The city of Lumberton, North Carolina utilized its Title X grant to remedy a variety of drainage problems. This project illustrates the long-term impact of a preventive nature that several other projects also achieved, and it paved the way for possible future economic development by providing improved services. Part of the $262,430 was used to aid three low-income residential areas, all serviced by unpaved streets lacking conventional storm sewers. Each area had a history of flooding, and stagnant waters created a health hazard, serving as a breeding ground for mosquitoes and a habitat for rodents. Mindful that the county population is about equally divided among whites, blacks, and Indians, the city chose to improve one neighborhood in which each group predominates. The clearance of drainage canals will last three-to-five years and has removed potential health and flooding hazards, possibly leading to an increase in the value of the land. The project was highly visible and extremely popular in the neighborhoods.

The second portion of the grant was used to excavate new drainage canals, principally around the municipal airport, an area zoned for future industrial expansion. While immediate development is not contemplated, the project has made future development more attractive by eliminating drainage problems at the site.

Talladega Project

The Title X project in Talladega County, Alabama created recreational facilities that will be used by children, and achieved preventive goals by repairing watersheds. Approximately 70 percent of the Title X grant of $352,430 was used to grade and landscape 18 county schoolyards for use as playgrounds. The rest of the grant was devoted to maintaining ten watersheds in the mountainous areas of the county.

The schoolyard work was in high demand among county residents. The 18 schools were originally black ones, but are now integrated, a factor believed to be connected with the high demand for improvements among county residents. The schoolyards had never been landscaped or graded, tasks that were accomplished under Title X. In addition, sidewalks were constructed, playing fields laid out, and county funds used to purchase playground equipment (swings, basketball hoops, backstops, bleachers). Community satisfaction with the work is high, and present and future generations of schoolchildren now have recreational space and equipment that were not available before.

The watershed work included preventive maintenance, the clearing of brush, opening of drainage ditches, and repairing of small flood-control dams. Maintenance is a relatively continuous activity, but the Title X grant made possible a more complete job than had been possible with county funds. The county water and soil conservation director acknowledged that, without such maintenance, there was a danger of dams bursting, which would flood farm land, drown livestock, and endanger residential dwellings. While it cannot be maintained that the Title X work, in itself, eliminated the cause of a potential disaster, it did contribute to decreasing the likelihood of major flooding.

Oconee Project

In Oconee County, South Carolina, $29,150 in Title X funds and $2,000 in other moneys were spent to fence and reclaim 200 acres of pasture land adjacent to the Oconee Prison Farm. In addition, a cattle feeder shed and corral were constructed. This very modest project will allow prison inmates to raise their own beef cattle. County officials estimate that several thousand dollars per year in meat costs will be saved in the county prison's operating budget. In addition, it is hoped that prisoners will develop some animal husbandry skills that may be useful in their employment search after their release. County residents supported the project because they favor the idea of an almost self-supporting prison farm.

Home Maintenance Service Project

The Home Maintenance Service project run by Florida's Division on Aging in Tallahassee was notable because all employees were over 50 years old. The employees provided home-maintenance services to seniors in 12 counties throughout the state and achieved significant improvements in the quality of life for those serviced, while providing themselves with a sense of pride and self-worth. The federal Administration on Aging has identified home-maintenance as one of its top four priorities for services for the elderly throughout the country. This project was funded as a joint effort that included programs providing clerical and food services. As a direct result of the Title X funds, the Florida Division on Aging has obtained funding under Title IX of the Older Americans Act to continue the home-maintenance projects in 13 communities.

Battleship Cove Project

The Battleship Cove project has contributed to the economic development of the waterfront area in Fall River, Massachusetts. The U.S.S. Massachusetts Memorial Committee is a nonprofit organization that operates Battleship Cove, a waterfront facility housing a battleship, PT boat, and submarine. The committee received $175,095 in Title X funds (supplemented by $58,365 from private sources) to repair, refurbish, and repaint the three vessels. General maintenance and operating costs of the educational and tourist facility are mainly covered by the gross revenues from ticket sales and the cove's store, which amount to approximately one-half million dollars annually. Major work, such as that accomplished under Title X, must be supported by bank loans. In the absence of Title X, some of the work would have been financed in this manner, but much of it would not have been completed.

The Battleship Cove maintenance work is significant because the facility has become an important economic factor in a city whose economy has been depressed for many years. Part of Fall River's development plan is to upgrade the waterfront area near and around Battleship Cove for tourism and commercial purposes. The cove has attracted more than one million visitors since its opening in the mid-1960s. The number of visitors has increased each year. Business has been generated for local service industries (restaurants, motels, gas stations) and recently a new restaurant was built adjacent to the cove to take advantage of the tourist activity. Thus, Title X has played a role in Fall River that is analogous to its role in Georgia's Agrirama project. The economic impact attributable to the project is, however, less clear-cut. At a minimum, the project saved the committee from incurring bank-loan interest, thus freeing funds for other purposes. It could also be argued that the project contributed to likely increased revenues from future visitors, or, by providing important rehabilitation, prevented the deterioration of an income-producing asset. Such arguments, however appealing, are as yet conjectural; it is too early to assess the impacts attributable to Title X.

Cherokee County Projects

Several Title X projects were pursued in Cherokee County, a relatively poor mountainous county in southwestern North Carolina. The county is an area eligible for EDA redevelopment, and is part of a five-county southwestern North Carolina economic-development district. The project visited as part of the impact-measuring sample supported renovation work on eight county schools. It is the most modest of the Title X projects pursued in the county. Three projects that were not part of this study deserve special mention because they provide economic returns for county residents. One project supported construction of facilities for a community produce market and cattle auction. This provided the first local outlet for the county's many part-time small farmers who previously had to market their products elsewhere. An estimated $100,000 in sales was realized in 1976 and represents a clear economic return from the Title X project. The same philosophy led to the construction of a community mountain-crafts center, funded by another Title X project. This cooperative center is the only local outlet for crafts produced by many older county residents. The third Title X project constructed ten neighborhood community centers in remote rural areas of the county to provide residents with a focal point for community affairs and indoor recreation. The centers also host services such as weekly bookmobiles and health clinics. Clearly, though the Title X projects under study are not outstanding or unique, the overall impact of the Title X program in Cherokee County has been significant.

NOTE

1. Under Title X, a project is considered labor intensive if "at least 60 percent of the project funds are to be expended for direct labor costs." Moreover, at least 50 percent of Title X funds were to be used to fund projects "in which no more than 25 percent of the funds will be used for nonlabor costs." See "Job Opportunities Program Interim Regulations" (parts 313.8 and 313.24), *Federal Register* Vol. 40; No. 101, p. 22537, and no. 118 (June 18, 1975), p. 25672.

APPENDIX A

NET LABOR-COST METHODOLOGY

INTRODUCTION

The objective of this appendix is to cite and discuss the exact procedures and underlying assumptions used to estimate the net labor costs of a program to taxpayers. Gross expenditures—actual outlays—should be reduced by the amount of primary and secondary cash returns to government, to arrive at net program costs. Primary returns originate from the earnings of Title X workers and the nonlabor expenditures incurred by the projects. The government receives personal income taxes, contributions to FICA, and excise- and sales tax revenue from earnings of Title X workers. Transfer payments, such as unemployment compensation and food stamps received by Title X employees prior to the program, may be reduced. Other budget savings result from sales and corporate income tax revenue generated by nonlabor purchases of goods and services by Title X projects. (The methodology and procedures for estimating returns from nonlabor expenditures of projects are discussed in Appendix C.) The direct labor returns examined in this appendix are shown in Table A.1.

Secondary, or indirect, returns occur because the expenditures made by individuals employed under Title X, as well as the outlays on program administration, and on nonlabor project expenditures can have multiplier effects within the local economy. These expenditures can affect employment in producing, wholesale, and retail industries; hence, secondary income tax, sales tax, and FICA effects may be traced to the Title X projects.

TABLE A.1

Sources of Direct Labor Returns to Government

Taxes	Transfers to Employees and Their Families
Employees:	Unemployment Compensation
Personal Income	Social Security
Sales and Excise	AFDC
FICA	Supplemental Security Income (SSI)
	General Relief
Employers:	Food Stamps
FICA	Medicaid
Unemployment Insurance	Subsidized Housing

Source: Compiled by the authors.

The net labor-cost calculations, based upon the Title X employee sample (totaling 1,969 workers from 195 projects), can be summarized in the following five equations.*

$$
\begin{aligned}
\text{Net additional earnings (NAE) of employee i} =\ & \left(\begin{array}{l} \text{employee i's} \\ \text{average weekly} \\ \text{earnings rate} \\ \text{under Title X} \end{array} \right) \times \left(\begin{array}{l} \text{employee i's} \\ \text{expected weeks} \\ \text{of Title X} \\ \text{employment} \end{array} \right) \\[2ex]
& - \left[\left(\begin{array}{l} \text{estimated number} \\ \text{of weeks that em-} \\ \text{ployee i would} \\ \text{have been em-} \\ \text{ployed in the ab-} \\ \text{sence of Title X} \end{array} \right) \times \left(\begin{array}{l} \text{employee i's} \\ \text{expected average} \\ \text{weekly earnings} \\ \text{in the absence} \\ \text{of} \\ \text{Title X} \end{array} \right) \right]
\end{aligned}
$$

$$
\begin{aligned}
\text{Net savings of transfers (NST) attributable to Title X} =\ & \sum_{i=1}^{\text{em-ployees}} \ \sum_{j=1}^{\text{8 types of transfers}} \left[\begin{array}{l} \text{average weekly} \\ \text{entitlements of} \\ \text{type j for which} \\ \text{employee i was} \\ \text{eligible} \end{array} \right. \\[2ex]
& \left. \times \left(\begin{array}{l} \text{employee i's} \\ \text{expected weeks} \\ \text{of Title X} \\ \text{employment} \end{array} - \begin{array}{l} \text{estimated number of} \\ \text{weeks that enrollee i} \\ \text{would have been em-} \\ \text{ployed in the absence} \\ \text{of Title X} \end{array} \right) \right]
\end{aligned}
$$

$$
\begin{aligned}
\text{Net additional taxes (NAT) attributable to Title X} =\ & \sum_{i=1}^{\text{employees}} \left[\text{AE(i)} \left(\begin{array}{l} \text{effective} \\ \text{tax rates} \\ \text{on earned} \\ \text{income} \end{array} \right) \right. \\[2ex]
& \left. + \begin{array}{l} \text{extra consumer} \\ \text{spending, out of} \\ \text{net additional} \\ \text{disposable income} \\ \text{of employee i} \end{array} \left(\begin{array}{l} \text{effective} \\ \text{sales and} \\ \text{excise} \\ \text{tax} \\ \text{rates} \end{array} + \begin{array}{l} \text{extra FICA} \\ \text{contributions} \\ \text{out of addi-} \\ \text{tional dis-} \\ \text{posable} \\ \text{income} \end{array} \right) \right]
\end{aligned}
$$

---

*The procedure used to weight the sample results to the universe of Title X projects is discussed in Appendix E.

$$\frac{\text{Net labor cost}}{\text{(NLC) of Title X}} = \frac{\text{gross labor}}{\text{expenditures}} - \text{NAT} - \text{NST}$$

Net cost per employee = NLC ÷ N

where N = number of employees

All the computations for tax revenues and reduction of transfer payments are dependent upon the estimated employment and earnings under Title X. A central question in the calculation of net Title X program costs is whether any measured increase in earnings and employment should be attributed to Title X or to other economic forces. There are two plausible approaches. The first is to assume that all labor and physical resources employed in the Title X projects would have remained idle in the absence of the program. This approach implies that all earnings from Title X should be used in the calculation of tax returns, and reductions in transfer payments should accrue to government for the duration of Title X employment.

In general, the assumption that all estimated returns are attributable to the program will overstate returns (and understate net cost), simply because some Title X employees would have been employed and would have earned income if they had not been working for Title X. (Such estimates are presented in Chapter 4 as unadjusted returns and are based only upon the weeks of employment and earnings under Title X.)

A more realistic and conservative assumption is that a portion of Title X employment and earnings would have occurred in the absence of the program. A participant in the program might have been employed for some length of time in the private or public sector during the period of Title X. The Title X employment and earnings must, therefore, be discounted by the estimated number of weeks and estimated earnings that each program participant would have received in the absence of Title X. The discounting of employment and earnings will reduce the returns from the program, thus increasing its net cost. Estimates of employment in the absence of Title X and average weekly earnings in the absence of Title X have been made for each individual in the employee sample. (A discussion of all aspects of the discount factor is given in Appendix B. Estimates using this discount methodology are presented in Chapter 4 as adjusted returns from Title X.)

This presentation of the net labor-cost methodology is divided into three sections. First we discuss the data and procedures used to calculate employees' average weekly earnings from Title X and the duration of Title X employment. Then we focus on the methodology used to calculate the savings in transfer payments. Finally, we present the data and procedures used to calculate tax revenues generated by Title X earned income.

EARNINGS AND DURATION OF EMPLOYMENT

The primary data required for the calculation of earnings and weeks of employment from Title X are derived from the survey instrument. An employee's average weekly earnings from Title X are obtained directly from questionnaire items on the Title X wage or salary, before any deductions, and on average hours worked per week. Wage/salary information was received in relation to the appropriate unit of pay for the individual (per hour, per week, biweekly, or per month). Thus, average weekly earnings calculations depend upon the particular pay period reported by the employee.

Duration of Title X employment is derived from actual starting dates and actual (or estimated) termination dates provided by each employee. In most instances, starting dates and actual termination dates could be confirmed by the Title X employer. However, since most interviews were conducted with employees who were still working at their Title X jobs, termination dates are usually expected dates. Expected dates of termination were estimated by employees and, in a number of cases, could be confirmed by employers. At most projects, too, there is internal consistency among the termination dates estimated by different employees. The relatively high internal consistency of these estimates is explained by the fact that many projects were nearing completion. Thus, employees usually knew when they were to be laid off.

There is, however, a distortion in the expected termination date for some employees, introduced by the fact that in many instances, only the employees' estimates of the termination date were available. In general, the bias should be in the direction of increasing the estimates of Title X employment duration. This is indicated by the fact that about 40 employees estimated termination dates that were actually after the projected termination date for the project. In such instances, the project's termination date was used as the employee's termination date.

The mean values of average weekly Title X earnings and duration of employment for the Title X employee sample are presented in Table A.2 for both persons who were still employed on projects when interviewed and persons who had terminated their Title X employment. Duration of Title X employment is derived from the start and actual (or expected) end dates of employment.

It should be noted that the duration of Title X employment reported for the employee sample, 35.2 weeks, is substantially longer than the average duration estimated by Abt and EDA for the universe of Title X employees. Using different data—the ED-736 project-completion reports received and processed by April 5, 1977—we estimated average employment duration at 19.5 weeks. The Economic Development Administration, using these completion reports and ED-110X payroll reports on completed projects, arrives at a comparable estimate. There are several reasons for the differences.

TABLE A.2

Earnings and Weeks of Employment from Title X: Mean Values

Measure	Employees Still Working	Terminees	Total
Average weekly earnings	135.50	136.60	135.80
Weeks of Title X employment	36.6	22.5	35.2
Hours worked per week	38.5	39.2	38.6
Earnings from Title X	4,914	3,089	4,753
Completed sample size	1,771	198	1,969

Source: Compiled by the authors.

First, the employee-sample information is likely to overestimate duration of employment. The survey was conducted in October–December, 1976, when many projects were finishing up their work. Since turnover on almost any type of project tends to be greater in its early stages than in its later stages, it is quite likely that the sample includes a substantial number of longer-term employees and an underrepresentation of employees with short periods of project employment. Moreover, seasonal factors may affect the estimates of employment duration. Since the survey was conducted in the fall and early winter, for several regions of the country it may have been too late to include workers whose jobs were confined to the warmer summer months. Finally, the phenomenon of employees overprojecting their likely termination date of Title X employment introduces a further, though probably a small, bias.

On the other hand, estimates of employment duration drawn from ED-736 completion reports and ED-110X payroll reports may be underestimates. The completion reports that had been received by the time this study was nearing completion were from projects which, on the average, were substantially smaller than the average Title X project. Thus, even though duration projections for the universe were based upon the relationship between planned duration and reported actual duration, there may be a downward bias caused by the fact that the completed projects are smaller, and of shorter duration, than the typical Title X projects. Even ED-110X payroll report data are subject to a bias in the same direction. This is caused by the fact that some Social Security numbers, used on the ED-110X form to transmit payroll information to EDA, are imperfectly recorded. Others are subject to keypunch error. Thus, a single employee may be counted as two (or more) employees, lowering the estimates of duration.

Given the data available, there is no defensible way to adjust estimates in order to derive a true figure for average duration of Title X employment. Suffice it to say that the true average lies somewhere between 35.2 weeks and 19.5 weeks, probably closer to 19.5 weeks.

It is important to stress that the clear overstatement of employment duration found in the employee sample should not significantly affect the net-cost analysis. First, net-cost projections for the universe, using the sample, rely upon weights based on person-months of employment, not on the number of employees, thus controlling for overestimates or underestimates of average employment duration. Second, careful testing shows that there are consistent relationships in the employee sample between employment duration and the incidence of losing, or receiving reduced, transfer payments during Title X employment. If there is a general relationship between employment duration and changes in transfer payments, it is more parabolic than hyperbolic. Generally speaking, persons who have been employed on a Title X project for less than 17 weeks or more than 52 weeks are less likely to have experienced a change in transfer status than those who have been employed 17–52 weeks. The highest incidence occurs between 27 and 52 weeks. One can hypothesize an interaction of two patterns: Those employed for a short period of time do not earn enough to be disqualified from means-tested programs; those employed for a long period of time are less likely to have been receiving transfers.

SAVINGS IN TRANSFER PAYMENTS

Reductions in transfer payments comprise a major component of financial benefits to governments that are stimulated by Title X labor expenditures. Eight different transfer programs are considered in this analysis: unemployment compensation, Social Security, Aid to Families with Dependent Children, Supplemental Security Income, General Assistance or General Relief, food stamps, Medicaid, and subsidized housing.

Estimated savings from transfer payments are based on data provided by workers in the sample on the types and amounts of transfer payments received before and during Title X employment. In general, transfer payments received during Title X employment should be the same as, or lower than, those received before Title X employment, due to the change in employment status. Title X participants receiving unemployment compensation before Title X employment, for example, were not eligible to receive payments during Title X employment.

Means-tested benefits may not change if Title X earnings are insufficient to alter eligibility status for each benefit. In a few cases, a participant could actually experience an increase in the benefit amount during the program period. For example, an employee may attain retirement age or experience a death or disability in the family, resulting in an increase in Social Security.

Possibly, another source of income has been lost. These increases, however, are not a result of Title X employment and thus are ignored in our calculations. We are interested in changes in benefit amount that are attributable to Title X employment. Therefore, we restrict our calculations to reductions in benefits received during Title X employment, presuming that all reductions may be limited to Title X employment. It is possible, of course, that other factors affecting income may have contributed to the benefit reduction. However, it is also likely that in some cases other factors contributed to the maintenance of, or increase in, a benefit that would otherwise have been lost under Title X employment. Thus, it is reasonable to assume that transfer-benefit reductions reported by employees are returns to the government from Title X projects.

The number of participants in the Title X employee sample experiencing a change in benefit amount during Title X employment as compared with before it are presented in Table A.3.

The calculation of the reduction in transfer payments attributable to Title X employment relies exclusively on those workers who experienced a decline in benefits during Title X employment. Social Security and food stamps are the only transfers with a noticeable number of recipients experiencing an increase in benefit amount during the Title X program as compared with before it. However, even for these benefits, the proportion of recipients reporting an increase is only 14.2 percent and 9.9 percent, respectively. It should be noted that in instances where change in benefit status is indicated, but information on benefit amount is incomplete, the average weekly (or monthly) benefit amount for the employee's state of residence is used. This situation occurs in about 5 percent of benefit cases. Given the low-income profile of most Title X employees, the use of the average benefit amount may serve to slightly understate estimates of transfer returns to government.

The specific procedures used to calculate the transfer savings are discussed according to the following categories: unemployment compensation; cash-transfer programs (Social Security, AFDC, SSI, and General Relief); and in-kind transfers (food stamps, public housing, and Medicaid assistance).

Unemployment Compensation

All workers in the sample were asked whether they were receiving unemployment compensation at the time of hire under Title X, the weekly benefit amount, if any, and the number of additional weeks to which they were entitled at the time they started the Title X job. For workers who were unemployed and collecting unemployment compensation before Title X employment, the calculation of the savings to government is a two-stage procedure. First, the saving in estimated benefit weeks attributable to Title X employment is calculated. The number of benefit weeks saved is the smaller of two figures: the weeks of Title X

TABLE A.3

Number of Employees Receiving a Change in Benefits during Title X Period Compared with Period before Title X

Type of Transfer	Did Not Receive a Change	Received During Period But Not Before	Experienced an Increase	Experienced No Change	Experienced a Decline
Social Security	1,772	6	28	130	33
Food stamps	1,543	22	20	79	305
AFDC	1,837	4	6	43	79
SSI	1,924	0	3	23	19
General Relief	1,879	0	3	13	74
Unemployment compensation	1,429	0	0	0	540
Public housing	1,758	0	0	154	57
Medicaid	1,566	0	0	286	117

Source: Compiled by the authors.

employment attributable to the program, or the weeks of benefits remaining. The savings to the government are equal to the estimated benefit weeks saved times the weekly benefit amount received prior to Title X employment. The following equations express the procedures used to calculate savings in unemployment compensation for those workers unemployed and receiving benefits before Title X employment:

$$
\begin{bmatrix} \text{Weeks of} \\ \text{Title X} \\ \text{employment} \\ \text{attributable} \\ \text{to program} \end{bmatrix} = \begin{bmatrix} \text{weeks worked} \\ \text{on Title X} & - & \text{estimated weeks of} \\ \text{job} & & \text{work in the absence} \\ & & \text{of Title X} \end{bmatrix}
$$

$$
\begin{bmatrix} \text{Estimated} \\ \text{benefit} \\ \text{weeks} \\ \text{saved} \end{bmatrix} = \begin{array}{c} \text{the smaller} \\ \text{of two} \\ \text{figures} \end{array} \begin{bmatrix} \text{weeks of} \\ \text{Title X} & \text{weeks of} \\ \text{employment} & \text{or} & \text{unemployment} \\ \text{attributable to} & \text{compensation} \\ \text{the program} & \text{benefits remaining} \end{bmatrix}
$$

$$
\begin{pmatrix} \text{Savings in unemployment} \\ \text{compensation for those} \\ \text{previously unemployed} \\ \text{and receiving benefits} \end{pmatrix} = \begin{pmatrix} \text{estimated} \\ \text{benefit} \\ \text{weeks} \\ \text{saved} \end{pmatrix} \times \begin{pmatrix} \text{weekly benefit} \\ \text{amount prior} \\ \text{to Title X} \\ \text{employment} \end{pmatrix}
$$

Unemployment-compensation savings are also imputed for those Title X employees who were employed prior to their Title X jobs, but are projected to experience some unemployment in the absence of their Title X jobs. It is assumed that these employees would have been eligible for unemployment compensation when they were unemployed. Just as persons unemployed prior to their Title X jobs are likely to have been employed for a certain number of weeks if they hadn't been hired under Title X, so also are previously employed persons likely to have been unemployed for a portion of time, if they hadn't accepted Title X employment. The assumption of eligibility for employment compensation is reasonable, given the fact that the persons were employed prior to their Title X jobs, and are projected to have been employed for most of the period of Title X employment, even if not hired for a Title X project.

Since no weekly benefit amounts are reported for these employees, they are assumed to have been eligible for the average weekly unemployment compensation benefit for their state of residence, a conservative assumption in light of their previous employment experience. The average weekly benefit amount ranges from $43 in Mississippi to $98 in the District of Columbia. The maximum benefit amount ranges from $49 in Mississippi to $110 for the District of Columbia, exclusive of allowances for dependents, which are paid in 11 states. Nationally,

TABLE A.4

Average Weekly Benefit Payments, July 1976

State/Area	Average Weekly Payment
Alabama	65.03
Alaska	79.61
Arizona	72.18
Arkansas	61.54
California	72.19
Colorado	82.41
Connecticut	73.91
Delaware	86.22
District of Columbia	98.32
Florida	63.34
Georgia	68.14
Hawaii	85.04
Idaho	64.15
Illinois	88.94
Indiana	60.36
Iowa	84.17
Kansas	67.59
Kentucky	65.69
Louisiana	65.62
Maine	62.45
Maryland	71.59
Massachusetts	75.30
Michigan	87.41
Minnesota	77.02
Mississippi	48.44
Missouri	71.51

State/Area	Average Weekly Payment
Montana	64.20
Nebraska	66.32
Nevada	74.14
New Hampshire	61.47
New Jersey	77.47
New Mexico	59.06
New York	72.06
North Carolina	64.19
North Dakota	66.10
Ohio	83.58
Oklahoma	59.92
Oregon	66.18
Pennsylvania	84.63
Puerto Rico	43.51
Rhode Island	66.24
South Carolina	64.92
South Dakota	62.47
Tennessee	60.69
Texas	54.85
Utah	71.55
Vermont	66.07
Virginia	66.78
Washington	74.11
West Virginia	55.81
Wisconsin	82.64
Wyoming	71.84

Source: U.S. Department of Labor, Employment and Training Administration, *Unemployment Insurance Statistics* (Washington, D.C.: November–December 1976), table 3a (mimeographed).

44 percent receive the maximum. The average weekly payment amount, by state and U.S. area, for July 1976 is presented in Table A.4.

The following equations express the procedures used to calculate savings in unemployment compensation for those workers employed prior to Title X:

$$\begin{bmatrix} \text{Estimated weeks of} \\ \text{unemployment in the} \\ \text{absence of Title X} \end{bmatrix} = \begin{bmatrix} \text{weeks worked} \\ \text{under} \\ \text{Title X} \end{bmatrix} - \begin{bmatrix} \text{estimated weeks of} \\ \text{work in the absence} \\ \text{of Title X} \end{bmatrix}$$

$$\begin{pmatrix} \text{Savings in unemploy-} \\ \text{ment compensation} \\ \text{for those previously} \\ \text{employed} \end{pmatrix} = \begin{pmatrix} \text{estimated weeks} \\ \text{of unemployment} \\ \text{in the absence of} \\ \text{Title X} \end{pmatrix} \times \begin{pmatrix} \text{average weekly} \\ \text{state payment} \\ \text{amount} \end{pmatrix}$$

It should be noted that the assumed imputing of a saving to those workers not receiving benefits before Title X employment does not apply to the means-tested transfers. Employed persons who were not receiving such transfers cannot be assumed to have been eligible for transfers as a result of projected unemployment. In general, such persons were employed prior to Title X employment, and would have worked, on the average, for about 28 of 35 weeks in the absence of Title X. It is not plausible to assume that such persons would have been eligible for means-tested transfers during the seven weeks of projected unemployment.

Allocation of the savings in unemployment compensation between the federal government and state governments depends upon the weeks of compensation remaining. The federal government, under the emergency Special Unemployment Assistance program, pays all the benefits for the last 26 weeks of the maximum claim of 65 weeks. The federal and the state governments share the cost of the 13 weeks that represent weeks 27-39 of the maximum claim of 65 weeks. The state pays all the basic benefit, which, in all but nine states, is a maximum of 26 weeks, but which varies among states according to individuals' prior work experience.

In lieu of data that would allow more precise allocation, we assume—only for purposes of calculating the federal-state split of savings—that each employee was originally eligible for the maximum duration of 65 weeks of benefits. Since we know how many remaining weeks of benefits on which the employee could have collected, we can allocate savings to the federal government or state governments. The effect of this assumption is to slightly overstate the federal share, because the federal government is presumed to pay the last 26 weeks of benefits.

Savings from Cash-Transfer Programs

In general, these transfer payments (Social Security, SSI, AFDC, and General Relief) will be reduced if the recipient has an increase in earned income, although they differ in that Social Security is earnings based, while the others are strictly needs based. The data needed to estimate the savings for each type of cash-transfer program come directly from the survey questionnaire. Each employee was asked to report the "average monthly benefit you or your family received," if any, prior to the Title X job and while on the Title X job. The difference is the direct estimate of average monthly benefit savings for each employee. These savings are converted to weekly savings, by simply dividing the monthly figure by 4.3 weeks per month, and then multiplied by the estimated weeks of employment attributable to Title X. Thus, the total for each cash transfer is derived, as shown in the equations below. Such equations are identical for each of the cash-transfer programs.

$$
\begin{array}{l}\text{Average monthly} \\ \text{savings in} \\ \text{Social Security}\end{array} = \left[\begin{array}{l}\text{average monthly} \\ \text{Social Security} \\ \text{benefit before} \\ \text{Title X employ-} \\ \text{ment}\end{array} - \begin{array}{l}\text{average monthly} \\ \text{Social Security bene-} \\ \text{fit during Title X} \\ \text{employment}\end{array}\right]
$$

$$
\begin{array}{l}\text{Total savings} \\ \text{in Social} \\ \text{Security}\end{array} = [(\text{average monthly savings}) \div 4.3]
$$

$$
\times \left[\left(\begin{array}{l}\text{weeks of} \\ \text{Title X} \\ \text{employment}\end{array}\right) - \left(\begin{array}{l}\text{estimated weeks of em-} \\ \text{ployment in the absence} \\ \text{of Title X}\end{array}\right)\right]
$$

The second equation is applied to all those workers in the sample experiencing a decline in benefit amount.

The federal-state split of the savings in cash transfers is determined separately for each cash transfer. Benefits are apportioned according to the percentage of total payments to recipients made by the federal government and state governments. Only payments to recipients are considered, not administrative or other costs of the transfer programs. Thus, all Social Security returns accrue to the federal government, while for General Relief the returns accrue to state governments. The federal-state split of returns from AFDC and SSI is presented, by state and U.S. area, in Tables A.5 and A.6 respectively.

Savings from In-Kind Transfer Programs

The primary data necessary to estimate the savings from the in-kind transfer programs (food stamps, public housing, and Medicaid assistance) also come directly from the sample of workers. With regard to food stamps, each worker was asked to report the average monthly value and cost of food stamps purchased,

TABLE A.5

Federal and State/Local Shares of AFDC Payments, Calendar Year 1975
(percent)

State/Area	Share of Federal Funds	Share of State and Local Funds
Alabama	76.2	23.8
Alaska	49.2	50.8
Arizona	59.5	40.5
Arkansas	74.3	25.7
California	47.3	52.7
Colorado	55.9	44.1
Connecticut	48.3	51.7
Delaware	50.5	49.5
District of Columbia	50.0	50.0
Florida	74.6	25.4
Georgia	73.8	26.2
Guam	50.0	50.0
Hawaii	50.0	50.0
Idaho	68.4	31.6
Illinois	49.2	50.8
Indiana	56.5	43.5
Iowa	57.7	42.3
Kansas	54.5	45.5
Kentucky	71.7	28.3
Louisiana	72.5	27.5
Maine	70.3	29.7
Maryland	49.6	50.4
Massachusetts	48.2	51.8
Michigan	49.5	50.5
Minnesota	54.2	45.8
Mississippi	83.1	16.9
Missouri	59.6	40.4
Montana	64.7	35.3

242

State/Area	Share of Federal Funds	Share of State and Local Funds
Nebraska	56.7	43.3
Nevada	47.7	52.3
New Hampshire	61.1	38.9
New Jersey	49.9	50.1
New Mexico	72.7	27.3
New York	46.3	53.7
North Carolina	69.0	31.0
North Dakota	63.4	36.6
Ohio	52.4	47.6
Oklahoma	67.4	32.6
Oregon	56.9	43.1
Pennsylvania	55.2	44.8
Puerto Rico	50.0	50.0
Rhode Island	56.0	44.0
South Carolina	77.1	22.9
South Dakota	68.7	31.3
Tennessee	73.5	26.5
Texas	73.0	27.0
Utah	69.6	30.4
Vermont	66.5	33.5
Virginia	58.1	41.9
Virgin Islands	50.0	50.0
Washington	51.2	48.8
West Virginia	72.6	27.4
Wisconsin	58.3	41.7
Wyoming	60.9	39.1
Total	53.3	46.7

Source: U.S. Department of Health, Education, and Welfare, Social and Rehabilitation Service, *Funds, by Source, Expended for Public Assistance Payments* (Washington, D.C.: mimeographed 1975), table 8.

TABLE A.6

Federal-State Shares of SSI Payments, December 1976
(percent)

State/Area	Federal Share	State Share
Alabama	.94	.06
Alaska	.55	.45
Arizona	.97	.03
Arkansas	.99	.01
California	.40	.60
Colorado	.71	.29
Connecticut	.76	.24
Delaware	.92	.08
District of Columbia	.98	.02
Florida	.99	.01
Georgia	.99	.01
Hawaii	.71	.29
Idaho	.81	.19
Illinois	.85	.15
Indiana	1.00	0
Iowa	.96	.04
Kansas	.99	.01
Kentucky	.92	.08
Louisiana	.99	.01
Maine	.80	.20
Maryland	.99	.01
Massachusetts	.41	.59
Michigan	.69	.31
Minnesota	.89	.11
Mississippi	.99	.01
Missouri	.85	.15
Montana	.94	.06
Nebraska	.84	.16
Nevada	.75	.25

State/Area	Federal Share	State Share
New Hampshire	.71	.29
New Jersey	.82	.18
New Mexico	1.00	0
New York	.66	.34
North Carolina	.91	.09
North Dakota	.99	.01
Ohio	.96	.04
Oklahoma	.79	.21
Oregon	.86	.14
Pennsylvania	.76	.24
Rhode Island	.73	.27
South Carolina	.99	.01
South Dakota	.96	.04
Tennessee	.99	.01
Texas	1.00	0
Utah	1.00	0
Vermont	.68	.32
Virginia	.98	.02
Washington	.81	.19
West Virginia	1.00	0
Wisconsin	.37	.63
Wyoming	1.00	0

Source: Social Security Administration, Office of Program Policy and Planning, *Supplemental Security Income for the Aged, Blind, and Disabled* (Washington, D.C.: mimeographed. March 1977), tables 5 and 9.

TABLE A.7

Average Monthly Medicaid Payment per Recipient, September 1976

State/Area	Dollar Amount
Connecticut	157
Maine	120
Massachusetts	114
New Hampshire	153
Rhode Island	141
Vermont	133
New York	176
New Jersey	128
Puerto Rico	32
Delaware	91
District of Columbia	145
Maryland	135
Pennsylvania	258
Virginia	119
West Virginia	89
Alabama	95
Florida	106
Kentucky	86
Mississippi	71
North Carolina	96
South Carolina	101
Tennessee	122
Illinois	99
Indiana	178
Michigan	176
Minnesota	329

State/Area	Dollar Amount
Ohio	118
Wisconsin	178
Arkansas	107
Louisiana	105
New Mexico	95
Oklahoma	232
Texas	150
Iowa	162
Kansas	147
Missouri	67
Nebraska	149
Colorado	143
Montana	179
North Dakota	219
South Dakota	160
Utah	157
California	129
Hawaii	115
Nevada	177
Alaska	103
Idaho	151
Oregon	161
Arizona[a]	—
Georgia	n.a.[b]
Washington	n.a.
Wyoming	n.a.

[a] Has no program.
[b] Data not available.
Source: U.S. Department of Health, Education, and Welfare, Social and Rehabilitation Service, *Medicaid Statistics* (Washington, D.C.: mimeographed. January 1977), table 4.

TABLE A.8

Federal-State Shares of Medicaid Payments, Calendar Year 1975

State/Area	Federal Funds	State and Local Funds
Alabama	74.7	25.3
Alaska	50.3	49.7
Arizona[a]	_b	—
Arkansas	81.0	19.0
California	43.6	56.4
Colorado	55.9	44.1
Connecticut	49.5	50.5
Delaware	50.5	49.5
District of Columbia	46.2	53.8
Florida	59.0	41.0
Georgia	66.0	34.0
Guam	37.5	62.5
Hawaii	42.3	57.7
Idaho	68.2	31.8
Illinois	47.2	52.8
Indiana	56.9	43.1
Iowa	57.9	62.1
Kansas	48.0	52.0
Kentucky	71.9	28.1
Louisiana	72.3	27.7
Maine	70.5	29.5
Maryland	41.9	58.1
Massachusetts	50.1	49.9
Michigan	49.8	50.2
Minnesota	56.2	43.8
Mississippi[c]	80.4	19.6
Missouri	55.5	44.5
Montana	64.4	35.6
Nebraska	56.9	43.1
Nevada	47.1	52.9
New Hampshire	60.4	39.6
New Jersey	48.2	51.8
New Mexico	73.8	26.2

State/Area	Federal Funds	State and Local Funds
New York	45.9	54.1
North Carolina	67.8	32.2
North Dakota	64.2	35.8
Ohio	53.7	46.3
Oklahoma	67.8	32.2
Oregon	56.3	43.7
Pennsylvania	42.5	57.5
Puerto Rico	24.4	75.6
Rhode Island	56.5	43.5
South Carolina	73.6	26.4
South Dakota	67.2	32.8
Tennessee	69.8	30.2
Texas	63.6	36.4
Utah	69.2	30.8
Vermont	68.1	31.9
Virginia	59.2	40.8
Virgin Islands	30.6	69.4
Washington	48.0	52.0
West Virginia	70.8	29.2
Wisconsin	58.7	41.3
Wyoming	60.7	39.3
Total	51.5	48.5

a Has no program.

b Data not available.

c Data represent expenditures for January 1–June 30, 1975; information not available for July 1–December 31, 1975 at time of writing.

Source: U.S. Department of Health, Education, and Welfare, Social and Rehabilitation Service, *Funds, by Source, Expended for Public Assistance Payments* (Washington, D.C.: mimeographed, 1975), table 9.

if any, prior to the Title X job and while on the Title X job. Thus the average monthly saving on food stamps is calculated as follows:

$$
\begin{array}{l}\text{Average monthly} \\ \text{savings on} \\ \text{food stamps}\end{array} = \left[\begin{array}{l}\text{(average monthly value of stamps before} \\ \text{Title X job)} - \text{(cost before Title X job)} \\ - \text{(value during Title X employment)} \\ - \text{(cost during Title X employment)}\end{array}\right]
$$

Total savings all of which accrue to the federal government, are calculated as follows:

$$
\begin{array}{l}\text{Total savings} \\ \text{on} \\ \text{food stamps}\end{array} = \left[\begin{array}{l}\text{(Average monthly savings} \div 4.3) \ \times \\ \text{(weeks of Title X employment} - \text{estimated weeks} \\ \text{of employment in the absence of Title X)}\end{array}\right]
$$

With regard to public housing, all participants were asked, first, whether they lived in public housing; second, whether their rent changed as a result of Title X employment; and, third, the approximate amount by which the monthly rent payments increased as a result of the Title X job. The monthly increase in rent payments is converted to a weekly amount and accrued for the duration of Title X employment, discounted by the estimated weeks of work in the absence of the program:

$$
\begin{array}{l}\text{Total savings} \\ \text{on} \\ \text{public housing}\end{array} = \left[\begin{array}{l}\text{(monthly increase in rent} \div 4.3) \ \times \\ \left(\begin{array}{ll}\text{weeks worked} & \text{estimated weeks of} \\ \text{on} \quad - & \text{work in the absence} \\ \text{Title X job} & \text{of Title X}\end{array}\right)\end{array}\right]
$$

The reduction in the public-housing rent subsidy due to Title X employment accrues only to the federal government.

For Medicaid assistance, all participants were asked whether they or their families were eligible for Medicaid before and during Title X employment. No benefit amount was asked for, since benefit amounts are not necessarily regular under Medicaid. Returns from Medicaid are defined only for those workers who were eligible before Title X employment, but not during it. Since no benefit amount is contained in the survey instrument, we must assume that those whose eligibility for Medicaid assistance has changed would have received benefits equal to the average monthly payment received by recipients in their state of residence. Since not all of those eligible are recipients in a given month, Medicaid returns are overstated. This is the only instance of clear overstatement in our methodology, and is caused by the lack of data on eligibles. Average monthly Medicaid payments for each state are shown in Table A.7. As can be seen, the average is $127 per month, ranging from $67 in Missouri to $329 in Minnesota.

Using the external data on benefit amount and the information on the change in eligibility from the survey, the formula for calculating Medicaid returns is:

$$
\begin{matrix}
\text{Total} \\
\text{savings} \\
\text{on} \\
\text{Medicaid}
\end{matrix}
=
\left[
\left(
\begin{matrix}
\text{weeks of} \\
\text{Title X} \\
\text{employment}
\end{matrix}
-
\begin{matrix}
\text{estimated weeks of employ-} \\
\text{ment in the absence of} \\
\text{Title X}
\end{matrix}
\right)
\times (\text{average monthly medicaid payment by state} \div 4.3)
\right]
$$

The federal and state shares of the Medicaid returns, which are calculated only for those participants experiencing a change in eligibility status during Title X employment, are based upon the percentage of payments provided by the federal and the state governments, as reported in Table A.8.

TAX REVENUES FROM TITLE X EMPLOYMENT

Title X earned income returns taxes to the federal treasury through income, excise, FICA, and unemployment insurance taxes, while the state governments receive increased income, sales, excise, and unemployment insurance taxes. The general algorithm for calculating these tax returns is:

$$
\text{Tax revenues} =
\left[
\begin{matrix}
\text{Earned income at-} \\
\text{tributable to Title X}
\end{matrix}
\right]
\left[
\begin{matrix}
\text{Income tax} \\
\text{rate}
\end{matrix}
\right]
$$

$$
+
\left[
\begin{matrix}
\text{consumption expendi-} \\
\text{ture out of disposable} \\
\text{income attributable} \\
\text{to Title X}
\end{matrix}
\right]
\left[
\begin{matrix}
\text{Sales- and Excise-} \\
\text{tax rate}
\end{matrix}
\right]
$$

$$
+
\left[
\begin{matrix}
\text{FICA contribution} \\
\text{from earned income} \\
\text{attributable to} \\
\text{Title X}
\end{matrix}
\right]
+
\left[
\begin{matrix}
\text{unemployment in-} \\
\text{surance contribution} \\
\text{from earned income} \\
\text{attributable to} \\
\text{Title X}
\end{matrix}
\right]
$$

In this calculation the earned income attributable to Title X employment is equal to actual Title X earnings minus the estimate of earnings in the absence of Title X (see Appendix B).

The algorithm is equally applicable to calculations of federal and state returns, with an appropriate modification of tax rates. In the following pages, the specific form of the general algorithm is defined for each type of tax, and simplifying assumptions are explained.

TABLE A.9

Projections of 1976 Federal Income Taxes

Adjusted Gross Income	Single Person	Married Couple	Couple with One Dependent	Couple with Two Dependents	Couple with Four Dependents
$3,000	63	0	0	0	0
5,000	381	170	29	0	0
6,000	551	326	178	35	0
8,000	924	642	505	347	50
10,000	1,331	982	855	709	372
12,500	1,804	1,395	1,245	1,114	796
15,000	2,315	1,810	1,660	1,510	1,191
17,500	2,905	2,276	2,089	1,925	1,625
20,000	3,544	2,795	2,608	2,420	2,045
25,000	4,990	3,930	3,720	3,510	3,090
30,000	6,610	5,228	4,988	4,748	4,268
35,000	8,385	6,698	6,428	6,158	5,618
40,000	10,275	8,303	8,011	7,718	7,133

Source: Compiled by the authors.

Personal Income Taxes

Personal income tax returns attributable to Title X employment are calculated as follows:

$$
\begin{bmatrix} \text{Personal} \\ \text{income} \\ \text{tax} \\ \text{revenue} \end{bmatrix} = \begin{bmatrix} \text{earned in-} \\ \text{come attrib-} \\ \text{utable to} \\ \text{Title X} \end{bmatrix} \times \begin{bmatrix} \left(\begin{array}{c} \text{effective} \\ \text{federal} \\ \text{income} \\ \text{tax rate} \end{array} \right) + \left(\begin{array}{c} \text{effective} \\ \text{state} \\ \text{income} \\ \text{tax rate} \end{array} \right) \end{bmatrix}
$$

Both federal and state tax rates are effective rates. The effective federal
rates are derived from projections of 1976 taxes paid for different levels of
adjusted gross income, as presented in a report of the House Ways and Means
Committee on the Tax Reform Act of 1975;[1] adjusted gross income is equal to
gross family income minus business and moving expenses, but before personal
exemptions and allowable deductions. These data are presented in Table A.9.

Effective federal income tax rates are calculated by simply dividing the tax
liability by adjusted gross income. A single person with an adjusted gross income
of $3,000, for example, is estimated to have a tax liability of $63; hence, the
effective income tax rate is .021 percent ($63 ÷ $3,000). Note that the information in Table A.9 permits the calculation of effective federal income tax rates for
only a single person and a married couple with one, two, or four dependents.

Conversion of the effective federal income tax rates to our survey data
required the following information and procedures for each participant: the
adjusted gross income of the participant plus others in the tax-reporting unit; the
interpolation of adjusted gross family income from the survey to coincide with
the income levels in Table A.9; the number of withholding exemptions in the
tax-reporting unit; the interpolation of the exemption data from the survey to
match the information in Table A.9.

All Title X workers were asked to estimate their 1976 gross family earnings
before deductions, as counted for tax purposes. The responses fell into seven
categories as summarized in Table A.10. The midpoint of each income range is
assumed as being representative of adjusted gross income. The midpoints, however, do not correspond to the adjusted gross income levels in Table A.10 upon
which the effective federal income tax rates are computed. Thus, interpolation
is necessary, as presented in Table A.11. In the table, there are three midpoints
of gross family income from the survey that are not matched by an adjusted
gross income level: $2,000, $7,000, and $9,000. The effective tax rate on an
adjusted gross income of $3,000 was selected as a proxy for the $2,000 family-
income midpoint. An average of the $6,000 and $8,000 effective tax rates, and

TABLE A.10

Gross Family Income of Title X Workers

Income Range	Percent of Workers	Midpoint of Range
$0–4,000	29.2	2,000
4,001–6,000	30.7	5,000
6,001–8,000	16.5	7,000
8,001–10,000	10.3	9,000
10,001–15,000	8.5	12,500
15,001–20,000	2.5	17,500
Over 20,000	2.3	25,000

Source: Compiled by the authors.

TABLE A.11

Conversion of Effective Tax Rates

Midpoint of 1976 Gross Family Income from Survey	Effective Federal Tax Rate for Levels of Adjusted Gross Income
$2,000	$3,000 rate
5,000	5,000 rate
7,000	$(6,000 + 8,000) \div 2$
9,000	$(8,000 + 10,000) \div 2$
12,500	12,500 rate
17,500	17,500 rate
Over 20,000	25,000 rate

Source: Compiled by the authors.

of the $8,000 and $10,000 rates, was used for the $7,000 and $9,000 family-income midpoints, respectively.*

---

*The selection of the $3,000 figure as representing the midpoint of the $0-$4,000 range may appear to be an overestimate. However, tax liabilities are zero for all but single individuals earning $3,000, and the rate for individuals is almost negligible. Moreover, it might be argued that a simple average of tax rates for $6,000 and $8,000 does not exactly represent the tax rate for $7,000, since effective tax rates are not linear with income (the

In addition to adjusted gross income, information on the number of exemptions counted for federal tax purposes is required to calculate federal income taxes for Title X participants. Participants were asked how many dependents they had, as counted for federal tax purposes. The effective federal tax rates, however, are based upon the number of exemptions, not the number of dependents. The number of exemptions for federal tax purposes is equal to the number of dependents plus one, where the additional exemption is the head of household. Confusion existed among respondents over the distinction between an exemption and a dependent; so the data from the survey instrument have been modified to create two measures. The conservative approach resulted in the addition of one dependent to every response; the second approach added one only to those participants that had no dependents—that is, they gave a zero-dependents response to the question. In both cases, the modified dependent/exemption data were collapsed into seven categories of exemptions: one, two, three, four, five, six, and seven or more.

However, federal income taxes are reported in Table A.9 for only one exemption and for two, three, four, and six exemptions. Thus, interpolation is required to match these data with Title X survey data. The interpolation of the effective tax rates was performed for the minimum, midpoint, and maximum ranges of gross family income categories, although only the results of the midpoint interpolation are discussed below.

The procedure used to interpolate an effective federal income tax rate for individuals with five and seven or more exemptions, at a given gross family income, is to make a multiple-regression estimate. The effective federal income tax rate is the dependent variable, with income the category from our survey and the number of exemptions being the independent variables. The sample size was 35, corresponding to the seven income categories multiplied by the five categories observed for exemptions. The result of the estimation is:

$$\text{Effective federal income tax rate} = .02 + \underset{(.0011)}{.0251} \text{(income category)} - \underset{(.0013)}{.014} \text{(exemptions)}$$

$R^2 = .94$
F-value = 286.14
N = 35

The regression equation was highly significant, explaining 94 percent of the variation in the effective federal income tax rate. The independent variables

---

same argument can be applied to the $9,000 tax rate). The effect, however, is only a minor understatement of effective rates, compensating for any minor overstatement in the $2,000 rate, and is consistent with the conservative approach in the methodology.

TABLE A.12

Effective Federal Income Tax Rates

Total Family Income	Exemptions						
	1	2	3	4	5	6	7
$3,000	.021	0	0	0	0	0	0
5,000	.076	.034	.006	0	0	0	0
7,000	.104	.067	.047	.025	.020	.003	.002
9,000	.125	.089	.075	.057	.050	.022	.015
12,500	.144	.112	.100	.089	.070	.064	.045
17,500	.166	.130	.119	.110	.100	.093	.070
25,000	.200	.157	.149	.140	.130	.124	.095

Source: Compiled by the authors.

were statistically significant at the 1-percent level or better. They also possess intuitively reasonable signs; that is, income increases the tax rate, while the number of exemptions decreases the tax rate. The effective federal income tax rates for five exemptions and seven or more exemptions were obtained by inserting substitute values in the estimated regression equation. For example, the tax rate for a family with five exemptions and an income of $9,000 (category number four) was obtained as follows:

$$\text{Effective federal income tax rate} = .02 + .0251(4) - .014(5) = .0504$$

The effective federal income tax rates corresponding to the midpoints of our family-income categories, for each number of exemptions, are presented in Table A.12.

The preceding discussion has focused on the derivation of effective federal income tax rates. These effective federal income tax rates are applied to the earned income attributable to Title X, to arrive at federal income tax revenue.* Recalling that three effective federal income tax rates exist, based upon the maximum, midpoint, and minimum ranges of the income categories found in the survey, and that two measures of the number of exemptions exist, we have made six distinct calculations of federal income tax revenue. The mean federal income tax revenues (per employee) for these six cases are contrasted in Table A.13.

TABLE A.13

Average Federal Income Tax Revenues for Title X Workers

Range of Income Category	Number of Dependents Plus One	Number of Dependents Plus One, Only for Zero-Dependents Responses
Maximum	$188	$250
Midpoint	147	204
Minimum	113	155

Source: Compiled by the authors.

---

*An underlying assumption is that all the earnings attributable to Title X originated in 1976. For most workers this will be the case; however, a few participants started Title X employment during November or December of 1975, and some participants continued with the program into 1977.

TABLE A.14

Effective State Personal Income Tax Rates for Selected Adjusted Gross Income Levels,
Married Couple with Two Dependents, by State, 1974

State/Area	Adjusted Gross Income							
	$2,500	$3,500	$5,000	$7,500	$10,000	$17,500	$25,000	$50,000
Alabama	—*	—	0.3	0.9	1.5	1.9	2.4	2.6
Alaska	—	—	0.5	1.4	1.8	2.1	2.7	4.2
Arizona	—	0.1	0.5	1.1	1.5	1.8	2.6	3.5
Arkansas	—	—	—	1.1	1.6	2.2	3.1	4.6
California	—	—	—	—	0.6	1.7	2.8	5.8
Colorado	—	—	0.1	1.0	1.6	2.2	3.1	3.9
Delaware	—	0.3	0.8	1.5	2.4	3.7	5.0	7.2
District of Columbia	—	—	0.5	1.7	2.5	3.3	4.4	6.5
Georgia	—	—	—	0.3	0.8	1.8	2.9	4.1
Hawaii	—	—	—	0.6	2.1	3.5	4.5	6.1
Idaho	0.4	0.3	0.2	0.5	1.4	2.7	3.9	5.3
Illinois	—	—	0.5	1.2	1.5	1.9	2.1	2.3
Indiana	—	0.6	1.0	1.3	1.5	1.7	1.8	1.9
Iowa	—	—	1.3	2.3	3.0	3.0	3.5	3.8
Kansas	—	—	0.5	0.9	1.3	1.7	2.2	3.0
Kentucky	—	—	0.6	2.0	2.4	2.5	3.0	3.2
Louisiana	—	—	—	0.1	0.5	0.7	0.9	1.5
Maine	—	—	0.1	0.4	0.6	0.9	1.4	2.4

258

Maryland	—	0.6	1.7	2.5	2.7	3.2	3.8
Massachusetts	—	—	2.1	2.8	3.7	4.1	4.5
Michigan	—	—	—	—	0.6	0.9	2.1
Minnesota	1.2	2.7	4.4	5.4	5.8	6.9	7.8
Mississippi	—	—	—	0.4	1.2	1.9	2.7
Missouri	—	0.1	0.7	1.1	1.5	2.3	2.9
Montana	0.3	1.0	2.0	2.8	2.9	3.8	5.0
Nebraska	—	—	—	0.4	0.9	1.3	2.3
New Mexico	—	0.1	0.5	0.8	1.4	2.1	4.0
New York	—	—	1.3	2.1	3.1	4.7	8.7
North Carolina	—	0.8	1.8	2.6	3.1	4.0	5.1
North Dakota	—	0.1	0.7	1.0	1.9	3.3	4.4
Ohio	0.1	0.3	0.4	0.6	1.1	1.6	2.4
Oklahoma	—	0.1	0.3	0.5	1.1	2.1	3.5
Oregon	—	2.2	0.9	2.4	3.6	4.7	6.8
Pennsylvania	—	—	2.0	2.0	2.0	2.0	2.0
Rhode Island	—	0.3	0.8	1.2	1.6	2.1	3.3
South Carolina	—	0.5	1.0	1.6	2.4	3.5	4.9
Utah	—	0.3	1.1	1.5	2.6	3.3	3.8
Vermont	—	—	1.5	2.2	3.0	3.8	6.0
Virginia	—	0.5	1.1	1.8	2.6	3.3	4.2
West Virginia	0.5	0.9	1.2	1.4	1.6	2.0	3.1
Wisconsin	—	0.5	2.6	3.7	4.6	6.0	7.5
Median rate	—	0.3	1.1	1.5	2.1	3.0	3.9

*Data not available.

Source: Compiled by the author.

TABLE A.15

Effective State Personal Income Tax Rates by Total Family Income, 1974

State/Area	Family Income						
	$2,000	$5,000	$7,000	$9,000	$12,500	$17,500	$25,000
Alabama	0	.003	.008	.013	.016	.019	.024
Alaska	0	.005	.012	.017	.019	.021	.027
Arizona	0	.005	.010	.014	.016	.018	.026
Arkansas	0	0	.009	.014	.018	.022	.031
California	0	0	0	.004	.010	.017	.028
Colorado	0	.001	.008	.014	.018	.022	.031
Delaware	0	.008	.014	.021	.028	.037	.050
District of Columbia	0	.005	.015	.022	.028	.033	.044
Georgia	0	0	.003	.006	.011	.018	.029
Hawaii	0	0	.005	.016	.026	.035	.045
Idaho	.04	.002	.004	.001	.018	.027	.039
Illinois	0	.005	.011	.014	.016	.019	.021
Indiana	0	.010	.012	.014	.016	.017	.018
Iowa	0	.013	.021	.028	.030	.030	.035
Kansas	0	.005	.008	.012	.014	.017	.022
Kentucky	0	.006	.017	.023	.024	.025	.030
Louisiana	0	0	.001	.004	.006	.007	.009
Maine	0	.001	.003	.005	.007	.009	.014

Maryland	0	.006	.015	.022	.026	.027	.032
Massachusetts	0	0	.017	.026	.031	.037	.041
Michigan	0	0	0	0	.002	.006	.009
Minnesota	0	.027	.041	.051	.055	.058	.069
Mississippi	0	0	0	.003	.007	.012	.019
Missouri	0	.001	.006	.010	.012	.015	.023
Montana	0	.010	.018	.025	.028	.029	.038
Nebraska	0	0	0	.003	.006	.009	.013
New Mexico	0	.001	.004	.007	.010	.014	.021
New York	0	0	.011	.018	.024	.031	.047
North Carolina	0	.008	.016	.023	.028	.031	.040
North Dakota	0	.001	.006	.009	.013	.019	.033
Ohio	.001	.003	.004	.005	.008	.011	.016
Oklahoma	0	.001	.003	.004	.007	.011	.021
Oregon	0	.022	.007	.019	.028	.036	.047
Pennsylvania	0	0	.016	.020	.020	.020	.020
Rhode Island	0	.003	.007	.011	.013	.016	.021
South Carolina	0	.005	.009	.014	.019	.024	.035
Utah	0	.003	.009	.014	.019	.026	.033
Vermont	0	0	.012	.019	.025	.030	.038
Virginia	0	.005	.010	.016	.021	.026	.033
West Virginia	0	.009	.011	.013	.015	.016	.020
Wisconsin	0	.005	.022	.033	.040	.046	.050

Source: Compiled by the author.

261

In the net-cost analysis in Chapter 4, income taxes are calculated for the midpoint of each employee's income range, and according to the conservative-exemption definition used in column two of Table A.13. This means that, for the employee sample, the average federal income tax revenue is $147. An examination of Table A.13 reveals that the average federal income tax revenues are quite sensitive to both the exemption and the income-range assumptions. The range among federal tax returns ($113–$250) amounts to fully 121 percent. The second lowest tax return is selected as the average because it is logically the most defensible and is consistent with the conservative stance of the methodology.

Effective state personal income tax rates have been compiled for 1974 by the Advisory Commission on Intergovernmental Relations.[2] The year 1974 is the most recent for which state personal income tax data are uniformly available. Since effective tax rates have increased in a number of states since 1974, the use of 1974 data understates somewhat the income tax returns to state governments as a result of Title X. These data are presented in Table A.14.

As was the case with federal effective income tax rates, the adjusted gross income levels in Table A.14 do not correspond exactly with the midpoints of our income categories; thus, interpolation is necessary. The interpolation for the midpoints is described below (calculations have also been made for the maximum and minimum values of the income categories). There are four midpoints of gross family income found in the survey that are not matched by an adjusted gross family income level in the state effective income tax table: $2,000, $7,000, $9,000, and $12,500. The effective state tax rate on an adjusted gross income of $2,500 was selected as a proxy for the rate corresponding to $2,000 in family income. The remaining rates for nonobserved family-income midpoint levels are approximated by a linear combination of adjusted gross income associated with effective tax rates. These procedures, again, will have the effect of slightly understating state income tax returns.

The effective state income tax rates corresponding to the midpoints of the gross family income categories are presented in Table A.15. Effective state income tax rates are available only for a family with four exemptions. This is also likely to cause a slight downward bias in our estimate of state income tax revenue, because the mean number of exemptions in our sample is approximately three.

The effective state income tax rates in Table A.15 are applied to the earned income attributable to Title X, to arrive at state income tax revenue. For each Title X employee, three state income tax revenue estimates are generated based upon the midpoint, maximum, and minimum ranges of the gross family income categories. For the employee sample, the mean state tax return attributable to Title X, using each of the three approaches, is presented in Table A.16. The estimate used in the calculation of net costs in Chapter 4 is the midpoint figure of $18. Similar to the case for federal income taxes, the selection of the midpoint, maximum, or minimum for the income ranges has a significant impact

TABLE A.16

Average State Income Tax Revenues from Title X Workers

Range of Income Category	Tax Revenue
Maximum	$23
Midpoint	18
Minimum	13

Source: Compiled by the authors.

on the estimate of state tax revenues. In the employee sample, this impact amounts to almost 28 percent of the midpoint mean, or $18 ± $5.

Sales and Excise Taxes

Title X employees are subject to state sales taxes, state excise taxes, and federal excise taxes, on the purchase of goods and services with their Title X earnings. Hence, earned income attributable to Title X generates tax revenues to government from expenditures on commodities subject to sales and excise taxes. Calculation of sales- and excise-tax revenue requires knowledge of individual state and federal sales and excise tax rates applicable to various types of expenditures; disposable income attributable to Title X; the distribution of disposable income attributable to Title X among taxable expenditures.

Sales-tax rates, for each state, applicable to the retail sale of tangible personal property have been tabulated by the Commerce Clearinghouse, and are reported in Table A.17. State excise-tax rates on gasoline are presented in Table A.18. The excise-tax rates are per gallon of gasoline; the rate is converted to a per-dollar basis by assuming that in 1974 a gallon of gasoline cost $0.60. Thus, a rate of eight cents per gallon means a rate of $0.133 per dollar of expenditure. The federal gasoline excise-tax rate is $0.04 per gallon, or $0.067 per dollar, assuming a $0.60 cost per gallon. State excise tax rates on cigarettes, per pack of 20 cigarettes, are presented in Table A.19. These rates are converted to a per-dollar basis by assuming that in 1974 a pack of cigarettes cost $0.60. The federal tobacco excise tax is equal to $8.40 per 1,000 cigarettes, or, assuming a cost of $0.60 per pack of 20 cigarettes, $0.28 per dollar of expenditure.

Disposable income is earnings attributable to Title X, minus personal income taxes, FICA, and any reduction in cash-transfer payments during Title X employment. The last term, reduction in cash-transfer payments, is included because transfer payments received prior to Title X employment generate sales- and excise-tax revenue to government. Consider an individual receiving

TABLE A.17

State Sales-Tax Rates
(percent)

State/Area	Sales-Tax Rate	State/Area	Sales-Tax Rate
Alabama	4	Missouri	3
Arizona	4	Nebraska	2.5
Arkansas	3	Nevada	3
California	4.75	New Jersey	5
Colorado	3	New Mexico	4
Connecticut	7	New York	4
District of Columbia	5	North Carolina	3
Florida	4	North Dakota	4
Georgia	3	Ohio	4
Hawaii	4	Oklahoma	2
Idaho	3	Pennsylvania	6
Illinois	4	Rhode Island	6
Indiana	4	South Carolina	4
Iowa	3	South Dakota	4
Kansas	3	Tennessee	4.5
Kentucky	5	Texas	4
Louisiana	3	Utah	4
Maine	5	Vermont	3
Maryland	4	Virginia	3
Massachusetts	5	Washington	4.6
Michigan	4	West Virginia	3
Minnesota	4	Wisconsin	4
Mississippi	5	Wyoming	3

Source: Compiled by the authors.

TABLE A.18

State Excise Tax on Gasoline
(cents per gallon)

State/Area	Cents/gal.	State/Area	Cents/gal.
Alabama	7	Montana	7.75
Alaska	8	Nebraska	8.5
Arizona	8	Nevada	6
Arkansas	8.5	New Hampshire	9
California	7	New Jersey	8
Colorado	7	New Mexico	7
Connecticut	11	New York	8
Delaware	9	North Carolina	9
District of Columbia	10	North Dakota	7
Florida	8	Ohio	7
Georgia	7.5	Oklahoma	6.58
Hawaii	12	Oregon	7
Idaho	9.5	Pennsylvania	9
Illinois	7.5	Rhode Island	10
Indiana	8	South Carolina	8
Iowa	7	South Dakota	8
Kansas	8	Tennessee	7
Kentucky	9	Texas	5
Louisiana	8	Utah	7
Maine	9	Vermont	9
Maryland	9	Virginia	9
Massachusetts	3.5	Washington	9
Michigan	9	West Virginia	8.5
Minnesota	9	Wisconsin	7
Mississippi	9	Wyoming	8
Missouri	7		

Source: Compiled by the authors.

TABLE A.19

State Excise Tax on Cigarettes
(cents per pack)

State/Area	Cents/pack	State/Area	Cents/pack
Alabama	12	Montana	12
Alaska	8	Nebraska	13
Arizona	13	Nevada	10
Arkansas	17.75	New Hampshire	12
California	10	New Jersey	19
Colorado	10	New Mexico	12
Connecticut	21	New York	15
Delaware	14	North Carolina	2
District of Columbia	13	North Dakota	11
Florida	17	Ohio	15
Georgia	12	Oklahoma	13
Hawaii	40	Oregon	9
Idaho	9.1	Pennsylvania	18
Illinois	12	Rhode Island	18
Indiana	6	South Carolina	6
Iowa	13	South Dakota	12
Kansas	11	Tennessee	13
Kentucky	3	Texas	18.5
Louisiana	11	Utah	8
Maine	16	Vermont	12
Maryland	10	Virginia	2.5
Massachusetts	21	Washington	16
Michigan	11	West Virginia	12
Minnesota	18	Wisconsin	16
Mississippi	11	Wyoming	8
Missouri	9		

Source: Compiled by the authors.

266

unemployment compensation of $100 weekly prior to Title X. A portion of this $100 cash-transfer payment is spent on goods and services subject to sales and excise taxes. During Title X employment this employee is not eligible to receive unemployment compensation; thus, sales and excise taxes are no longer generated on a portion of the $100 cash transfer.

It is assumed that disposable earnings attributable to Title X employment are spent, not saved, a reasonable assumption considering the low family earnings and the duration of employment of Title X employees. It is further assumed that spending of disposable income follows the distribution of spending reflected in the Consumer Expenditure Survey, conducted by the Bureau of Labor Statistics.[3] The distribution of expenditures selected from the CES for net-cost calculations is that for the median family income of the Title X employee sample, $5,000-$5,999. These expenditures are shown in Table A.20.

For purposes of net-cost calculations, we assume that expenditures on gasoline and tobacco are subject to the appropriate excise taxes. Moreover, we assume that the following items are subject to state sales tax: tobacco, fuel and utilities, house furnishings, clothing, vehicle purchases, vehicle operation, and gifts.* If disposable income is spent according to the CES data presented in Table A.20, then the portions of disposable income subject to gasoline and tobacco excise taxes are 7.2 percent ($228.69 ÷ $3,177.84) and 2.9 percent ($92.75 ÷ $3,177.84), respectively. Sales tax is taken on 66.1 percent ($2,101.06 ÷ $3,177.84) of disposable income.

Given the three components required for the calculation of sales- and excise-tax revenues, the algorithms are:

$$\begin{array}{l} \text{Sales-tax} \\ \text{revenue} \end{array} = \left[\begin{array}{l} \text{disposable earnings attributable} \\ \text{to Title X} \end{array}\right]$$

$$\times \left[\begin{array}{l} \text{percent of disposable earnings} \\ \text{subject to sales tax (.661)} \end{array}\right]$$

$$\times \left[\begin{array}{l} \text{individual state sales tax} \\ \text{rate from Table A.16} \end{array}\right]$$

---

*This is a simplifying assumption, since different states impose sales taxes on different expenditures. Some states, for example, impose taxes on food purchases, a substantial portion of expenditures but one which is not included as taxable in our methodology. Conversely, some states exempt clothing or other items from sales tax. The simplifying assumption probably results in a slight understatement of state sales tax returns, but the assortment of sales tax provisions across states makes this assertion difficult to defend with complete confidence.

TABLE A.20

Selected Expenditures by a Family with Total Income, before Taxes, of $5,000–5,999

Item	Expenditure
Food	$1,028.32
Tobacco	92.75
Fuel and utilities	324.44
Home furnishings, etc.	252.94
Clothing, etc.	393.28
Vehicle—purchases	350.39
Vehicle—gasoline	228.69
Vehicle—other	243.10
Reading and education	48.46
Gifts	215.47
Total	3,177.84

Note: Two significant items are not counted in the CES—housing and alcoholic beverages. In the case of housing, it is reasonable to assume that no major changes in housing expenditures will result from the temporary increased disposable income attributable to Title X employment. A change in housing involving any substantial change in monthly costs is extremely unlikely to result in the short run and as a result of a short-term increase in disposable income. Some change may occur as a result of rent increases for public housing, but, in the Title X employee sample, these changes account for only 0.3 percent of increased disposable income. Thus, for purposes of calculating sales and excise taxes, the omission of housing (an untaxed item) from CES selected expenditures can be ignored. The omission of spending on alcohol is unfortunate, given the substantial excise taxes on this item. Lacking another source of comparable data, we must ignore excise-tax returns on alcohol to governments. Thus, excise-tax estimates in the study are conservative underestimates of the actual returns to government.

Source: Compiled by the authors.

$$
\begin{array}{c}
\text{Gasoline} \\
\text{excise tax} \\
\text{revenue}
\end{array}
=
\begin{bmatrix}
\text{disposable earnings} \\
\text{attributable to} \\
\text{Title X}
\end{bmatrix}
\times
\begin{bmatrix}
\text{percent of disposable} \\
\text{earnings subject to gaso-} \\
\text{line excise tax (.072)}
\end{bmatrix}
$$

$$
\times
\begin{bmatrix}
\text{individual state gasoline} \\
\text{excise tax per dollar,} \\
\text{based on Table A.18}
\end{bmatrix}
+
\begin{bmatrix}
\text{federal gasoline excise} \\
\text{tax rate per dollar} \\
(\$0.067)
\end{bmatrix}
$$

$$
\begin{array}{c}
\text{Tobacco} \\
\text{excise tax} \\
\text{revenue}
\end{array}
=
\begin{bmatrix}
\text{disposable earnings} \\
\text{attributable to} \\
\text{Title X}
\end{bmatrix}
\times
\begin{bmatrix}
\text{percent of disposable} \\
\text{earnings subject to to-} \\
\text{bacco excise tax (.029)}
\end{bmatrix}
$$

$$
\times
\begin{bmatrix}
\text{individual state tobacco} \\
\text{tax per dollar,} \\
\text{based on Table A.19}
\end{bmatrix}
+
\begin{bmatrix}
\text{Federal tobacco} \\
\text{tax per dollar} \\
(\$0.28)
\end{bmatrix}
$$

FICA and Unemployment Insurance Taxes

All Title X employees and their employers are subject to the standard 5.85 percent annual Social Security deduction on the first $15,300 of earnings. Hence, 11.7 percent (2 $\times$ 5.85) of the earnings attributable to Title X, for all Title X income earned prior to an individual's reaching the $15,300 limit, is credited as a tax return attributable to the Title X program.*

It is unlikely that a Title X employee will have gross earnings (from all sources) greater than $15,300. Only 4.8 percent of the participants reported gross family income greater than $15,000. If a Title X participant did have earnings greater than $15,300, including sources other than Title X employment, the FICA tax return calculation will be slightly overstated, depending upon the timing of Title X and other employment throughout the year. We expect this bias to be negligible, because of the small number of sample members reporting income above $15,000, and because the gross income figure reported by respondents includes earnings of other family members, whose wages are separately subject to FICA taxes.

With regard to unemployment insurance, states impose an assessment on employers that ranges between 0 and 6 percent of an employee's earnings up to a maximum, which varies from $4,200-$10,000 by state. Any earnings attribut-

---

*The employer's 5.85 percent share of FICA tax contributions on incremental earned income is credited to the program under the assumption that the project sponsor would not have undertaken the project without Title X funds; hence, employers' FICA contributions would have been based on the individual employee's alternative-earnings income in the absence of the program.

able to Title X that comprise part of the base to which this tax applies (for example, earnings that occur prior to the applicable maximum being reached) should be taxed, and the return credited to states. Since the mean amount of earnings attributable to Title X, $3,322, is below the lowest maximum earnings to which the state unemployment insurance rate is applicable, we assume that all earnings attributable to Title X are subject to the state unemployment insurance assessment. The individual state insurance rate applied is the average of the minimum and maximum rates for the particular state.

In addition to the state tax, employers must pay federal unemployment tax. The federal tax rate is 3.2 percent, but the employer's net tax for the year is normally .5 percent due to credits granted for paying state unemployment tax. The tax is paid on the first $4,200 of wages paid to an employee during the year.[4]

It should be noted that, to the extent that Title X workers are employed directly on federal, state, or local payrolls, assumptions regarding FICA and unemployment insurance taxes may be questionable. Generally, federal, state, and local permanent employees are not covered under FICA, but are, instead, subject to government pension plans. However, temporary employees such as those supported by Title X usually are covered, a fact confirmed by a check of ED-110X payroll forms. And, if a few are, instead, covered by other government plans, employers' payments to these plans may be assumed to be roughly comparable to FICA payments. Thus, the impact upon estimates of employers' FICA payments is likely to be minor.

Employers' unemployment insurance payments are potentially of more serious concern. For federal employees, there is no federal tax, and payments to state funds are on a reimbursement basis. In other words, the federal government transfers moneys to state funds to cover whatever unemployment compensation payments may eventually be made that are earned from federal employment. Technically, these payments should not be counted as returns to government. In fact, a case could be made for calling them potential liabilities incurred as a result of the program. State and local governments are also exempted from federal UI taxes. Moreover, a majority of state and local governments pay unemployment insurance taxes for their employees on a reimbursable basis. As of December 1975, only 13 state governments and the local governments in 14 states paid UI taxes on a contributory basis similar to that required of most private employers. And in most of these jurisdictions, contributory payments were not mandatory. Thus, it is quite possible that estimates of unemployment insurance tax returns to governments are overestimated.

Nonetheless, a decision has been made to retain the estimates which are based upon original assumptions, a decision motivated by the fact that there is no reliable basis for ascertaining an accurate adjustment. First, data are not available on the proportion of Title X workers who have been directly employed by governments. Second, there is some doubt regarding the UI tax procedures for temporary government employees of government programs in a number of states. Lacking better information, one can only use original estimates and assume that they somewhat overstate the actual returns to government. However, because conservative assumptions have been applied throughout our net-cost methodology, this instance of likely overstatement is probably more than compensated for by underestimates elsewhere.

NOTES

1. *Tax Reform Act of 1975: Together with Supplemental, Separate, Minority and Dissenting Views on HR10612*, Report of the House Committee on Ways and Means, U.S. House of Representatives, November 12, 1975, p. 23. Note that the tax liabilities presented in Table A.9 are those projected to result from the implementation of HR10612. The final Tax Reform Act of 1975 did not include all tax provisions of HR10612, but it did embody almost all provisions which could significantly affect personal income taxes. Correspondence with the Joint Committee-IRS staff, currently working on a report on the impacts of tax reform, confirms that the figures in Table A.9 are as accurate as can be projected at this writing. If anything, the figures slightly understate the tax liability and thus would have the effect of slightly understating the federal tax returns from Title X income. Again, this possible understatement is consistent with the conservative approach adopted throughout our net-cost methodology.

2. Advisory Commission on Intergovernmental Relations, cited in *Significant Features of Fiscal Federation, 1976 Edition, I: Trends* (Washington, D.C.: Government Printing Office, 1976), table XVII.

3. Bureau of Labor Statistics, *Consumer Expenditure Survey Series: Interview Survey, 1972 and 1973* (Washington, D.C.: Government Printing Office, March 1976).

4. *Commerce Clearinghouse Index-Standard Federal Tax Reports* (Washington, D.C.: Government Printing Office, 1976), p. 7727.

APPENDIX B

ESTIMATED WEEKS OF
WORK AND EARNINGS IN
THE ABSENCE OF
TITLE X:
A STATISTICAL CONTROL

INTRODUCTION

The gross expenditures under Title X are not an accurate or fair measure of the net public cost of Title X, since at least some of the work (and the earnings from that work), and some nonlabor expenditures financed by the program, would not have existed without Title X.* Net program costs, taking into account both savings in transfer payments and increases in tax revenues generated by the program, are a better measure of the social-opportunity cost of any program like Title X.

The estimation of net program costs is not an altogether new idea, and several simulations have been carried out for policy purposes. Recently, the Congressional Budget Office employed various national econometric models to estimate the increase in jobs, the reduction in the national unemployment rate, and the net budget costs for a variety of employment-generating programs.[1] The CBO simulation most closely akin to the cost estimates for the Title X program is called the "accelerated public works" simulation. Taking into account taxes generated and transfers saved (based on a $1 billion expenditure), the CBO estimated that the net costs involved in the initial impact of the public-works expenditures ranged from 79.3 percent to 91.5 percent of gross costs, and after 12 months they dropped to between 51 and 53.7 percent. This means that for each $1 billion in public expenditure for accelerated public works, various government levels would have experienced a net return (saved transfers plus additional taxes) in the range of $463–$490 million.[2] The net budget costs drop even further after 24 months. The CBO estimates have generated some controversy, as have other efforts to estimate net costs and related measures of displacement.[3]

All prior studies have been based upon simplifying assumptions and aggregate data, with the intention of yielding rough estimates of net cost. This study provides the first opportunity to develop a precise net-cost methodology and apply it to empirical data on participants of a current employment-generating program. Data from samples of participants and projects funded under the auspices of Title X allow for a valid estimate of the net costs of the Title X program. The study is carefully designed to generate data which can be combined with additional published data, to arrive at net-cost estimates; these data can then be used to generalize about the entire universe of Title X projects.

---

*The nonlabor-expenditure calculations are based on a sample of 50 project sites. The issues and calculations are discussed in Appendix C.

The equations presented in Appendix A summarize the net-cost calculations. The variables in the equations fall into three categories: (1) information
about the stratified cluster sample of 2,000 Title X employees, obtained through
personal interviews (and including weekly earnings, actual or projected weeks of
employment under Title X, transfers received); (2) published information (or
data derived from published tables) on effective rates of income tax, sales tax,
excise tax, FICA, and so on; (3) unobservable variables, that is, the estimated
number of weeks that employee i would have been employed in the absence of
the program, and the associated earnings. Data sets 1 and 2 (the observable variables) and the methodologies incorporating them are presented fully in Appendixes A and C. This appendix is mainly concerned with the unobservable variables, which are crucial to the estimation of the net costs of Title X. These variables are critical because they reduce the gross estimates of tax and transfer
returns from Title X labor expenditures. They control for the possibility that a
Title X employee would have worked in the absence of Title X, thus reducing
the tax and transfer savings attributable to Title X.*

ESTIMATED WEEKS OF WORK
IN THE ABSENCE OF TITLE X

There are two possible extremes: that Title X creates no additional employment experience for the individuals involved (everyone enrolled would have
worked for the same total number of weeks over the program period) or that all
the employment experience is additional (none of the participants would have
found any work without the program, over the Title X period).† This latter
assumption might hold for those who were either structurally unemployed or
brought back into the labor force as a result of Title X, thus making the whole
Title X experience an addition to their employment experience. The former
might hold true for participants who were either employed prior to Title X or
unemployed for a very short time prior to Title X. The actual situation, of
course, lies somewhere between the extremes.

The ideal solution to this unobservable-variable problem would have been
to set up a control group of non-Title X participants at each project site, matched
to our sample by age, race, sex, labor-market experience, and so on; and then to
compare their experiences during the Title X project period with those of partic-

---

*The other "unobservable" variable in equation 1, employee i's expected earnings in
the absence of Title X, is discussed briefly at the end of this appendix.
†Note that this methodology does not directly address the issues of budget substitution, displacement, or vacuum effects of the program. The perspective here centers on the
aggregate of the net benefits to the enrollees themselves.

ipants.* Budget constraints on the initial design of the evaluation did not permit construction of a control group.† Thus, it was necessary to find another method of estimating the expected weeks of employment that each enrollee would have experienced in the absence of Title X.

A simplistic approach of using prior employment status as a proxy for future employment (for example, the unemployed would have remained unemployed; those working full time would have remained employed full time) was rejected as being unreliable and untestable. A multivariate analysis—using variables such as an individual's occupation, personal characteristics, employment status, duration of prior unemployment, and reason for leaving the last job, along with regional data and seasonal information, to predict the expected amount of future unemployment—was rejected, after preliminary testing, as being unworkable and too imprecise to provide meaningful output.

We then turned to the burgeoning literature on expected duration of unemployment and employment,[4] stocks and flows in the labor market,[5] longitudinal cohort analysis,[6] and previous evaluations of public-works and public-service employment programs.[7] This led to the job-search-theory-based work at the Urban Institute, specifically the institute's Inflation and Unemployment Project, directed by Charles Holt, and funded by the Office of Research and Development of the U.S. Department of Labor. With the enthusiastic support and advice of Holt, and especially Ralph Smith and Jean Vanski, we proceeded to adapt the work done under the auspices of the Urban Institute to formulate a statistical control group.

Smith, Vanski, Holt, and their colleagues had collected month-to-month "gross-flows" data from the Current Population Survey of the Bureau of the Census, covering the period between July 1967 and December 1973 (5.3 years $\times$ 12 months per year = 66 months worth of data), a period including one complete short business cycle. They focused on 16 demographic groups, broken down by sex, race, and age: male whites in each of four age groups—16-19, 20-24, 25-59, and 60 or over; and male nonwhites, female whites, and female nonwhites in each of the same age groups. For each of these 16 demographic groups, the Urban Institute research team constructed a string of month-to-month "employment status transition matrixes," using the following structure:

---

*If, say, Joe Smith is employed full time on a Title X project as a carpenter, while other local men similar to Joe in background and personal characteristics are unemployed (part or all of the time of the project), then we would be able to calculate the additional weeks of employment that are attributable to Title X.

†Development of a control group (and the subsequent followup necessary) is the single most expensive and difficult program-evaluation design problem. In addition, the program was operating prior to the beginning of the evaluation.

	Status in Current Month (j)		
Status in Previous Month (i)	Employed	Unemployed	Not in the labor force
Employed	P_{11}	P_{12}	P_{13}
Unemployed	P_{21}	P_{22}	P_{23}
Not in the labor force	P_{31}	P_{32}	P_{33}

Each element (P_{ij}) represents the probability that a person with a profile of corresponding age/race/sex characteristics will have a particular employment status in the current month, given his or her status in the previous month. The probabilities sum to 1.0 (or 100 percent) along the rows. Thus, for example, of everyone employed in the previous month, P_{11} is the number that were employed in the current month, P_{12} is the number of unemployed, and P_{13} is the number that dropped out of the labor force. Obviously, $P_{11} + P_{12} + P_{13} = 1.0$. For each demographic group, we therefore have a string of 65 (66 - 1) transition matrixes that describe how people of given age/race/sex move in and out of jobs, and in and out of the labor market, from month to month.

The Urban Institute team uses multivariate-regression analysis to explain the causes of these month-to-month variations in the Ps.[8] Simplifying their presentation somewhat, we have the equivalent of 144 (9 X 16) equations, one for each type of transition for each demographic group:

P_{dijt} = f (the time trend, seasonal-adjustment factors, and the ratio of the Conference Board's estimated level of job vacancies to the Current Population Survey unemployment level, lagged one month; the ratio is called V/U)

where d = one of 16 demographic groups
       i = one of three previous-month statuses
       j = one of three current-month statuses
and   t = one of 65 month-to-month changes being observed

The ratio V/U in month t - 1 is an important variable measuring the tightness of the labor market, that is, "the availability of jobs in relation to the availability of people to fill them."[9]

We already know the age, race, sex, program entry and exit months, and season of enrollment for each Title X employee. From CPS and Conference Board data, we can measure $(V/U)_{t-1}$, the labor-market conditions in each of the employee's enrollment months (with a one-month lag). By substituting the appropriate Title X project period data for data in the Urban Institute equations, we can forecast the expected pattern (time path) of transition probabilities for each Title X employee. Appropriate cumulation of the forecasted conditional probabilities of being employed in each month,* counted over the range of months in the program, then yields the needed estimate of the unobservable variable in our Abt net-cost methodology: the estimated number of weeks that employee i would have worked in the absence of Title X.

In fact, the Urban Institute model is not quite as straightforward as we have presented it above. In particular, recalling that the Urban Institute model uses an aggregate of cohorts (that is, it does not literally forecast the mobility patterns of individuals), we note that the population of each cohort varies from month to month, changing the size of the pool of people entering the system being simulated (in other words, the system is not closed). Operationally, this means that the transition process is not strictly Markovian, so that nine transition probabilities (P_{ij}) cannot in fact be consistently estimated by nine equations.

The Urban Institute solution is to estimate the nine transition probabilities (for each of the 16 demographic groups) with six equations and five identities that allow for an intermediate state called "labor force reentry" (which may or may not be successful), and account for month-to-month variations in the size of the population in the system. The six behavioral equations that, together with two identities, permit estimation of the off-diagonal probabilities are of the following form:

$$P_{ijt} = a(\frac{V}{U})^{\beta}_{t-1} e^{\gamma T} e^{\sum_{t=1}^{11} \delta_t S_t}$$

For example, for the unemployment-to-employment transition:

$$\ln_e\left(\frac{UE_t}{U_{t-1}}\right) = \ln_e a + \beta \ln_e (\frac{V}{U})_{t-1} + \gamma T + \sum_{t=1}^{11} \delta_t S_t$$

Here, the Ss are seasonal dummies, indexing the particular month, and T is an annual time trend, indexing the year. There are three identities for the diagonal probabilities, constructed to allow for changes in the various stocks of persons in the model (population, total labor force, etc.).

The team develops their model by inputting initial stock values, simulating one month's flows, and then observing the new stock values. These endogenously generated stocks then become input into the next month's simulation, and so on. Since we have exogenous vacancy and unemployment data for each month of

---

*The algorithm for this cumulation assumes that the transition from one month to the next is a first-order Markovian process. This is a simplification of the transition process, but it is the only assumption consistent with the first-order-difference equation form of the Urban Institute model.

our simulation period, drawn from Conference Board and CPS records, we chose to use the Urban Institute model to compute wholly self-contained month-by-month forecasts. That is, instead of simulating new stocks each month, we entered them anew, from outside the model. The mechanics were simplified in this way, but our forecasts became inconsistent, occasionally producing transition matrixes whose row sums exceeded unity. To adjust for this, we decided to use only the six behavioral equations and two identities that generate the off-diagonal probabilities, and to constrain the diagonal probabilities to values that would preserve the condition that row elements sum to unity. There is some loss of information here, because the six behavioral equations do not take into account the levels of stocks of employed persons, unemployed persons, and so on. But since our subsequent simulation of cumulative weeks worked (done below) requires that the strings of forecasted transition matrixes be consistent with a first-order Markovian transition process (that is, row elements sum to unity), we really had no choice.*

In sum, then, for each of 16 cohorts, for the Title X enrollment period from November 1975 to July 1977, we insert current values of T, S, and V/U into the Urban Institute model (modified as indicated) and forecast a string of transition matrices.† Casual inspection of the tables (on pp. 282-285) reveals realistic patterns, especially in terms of seasonality (for example, young workers show the most volatile changes in entering and leaving the labor force at the beginning and end of summer). It remains now to explain how we use these forecasted transition tables to estimate weeks worked in the absence of Title X.

We have a sample of 2,000 Title X workers. We know each person's age (at time of program entry), race, sex, employment status in the month prior to program entry, month of program entry, and an actual (or planned) duration in the program (in other words, an exit month). The person's age, race, and sex tell us which of the 16 transition-matrix strings to consult. The entry and exit

---

*It is hard to pin down the cause of our inability to produce consistent forecasts with the Urban Institute model in its original form, because the behavioral equations in that model were estimated by using ordinary least squares. Since the dependent variables are probabilities bounded by 0 and 1, ordinary least squares produce estimates which are heteroschedastic, and which do not rule out forecasts that fall outside the 0-1 interval. The correct estimation technique is probit analysis (since those left-hand variables, at the Urban Institute model's level of aggregation, are ratios). We considered reestimating the basic equations themselves, but the cost would have been prohibitive. The upshot is that forecasts of transition probabilities that do not sum to unity across rows are quite possible with the system that the Urban Institute has generated.

†Actually, since we only had the exogenous V/U data for the period November 1975–November 1976, we assumed that the transition tables for each month in the period December 1976 to July 1977 would be identical to those for the year before. Equipped with the requisite V/U data, we could easily make this assumption.

months tell us where to enter and from which point to leave the string. The preenrollment status tells us through which row (or "window") of the entry-month matrix we are to enter (row 1 = employed, row 2 = unemployed, and row 3 = not in the labor force). We then "walk" the person through the sub-system of transition probabilities so selected, compute the cumulative number of expected months spent being employed, and multiply that number by 4.3 (average weeks in a month).

For each cohort, it is possible to compute a table of expected weeks of employment for all possible entry- and exit-month pairs, for each of the three possible preenrollment statuses. For each Title X worker, we can then consult the appropriate precomputed table, as an alternative to actually computing the month-by-month expectations for each of the 2,000 workers in our sample. A sample of tables for white women aged 20-24 (one of the 16 cohorts) is shown in this Appendix .

What does this methodology assume? It assumes that month-to-month and season-to-season changes (not levels) in the employment-status/demography/labor-market nexus during the Title X period are likely to have about the same shape as those in the Urban Institute sample period 1967-73. And it assumes that Title X is generally too small a program to feed back and actually affect the national levels of the instrumental variables (unemployment and vacancy rates). These seem to us to be reasonable assumptions.

However, there are other assumptions underlying the model that make it imperfectly applicable to some Title X employees. The search theory of unemployment is central to the formulation (and use) of the model. As developed by Holt and others,[10] the search theory turns on several separate but related assumptions. First, it posits that the duration of unemployment is dependent on the time it takes workers to search firms for vacancies, as well as the time it takes them to search vacancies for suitable wages.

The individual job searcher is assumed to have an asking wage that falls with the individual's unemployment duration. Robert Crosslin and David Stevens address this issue with a two-equation model where the asking wage and the duration of unemployment are endogenous. Their results show that a significant downward flexibility in asking wages over time does exist. They go on to say: "However, this downward flexibility can be significantly impeded by statutory and institutional restrictions, such as legal minimum wages."[11] We would add that the level of transfers available and the available assets of the person would also be important constraints on the lower level of wages a person would accept. And, of course, there are a host of labor-market, demand-side factors that affect the outcome of any job search.*

---

*The point at which a person ceases the search completely, and therefore has a zero or non-zero probability of finding employment, turns on a series of personal, institutional,

Expected Transition Probabilities of White Women Aged 20–24

NOV 1975

0.94	0.01	0.05
0.29	0.57	0.14
0.06	0.06	0.88

DEC 1975

0.93	0.01	0.06
0.26	0.60	0.14
0.06	0.06	0.88

JAN 1976

0.92	0.02	0.06
0.23	0.61	0.16
0.05	0.06	0.90

FEB 1976

0.94	0.01	0.05
0.25	0.61	0.14
0.06	0.07	0.88

MAR 1976

0.95	0.01	0.05
0.22	0.63	0.15
0.05	0.06	0.89

APR 1976

0.94	0.01	0.05
0.24	0.61	0.16
0.05	0.06	0.89

MAY 1976

0.94	0.01	0.05
0.24	0.61	0.15
0.05	0.06	0.89

JUNE 1976

0.92	0.01	0.06
0.26	0.61	0.13
0.10	0.10	0.81

JULY 1976

0.93	0.01	0.06
0.31	0.56	0.13
0.07	0.07	0.86

AUG 1976

0.93	0.01	0.06
0.28	0.59	0.13
0.06	0.07	0.86

SEP 1976

0.89	0.01	0.09
0.28	0.59	0.13
0.08	0.08	0.84

OCT 1976

0.94	0.01	0.05
0.30	0.58	0.12
0.07	0.07	0.86

NOV 1976

0.94	0.01	0.05
0.29	0.56	0.14
0.06	0.06	0.83

DEC 1976

0.93	0.01	0.06
0.26	0.60	0.14
0.06	0.06	0.88

JAN 1977

0.92	0.02	0.06
0.23	0.61	0.16
0.05	0.06	0.90

FEB 1977

0.94	0.01	0.05
0.25	0.61	0.14
0.06	0.07	0.88

MAR 1977

0.95	0.01	0.05
0.22	0.63	0.15
0.05	0.06	0.89

APR 1977

0.94	0.01	0.05
0.24	0.61	0.16
0.05	0.06	0.89

MAY 1977

0.94	0.01	0.05
0.24	0.61	0.15
0.05	0.06	0.89

JUNE 1977

0.92	0.01	0.06
0.26	0.61	0.13
0.10	0.10	0.81

JULY 1977

0.93	0.01	0.06
0.31	0.56	0.13
0.07	0.07	0.86

WHITE FEMALES AGED 20-24
Previously Employed
Estimated Weeks Worked: Entry Months (Down) by Exit Months (Across)—Previously Employed Workers

4.06																				
7.62	4.02																			
11.26	7.44	3.96																		
15.35	11.42	7.52	4.05																	
19.30	15.31	11.34	7.71	4.07																
23.06	19.06.	15.06	11.51	7.72	4.06															
26.72	22.72	18.70	15.24	11.50	7.64	4.03														
30.22	26.23	22.23	18.86	15.17	11.33	7.51	3.98													
34.08	30.05	26.00	22.68	19.01	15.15	11.30	7.45	3.99												
37.95	33.87	29.76	26.52	22.86	18.97	15.09	11.19	7.48	4.00											
40.17	36.23	32.24	29.16	25.66	21.91	18.16	14.37	10.79	7.22	3.85										
45.95	41.78	37.56	34.40	30.75	26.80	22.85	18.83	15.09	11.35	7.30	4.03									
50.08	45.85	41.55	38.46	34.81	30.82	26.81	22.73	18.97	15.22	11.01	7.67	4.06								
53.35	49.13	44.82	41.84	38.26	34.29	30.31	26.22	22.52	18.82	14.52	11.37	7.63	4.02							
56.28	52.09	47.79	44.95	41.44	37.52	33.57	29.50	25.86	22.24	17.86	14.93	11.28	7.44	3.96						
61.40	57.09	52.66	49.80	46.24	42.21	38.15	33.95	30.24	26.54	21.94	19.09	15.38	11.42	7.52	4.05					
65.62	61.25	56.72	53.95	50.38	46.32	42.21	37.93	34.21	30.50	25.73	23.04	19.33	15.31	11.34	7.71	4.07				
69.18	64.79	60.25	57.55	54.02	49.96	45.85	41.54	37.84	34.16	29.28	26.77	23.10	19.06	15.06	11.51	7.72	4.06			
72.54	68.15	63.59	60.98	57.50	53.45	49.34	45.02	41.36	37.71	32.72	30.39	26.77	22.72	18.70	15.24	11.50	7.64	4.03		
75.55	71.21	66.69	64.11	60.67	56.66	52.58	48.30	44.68	41.07	36.07	33.04	30.27	26.23	22.23	18.86	15.17	11.33	7.51	3.98	
79.52	75.13	70.58	68.04	64.62	60.58	56.48	52.15	48.50	44.91	39.74	37.68	34.14	30.05	26.00	22.68	19.01	15.15	11.30	7.45	3.99

WHITE FEMALES AGED 20-24

Previously Unemployed

Estimated Weeks Worked: Entry Months (Down) by Exit Months (Across)—Previously Unemployed Workers

1	2	3	4	5	6	7	8	9	10	11	12	13	14	15	16	17	18	19	20	21
1.23	3.66	5.21	7.28	8.64	10.66	12.43	14.67	17.51	18.72	20.17	23.39	24.97	25.62	26.04	29.13	29.39	31.97	33.73	36.66	40.85
	1.12	3.33	5.24	6.60	8.51	10.21	12.34	15.04	16.23	17.69	20.71	22.22	22.86	23.29	26.21	26.41	28.92	30.63	33.49	37.61
		1.00	3.29	4.64	6.39	8.00	10.00	12.48	13.63	15.08	17.84	19.26	19.89	20.31	23.04	23.19	25.56	27.18	29.99	33.89
			1.09	3.26	5.04	6.73	8.72	11.18	12.50	14.02	16.79	18.34	19.14	19.73	22.47	22.82	25.22	26.91	29.64	33.54
				0.93	3.10	4.66	6.49	8.73	9.98	11.46	13.96	15.40	16.15	16.69	19.22	19.46	21.72	23.30	25.95	29.68
					1.02	3.23	5.05	7.20	8.60	10.14	12.60	14.14	15.07	15.79	18.29	18.76	20.99	22.62	25.23	28.79
						1.03	3.39	5.45	6.94	8.53	10.90	12.49	13.52	14.34	16.77	17.35	19.56	21.20	23.74	27.23
							1.11	3.76	5.41	7.08	9.42	11.12	12.31	13.30	15.73	16.49	18.70	20.41	22.89	26.35
								1.32	3.89	5.71	8.09	9.97	11.43	12.68	15.17	16.26	18.53	20.37	22.86	26.22
									1.20	3.65	5.83	7.65	9.10	10.35	12.67	13.72	15.88	17.65	20.04	23.28
										1.20	3.88	5.74	7.28	8.62	10.86	12.00	14.11	15.87	18.21	21.33
											1.31	3.99	5.70	7.23	9.46	10.80	12.94	14.77	17.10	20.15
												1.26	3.69	5.26	7.35	8.74	10.76	12.55	14.80	17.64
													1.12	3.33	5.24	6.60	8.51	10.21	12.34	15.04
														1.00	3.29	4.64	6.39	8.00	10.00	12.48
															1.09	3.26	5.04	6.73	8.72	11.18
																0.93	3.10	4.66	6.49	8.73
																	1.02	3.23	5.05	7.20
																		1.03	3.39	5.45
																			1.11	3.76
																				1.32

WHITE FEMALES AGED 20-24

Previously Not in the Labor Force
Estimated Weeks Worked: Entry Months (Down) by Exit Months (Across)—Previously Not in the Labor Force

Entry \ Exit	1	2	3	4	5	6	7	8	9	10	11	12	13	14	15	16	17	18	19	20	21
1	0.24	1.04	1.40	2.05	2.43	2.87	3.38	5.23	5.28	5.39	6.41	7.03	6.90	7.25	7.00	8.18	8.25	8.61	9.18	13.07	12.31
2		0.26	0.97	1.59	2.02	2.49	3.01	4.70	4.84	5.02	6.00	6.85	6.60	6.97	6.79	7.95	8.06	8.45	9.03	12.75	12.10
3			0.21	0.96	1.37	1.80	2.27	3.76	3.90	4.08	5.00	5.57	5.51	5.87	5.70	6.75	6.86	7.19	7.72	11.29	10.59
4				0.25	1.00	1.48	1.99	3.34	3.61	3.88	4.77	5.41	5.46	5.86	5.77	6.84	7.00	7.40	7.96	11.34	10.83
5					0.23	0.94	1.42	2.58	2.88	3.17	4.01	4.60	4.68	5.07	5.02	6.01	6.19	6.55	7.09	10.31	9.79
6						0.22	0.92	1.90	2.26	2.59	3.37	3.95	4.07	4.46	4.45	5.38	5.57	5.93	6.46	9.50	9.03
7							0.22	1.28	1.71	2.10	2.84	3.43	3.61	4.02	4.07	4.96	5.18	5.56	6.08	8.96	8.57
8								0.41	1.54	2.17	3.02	3.86	4.33	4.91	5.18	6.27	6.67	7.30	8.00	10.71	10.80
9									0.32	1.24	1.98	2.67	3.07	3.59	3.83	4.74	5.10	5.60	6.21	8.75	8.67
10										0.28	1.25	1.89	2.31	2.81	3.06	3.89	4.23	4.70	5.27	7.63	7.58
11											0.34	1.38	1.91	2.48	2.83	3.68	4.10	4.64	5.26	7.48	7.57
12												0.32	1.22	1.79	2.18	2.95	3.38	3.90	4.49	6.54	6.64
13													0.26	1.07	1.45	2.12	2.52	2.98	3.51	5.36	5.43
14														0.26	0.97	1.59	2.02	2.49	3.01	4.70	4.84
15															0.21	0.96	1.37	1.80	2.27	3.76	3.90
16																0.25	1.00	1.48	1.99	3.34	3.61
17																	0.23	0.94	1.42	2.58	2.88
18																		0.22	0.92	1.90	2.26
19																			0.22	1.28	1.71
20																				0.41	1.54
21																					0.32

The truncation of the downward flexibility, whether it be caused by institutional or personal constraints, can be viewed as the point where a person's unemployment turns from frictional or cyclical, to structural. The implications of this point for the Title X evaluation are important. If a person passes the point where his or her unemployment has become long term or structural, it is unlikely that the person will find work until such time as there is a significant shock to the local demand for labor. That shock could take the form of a large new firm opening up in the area or, perhaps, the injection of substantial funds into the area in the form of a public-works project or a public-service employment program. The shock in reference to this evaluation is, of course, the Title X program.

How then does one treat long-term or structurally unemployed persons when estimating the expected number of weeks of unemployment in the absence of Title X? A comprehensive review of the job-search literature and related studies was undertaken to ascertain a method whereby one might "discount the discount factor." Clearly, a person who has been unemployed for 26 weeks will be less likely to have the same employment experience (over the Title X period) as a person who was unemployed for only five weeks prior to Title X.

---

and labor-market-mobility constraints. The personal constraints may simply be an individual's perception of his or her worth in the market, and the point at which the market offerings are such that the person will simply not accept the wage or type of job offered (or that, in the person's mind, would be offered) and therefore stops looking. This, in part, depends on the assets of the individual, and possibilities for transfers and alternative sources of support, such as family or friends. The institutional constraints center on the following areas:

1. Transfer levels available, primarily UI and welfare: In the case of UI, the person must maintain the guise of looking for work in order to keep on collecting benefits, even if he or she has given up the search; and the UI benefits must be large enough to sustain the person. The welfare level follows the same rationale, except that one may not have to remain officially unemployed unless one is subject to the WIN II provisions of the law.
2. Legal and job-protection constraints: This issue centers on the minimum wage laws, where a person's asking wage is definitely truncated on the down side by the legal minimum the law allows him or her to accept. Other possible constraints have to do with union regulations (a la the Davis-Bacon Act or hiring-hall priorities) and certain licensing requirements that may prevent a person from taking a position at a wage lower than the normal market wage.
3. Mobility constraints: No matter what a person is willing to accept as a lowest wage, it may be constrained by the fact that, if migration is necessary to take the job, the wages offered will have to be high enough to compensate for the explicit and implicit costs of moving.
4. Race and sex discrimination: Minority and women workers may have to be willing to reduce their asking-wage rates below those of men, in order to be competitive for similar jobs. In the case of jobs which are, by custom, substantially reserved for white males (as per the crowding hypothesis), no asking wage, however low, will make the job searcher eligible for hire.

However, the Smith-Vanski-Holt model presented previously has as its starting point the labor-force status of the person in the month prior to "entrance into the model." None of the movement in the model depends on the past history of the individual (before month t - 1).* Duration-of-previous-employment status is not considered.[12]

If all Title X participants were entered into the model without regard to their employment histories, we believe we would seriously distort the net-cost calculations by overestimating the number of weeks a person would have been employed in the absence of the program. We have therefore adjusted entrance into the model in the following manner: First, all persons employed at the time of their entry into the Title X program, or either unemployed or not in the labor force for a period of 26 weeks or less prior to Title X, are entered into the model as discussed above—that is, according to their status in the month prior to Title X hiring. Second, all persons who were unemployed or out of the labor force for more than 26 weeks are not entered into the model at all. The result of this qualification is to count all of the Title X employment of these persons as an addition to their work experience.

This decision is, of course, arbitrary. But there has been no compelling empirical work relating probabilities of future employment to duration of past unemployment or non-participation in the labor force. The 26-week cutoff point is a simplifying assumption, made in the absence of other relevant research, and consistent with BLS definitions of the long-term unemployed. BLS publications sometimes define as long-term unemployed persons those unemployed for longer than 15 weeks, and sometimes those unemployed longer than 26 weeks. The 26-week point was chosen because it both fits better with the economic downturn of the mid-1970s and is consistent with the conservative stance taken in our study when making net-cost calculations. In our opinion, the 15-week cutoff would overestimate the net additions to the employment experience of individuals in the program, since all Title X employment would be new employment. This, we believe, is unrealistic, since 15 weeks is not very far above the average duration of unemployment during 1976 (15.8 weeks). Twenty-six weeks, on the other hand, is accepted as a point where the person is having severe (often referred to as structural) employment problems. It is a conservative decision rule, with 81.7 percent of the unemployed during 1976 having experienced 26 weeks of unemployment or less.[13]

---

*For the U.S. population sampled randomly, the assumption that history doesn't count may not matter; the long-term unemployed are probably a small-enough proportion of the total labor force for the Urban Institute model to have unbiased coefficients. For our Title X sample, on the other hand, the group of workers who were previously unemployed for 26 weeks or longer is the model group. Thus, duration of prior unemployment is likely to be an important variable in projecting employment in the absence of Title X.

This decision rule fits well with the intent of the Title X program. Since Title X is a countercyclical program and targeted at those who were unemployed due to the economic slump dating to mid-1974, the degree to which the structural or long-term unemployed were aided by the program can be viewed as a desirable side benefit. The data collected show, somewhat surprisingly, that approximately one-third of those working on Title X projects had been unemployed for over 26 weeks. In fact, over 15 percent of the participants had been unemployed for longer than 52 weeks, clearly in the structural category. These figures show that the program, even though not required to do so by legislation or regulations, employed many who were most in need of work.

One final aspect of the discount methodology should be mentioned. The Smith-Holt model is a national model, relying upon national data from the CPS and the Conference Board. Although Title X is a national program, its projects are concentrated in areas of high unemployment and lagging economies. It is likely, therefore, that the transition probabilities produced by the model somewhat overstate the likelihood of employment in the local areas served by Title X. In other words, the number of weeks of employment in the absence of Title X is probably somewhat overestimated. As a result, net-cost and net-employment estimates that are based upon these discounts are conservative.

EXPECTED WEEKLY EARNINGS
IN THE ABSENCE OF TITLE X

In the net-cost study, the estimated weeks of work in the absence of Title X are calculated for each individual utilizing the methodology described above. Having estimated a discount to cover weeks employed under Title X, it is only necessary to couple it with an estimate of expected weekly earnings in order to complete the statistical control on Title X costs.

The estimate of each employee's average weekly earnings in the absence of Title X is based upon his or her earnings and employment history. The Title X employee survey collected data on average weekly earnings from each employee's usual and prior employment, and, in the case of a terminee who was subsequently employed, average weekly earnings from the subsequent job. Employment status prior to Title X and the duration of unemployment, when applicable, are available for all workers. Prior, usual, and subsequent earnings, as well as employment status, are used to impute a figure for earnings in the absence of Title X. A participant's earnings from his or her prior and usual employment can be considered a proxy for the returns to each worker's human capital. Since it is unlikely that a worker's human-capital stock will be drastically altered during the period of the program, past labor-market experience is a reasonable proxy for earnings in the absence of Title X.

TABLE B.1

Calculation of Average Weekly Earnings in the Absence of Title X

Case	Employment Status prior to Title X	Employment Status at Time of Study	Average Weekly Earnings in the Absence of Title X
1	employed	not employed or still working on project	prior weekly earnings
2	employed	employed elsewhere	prior weekly earnings and subsequent weekly earnings $\div 2$
3	not employed	employed elsewhere	deflated subsequent weekly earnings
4	not employed	not employed or still working on project	prior weekly earnings and usual weekly earnings (inflated) $\div 2$

Source: Compiled by the authors.

Based upon each participant's employment status prior to Title X (employed or not employed), and the employment status at the time of our study (not employed, still working on the project, or employed elsewhere), four cases are presented in Table B.1 to impute the estimated average weekly earnings in the absence of Title X.

Case 1 corresponds to those participants who were employed when hired under Title X, and who were not employed elsewhere at the time of our study or were still employed under Title X. We assume that, in the absence of the program, these persons would have received weekly earnings comparable to those received from their prior jobs.

The second case includes those participants who were employed when hired under Title X and were employed elsewhere at the time of the study. Given weekly earnings data for periods just before and just after Title X, we assume that, in the absence of the program, expected weekly earnings are the average of prior and subsequent weekly earnings.

The third case includes those participants who were not employed when hired under Title X and were employed elsewhere at the time of the study. Although earnings data exist for periods before and after Title X, we use only the subsequent earnings because these workers were unemployed immediately prior to the program. Average weekly earnings in the absence of Title X are

TABLE B.2

Average Earnings

Case	Sample Size	Average Estimated Weekly Earnings in the Absence of Title X	Average Actual Earnings from Title X
1	342	$134	$148
2	16	147	163
3	60	137	125
4	1,551	144	133

Source: Compiled by the authors.

designated as the subsequent weekly earnings, deflated to account for the antici-pated normal increases in wages from the primary period of Title X employment to the time when subsequent earnings were measured. The average time span between when these workers left the program and when subsequent earnings were measured is 32 weeks. The deflation factor used is one minus .0758 (the 1975 increase in average hourly earnings of production or nonsupervisory work-ers on private payrolls), or .9242.

The final case includes all participants who were not employed when hired under Title X and were either still employed under Title X or not employed at the time of the study. This case accounts for more than 78 percent of the sample. For these workers, earnings data exist for their usual and prior jobs. We assume that expected weekly earnings are the average of prior and usual weekly earnings. Moreover, earnings from a prior and/or usual job that was held more than one year prior to their starting date under Title X are inflated to account for the normal increases in wages experienced by all production or nonsupervisory workers during 1975 (that is, inflated by 7.58 percent).

The estimated average weekly earnings in the absence of Title X and actual average weekly earnings from the program are reported for the four cases in Table B.2.

Table B.2 shows that there is actually very little variation between esti-mated average weekly earnings for the four cases. However, average weekly Title X earnings are substantially higher for the previously employed (cases 1 and 2) than for the previously not employed (cases 3 and 4). Prior employment status is thus correlated with Title X weekly earnings. One can hypothesize that higher earnings motivated the previously employed to leave their jobs for a Title X job. Those not previously employed, on the other hand, had lower asking wages and were willing to accept positions which actually paid less than they would have made if they could have found other employment.

Once weekly earnings in the absence of Title X are estimated for each employee, they are simply multiplied by the weeks of employment in the absence of Title X to arrive at an estimate of employee earnings in the absence of the program. This earnings-discount figure is then subtracted from the actual Title X earnings of the employee to arrive at the earnings directly attributable to the Job Opportunities Program. These adjusted earnings serve as the basis for the calculation of adjusted net cost in Chapter 4.

As an epilogue to this appendix, it is useful to point out to the reader what the methodology presented does not do. The particular question we had to answer as accurately as possible was the following: How much of the labor demand created by the Title X program would have made jobs available to the enrollees anyway, even if the program never existed? Our statistical control group addresses this question directly, but does not answer a legitimate question posed by economists and policy makers concerning the net social program benefits, or how many jobs are really created. In order to do this, a detailed study of local budget substitution and displacement would have to be undertaken. Further, the issue of the program's vacuum effects is not germane to our analysis even though it is important from a microeconomic viewpoint.

Our derived measure of the program enrollee's expected work in the absence of the program allows us to better estimate the net benefits of the program to the enrollee as well as to those officials who are in charge of the program.

NOTES

1. See Congressional Budget Office, *Temporary Measures to Stimulate Employment: An Evaluation of Some Alternatives* (Washington, D.C.: Government Printing Office, 1975).

2. Ibid., summary table 1.

3. See for example, George Johnson and James Tomola, "The Efficacy of Public Service Employment Programs," *Technical Analysis Paper 17A* (Washington, D.C.: U.S. Department of Labor, ASPER, 1975); National Planning Association, *An Evaluation of the Economic Impact Project of the Public Employment Program* (Washington, D.C.: National Planning Association, May 1974); Michael Wiseman, "Public Employment as Fiscal Policy," *Brookings Papers on Economic Activity*, vol. 1 (Washington, D.C.: Brookings Institution, 1976), pp. 67–114. Furthermore, a study recently funded by the Department of Labor will examine the costs and feasibility of several large-scale countercyclical public job-creation options.

4. For example, see "Work Experience of the Population in 1975," Special Labor Force Report 192, mimeographed (Washington, D.C.: U.S. Department of Labor, Bureau of Labor Statistics, 1976); *Employment and Earnings* (Department of Labor, BLS) and *Employment and Training Report of the President, 1976* (Washington, D.C.: Government Printing Office, 1976).

5. There has been much research done on these issues, especially in reference to national employment policy. See, for example, George L. Perry, "Unemployment Flows in the U.S. Labor Market," *Brookings Papers on Economic Activity*, vol. 2 (1972); Robert E. Hall, "Turnover in the Labor Force," *Brookings Papers on Economic Activity*, vol. 3 (1972); Stephen Marston, "Employment Instability and High Unemployment Rates," *Brookings Papers on Economic Activity*, vol. 1 (1976); Robert L. Crosslin and David W. Stevens, "The Asking Wage-Duration of Unemployment Relation Revisited," *Southern Economic Journal* 43, no. 3 (January 1977).

6. See, for example, Carol Jusenius and Richard Shortledge, *Dual Careers: A Longitudinal Study of Labor Market Experience of Women*, Manpower Research Monograph No. 21, vol. 3 (Columbus: Ohio State University, Center for Human Resource Research, 1976).

7. See Sar Levitan and Joyce Zickler, *Too Little But Not Too Late: Federal Support to Lagging Areas* (Lexington, Mass.: Lexington Books, 1976); Anthony Sulvetta and Norman Thompson, *An Evaluation of the Public Works Impact Program* (Washington, D.C.: U.S. Department of Commerce, Economic Development Administration, 1975); and Sar Levitan and Robert Taggart, *Emergency Employment Act: The PEP Generation* (Salt Lake City, Utah: Olympus, 1973).

8. See Ralph E. Smith, "A Simulation Model of the Demographic Composition of Employment, Unemployment, and Labor Force Participation," Urban Institute Working Paper (Washington, D.C.: Urban Institute, June 1976), published in *Research in Labor Economics*, vol. 1, ed. Ronald Ehrenberg, forthcoming, 1979.

9. Ibid., p. 17. Smith notes:

> The U.S. does not have comprehensive vacancy statistics. We assume an average vacancy level during the 1967–73 estimation period of about 2 million and use the Conference Board's *Index* to measure the variation (from month to month) in the level (p. 19).

10. See Charles Holt, "Job Search, Phillips' Wage Relation, and Union Influence: Theory and Evidence," in Edmund S. Phelps et al., *Microeconomic Foundations of Employment and Inflation Theory* (New York: W. W. Norton, 1970), pp. 53–123.

11. Crosslin and Stevens, op. cit., p. 1301.

12. Note that none of the studies done on the flows in the labor market have explicitly taken into account individuals' previous labor-market experience. See Hall, op. cit., and Marston, op. cit. It should be mentioned that the Marston paper contains conclusions about the determinants of employment instability that have serious public-policy implications and that, we believe, are unsubstantiated by the analysis and data presented. He has no variable for measuring job quality or job tenure, and still concludes that personal characteristics are responsible for employment instability, because his industry-occupation variables failed to explain the variance among sex, age, and race groups. June O'Neill makes a similar criticism, in part, in her comments following the paper.

13. *Wages and Earning* (January 1977), p. 149.

APPENDIX C

RETURNS FROM
NONLABOR EXPENDITURES

Title X projects purchase a variety of nonlabor items, usually from private-sector producers of goods and services. The extra taxes paid to all levels of government from these contracts/procurements constitute a "social" return, which must be netted separately from these gross EDA nonlabor costs to get a truer picture of the real net costs of Title X.

Conceptually, there are two major issues of concern: Which taxes count (and how are they to be measured?)? And which nonlabor expenditures of projects count, that is, which are directly attributable to Title X's existence? Our methodology makes a series of assumptions in order to make the net-cost estimate operational.

First, there are literally thousands of federal, state, and local business tax rates in the United States; counting and employing them all would be simply impossible. Also, the use of published tax rates (or schedules) applied to before-tax business profits is unsatisfactory, since the tax system is replete with incentives, allowances, and other so-called loopholes. Instead, it is preferable to know the effective tax rate applicable to each contractor/supplier, that is, actual taxes paid by producers as a proportion of the value of their total output.

Our method makes use of readily available published data, by industry, in the Commerce Department's monthly *Survey of Current Business*. There, direct corporate tax payments by each industry to all levels of government are regularly identified in table 6.20. Indirect taxes paid by the business sector—sales, excise, property, and other such taxes—are identified (again, by industry) in table 6.1. And the gross domestic product (GDP) originating in (or contributed by) each industry is also reported in table 6.1. Thus, for each industry, effective direct and indirect tax rates can be estimated as the ratio of taxes actually paid to the market value of its net output (GDP). By applying these computed rates to the actual industry-by-industry expenditures of Title X projects, the additional tax returns to the government sector that are attributable to Title X can be calculated.*

Reliance on data from the *Survey of Current Business* necessitates several modest compromises and assumptions:

---

*A small portion (about 3.7 percent industrywide) of the indirect taxes included in table 6.1 are not taxes, but fees and licenses paid to federal, state, and local sources. These payments, which are not a function of marginally increasing GDP, can be excluded from the net-cost calculations, which rely upon unpublished data from the Bureau of Economic Analysis.

1. Tax and GDP data are for 1975, the most recent complete data available.
2. Industry data can only be disaggregated to the two-digit SIC level, for example, contract construction, durable-goods manufacturing.
3. Since the direct tax payment data are only reported for corporations, we must assume that the effective tax rates for partnerships and sole proprietorships in any industry are the same (on the average) as those for corporations in that same industry.
4. Average, rather than marginal, tax rates must be relied upon, since data are not available from which marginal rates can be calculated.

The second issue concerns the attribution of nonlabor expenditures to Title X. Nonlabor expenditures come from three general sources: Title X and other federal grants; locally incurred debt, i.e., borrowing via bond issues or short-term notes; and state, local, and private complementary funds that are procured from regular operating revenues.* Depending upon the source of funds, one may presume that different patterns of fiscal substitution take place at the local level. Thus, there is a question of which nonlabor expenditures should be counted. The answer depends upon whether one is estimating the net nonlabor costs to various levels of government or the net stimulus to the economy due to Title X spending.

For purposes of net-cost estimates, all nonlabor expenditures of Title X projects must be counted. Displacement is not an issue. All moneys which are appropriated and spent on nonlabor purchases are included in the total gross cost of Title X; tax returns from these expenditures are part of the returns to government from the program. We are interested in the net cost of the program as it has been implemented, not in a comparison of program returns with hypothetical returns from possible alternative uses of funds. This is consistent with the methodology applied to labor expenditures, where the focus is also on returns attributable to actual Title X expenditures, not on returns relative to alternative uses of funds. In the case of labor expenditures, however, the efficiency of using Title X funds to pay workers who might have been employed in the absence of the program is an issue. This is not the case for nonlabor expenditures.

In contrast, displacement effects must be considered when estimating the net stimulus to local economies attributable to Title X. Such an estimate is important to calculations of indirect and induced effects (discussed in Chapter 5). For purposes of estimating net stimulus, any expenditures out of federal grant money are clearly new expenditures, since the federal portion of the program is debt financed. Similarly, one can assume that nonlabor expenditures from

---

*A small proportion of Title X funds was generated from private sources, usually foundations, and often of an in-kind nature.

locally incurred debt represent a net stimulus to the economy, presuming that local grant recipients would not have incurred the debt in the absence of the Title X grant. Nonlabor expenditures from state or local operating revenue, however, are very likely to have been spent in the local area, regardless of Title X. Thus, one cannot count them as part of the net stimulus to the economy.

In sum, all expenditures made on nonlabor items are included in the net nonlabor-costs calculations. However, when making an assessment of the net stimulus to the economy resulting from Title X, that portion of Title X project funds that comes directly out of local operating budgets should not be included.

The basic calculations are shown in the following algorithm:

$$
\begin{bmatrix} \text{net additional} \\ \text{taxes on non-} \\ \text{labor expendi-} \\ \text{tures (NATNL)} \end{bmatrix} = \sum_{v=1}^{m \text{ projects}} \sum_{l=1}^{k \text{ industries}} \begin{bmatrix} \text{project j's nonlabor} \\ \text{purchases from} \\ \text{industry l that are} \\ \text{subject to taxation} \\ \text{(NET PNE}_{jl}) \end{bmatrix}
$$

$$
\times \begin{bmatrix} \text{direct effective federal,} & \text{indirect effective} \\ \text{state, and local implicit} & + & \text{federal (sales, excise,} \\ \text{tax rate applicable to} & & \text{etc.) implicit tax} \\ \text{industry l} & & \text{rate applicable to} \\ & & \text{industry l} \\ & DTR_l + ITR_l & \end{bmatrix}
$$

where

NET PNE_{jl} =   nonlabor expenditures for the products or services of industry l that are directly financed out of EDA funds plus local contributions to PNE.

$$
DTR_l = \left[\frac{\text{1975 federal, state, and local corporate taxes paid by industry l}}{\text{1975 Gross Domestic Product originating in industry l (GDP}_l)} \right]
$$

$$
ITR_l = \left[\frac{\text{1975 federal, state, and local indirect business taxes paid by industry l}}{GDP_l} \right]
$$

A hypothetical example will illustrate the application of this methodology:

Assume gross Title X expenditure = $10 million
               labor cost= $ 6 million
              nonlabor   = $ 4 million

And the $4 million nonlabor cost includes $2 million for contract-construction sector (const); $1 million for wholesale and retail trades (wrt)—materials, equipment, etc.; $1 million for manufacturing of durable goods (mfg)

Then

$$\text{NATNL} = (\text{DTR}_{const} + \text{ITR}_{const})\ \overset{net}{\text{PNE}}_{const}$$

$$+ (\text{DTR}_{wrt} + \text{ITR}_{wrt})\ \overset{net}{\text{PNE}}_{wrt}$$

$$+ (\text{DTR}_{mfg} + \text{ITR}_{mfg})\ \overset{net}{\text{PNE}}_{mfg}$$

Direct corporate taxes are located in table 6.20 of the *Survey of Current Business*.
Indirect business taxes are located in table 6.1 of the *Survey of Current Business*.
Gross domestic product, by industry, is given in table 6.1 of the *Survey of Current Business*.

$$\text{NATNL} = \left(\frac{896\ \text{million}}{66.5\ \text{billion}} + \frac{1.6\ \text{billion}}{66.5\ \text{billion}}\right)\ \$2\ \text{million}$$

$$+ \left(\frac{8.3\ \text{billion}}{272.4\ \text{billion}} + \frac{55.4\ \text{billion}}{272.4\ \text{billion}}\right)\ \$1\ \text{million}$$

$$+ \left(\frac{9.993\ \text{billion}}{203.7\ \text{billion}} + \frac{5.7\ \text{billion}}{203.7\ \text{billion}}\right)\ \$1\ \text{million}$$

$$= (.013 + .020 = .033)\ (\$2{,}000{,}000) = \$66{,}000$$

$$+ (.030 + .203 = .233)\ (\$1{,}000{,}000) = \$233{,}000$$

$$+ (.049 + .025 = .074)\ (\$1{,}000{,}000) = \$74{,}000$$

$$= \$373{,}000 = 9.32 \text{ percent of } \$4 \text{ million in nonlabor expenditures}$$

TABLE C.1

Direct Taxes on Nonlabor Expenditures

SIC Codes	Industry Category	Direct Tax Rate	Federal Share[a]	Nonfederal Share[a]
10–14	Mining	.034	85%	15%
15–17	Contract con-struction	0.13	85	15
20–23, 26–31	Nondurable goods	.093	85	15
19, 24, 25, 32–39	Durable goods	.049	85	15
40–47	Transporation	.015	85	15
48–49	Communication and utilities	.037	85	15
50	Wholesale trade	.043	85	15
52–59	Retail trade	.027	85	15
60–67	Finance, insurance, real estate	.048	85	15
70–89	Services	.006	85	15
	All industries[b]	.033	85	15

[a] Breakdowns of direct taxes returned to the federal government and nonfederal governments are not available at the industry level.

[b] Returns from nonlabor expenditures that are described too vaguely to be allocated to an industry are calculated at the all-industry rate. These represent 3.7 percent of nonlabor expenditures of our sample projects.

Source: Compiled by the authors.

TABLE C.2

Indirect Taxes on Nonlabor Expenditures

SIC Codes	Industry Category	Indirect Tax Rate	Federal Share	Nonfederal Share
10–14	Mining	.074	0%	100.0%
15–17	Contract construction	.020	0	100.0
20–23, 26–31	Nondurable goods	.106	77.4	22.6
19, 24, 25, 32–39	Durable goods	.025	13.8	86.2
40–47	Transportation	.062	25.9	74.1
48–49	Communication and utilities	.120	39.0	61.0
50	Wholesale trade	.213	26.2	73.8
52–59	Retail trade	.179	1.7	98.3
60–67	Finance, insurance, and real estate	.171	0	100.0
70–89	Services	.026	0.3	99.7
	All industries[a]	.089	16.7	83.3

[a] Returns from nonlabor expenditures that are described too vaguely to be allocated to an industry are calculated at the all-industry rate.

Source: Compiled by the authors.

Having calculated additional taxes attributable to nonlabor expenditures, the next step is to allocate returns to federal and state/local governments. The *Survey of Current Business* does not disaggregate data in a way permitting such allocations. Unpublished BEA data do, however, provide federal vs. nonfederal breakdowns for indirect taxes. For direct taxes, the *Statistical Abstract of the United States* contains information upon which an approximate allocation of federal and nonfederal returns may be estimated.[1]

In Tables C.1 and C.2, the rates utilized in this study are summarized.

This methodology is admittedly less precise and sophisticated than the methodology applied to labor costs. The principal reason is that data on the nonlabor expenditures of Title X projects are too rough to support a more elegant approach. Projects are not required to submit an ongoing record of expenditures to EDA, or to report funds spent on nonlabor purchases. The only sources of data are the local records of individual projects, and even these are often not of a form or level of specificity to support precise analysis. Faced with this problem and the resource constraints of the study, Abt Associates was able to examine local records of all projects visited for purposes of estimating long-term impacts. Nonlabor-expenditure information at the two-digit SIC Code level was obtained from 50 projects, and reflects actual nonlabor expenditures plus estimates of future nonlabor purchases cited by the project director and/or responsible agent. It is on these data that the nonlabor analysis must be based, data which do not justify an investment in more sophisticated methodology development.

NOTE

1. See *Statistical Abstract of the United States, 1975* (Washington, D.C.: Government Printing Office, 1975), table no. 416, "Tax Revenues, by Source and Level of Government," p. 252.

APPENDIX D

RETURNS ON
LABOR EXPENDITURES:
THE EMPLOYEE SAMPLE

Projections of returns to government from Title X labor expenditures are based upon data from the Title X employee survey. As a supplement to the analysis in Chapter 4, Tables D.1-D.5 present data from the sample of 1,969 respondents.

TABLE D.1

Unadjusted Tax Revenues from Title X Labor Expenditures: Employee Sample

Type of Tax	Increased Tax Revenue	Percent of Total Tax Return	Federal Share	State Share
Income	$503,440	22.5	$448,501	$ 54,939
FICA—employee	548,147	24.5	548,147	–
FICA—employer	548,147	24.5	548,147	–
Sales	191,140	8.5	–	191,140
Excise, on gasoline	93,644	4.2	21,527	72,117
Excise, on tobacco	113,311	5.1	64,582	48,729
Unemployment insurance	238,963	10.7	33,953	205,010
Total revenue from taxes	$2,236,792	100.0	1,664,857	571,935

Source: Compiled by the authors.

TABLE D.2

Unadjusted Reductions in Transfer Payments from Title X Labor Expenditures: Employee Sample

Transfer Payment	Reduction in Payment	Percent of Total Transfer Savings	Federal Share	State Share
Unemployment compensation	$392,187	36.1	$322,353	$ 69,834
Social Security	40,067	3.7	40,067	–
AFDC	123,738	11.4	103,075	20,663
General Relief	124,144	11.4	–	124,144
SSI	15,964	1.5	15,562	402
Food stamps	203,709	18.8	203,709	–
Medicaid	167,185	15.4	90,788	76,397
Public housing	18,185	1.7	18,185	–
Total savings from Transfers	1,085,178	100.0	793,738	291,440

Source: Compiled by the authors.

TABLE D.3

Total Adjusted Returns to the Government from Title X: Employee Sample

Measure	Total	Tax Revenues	Reduction in Transfers
Total Title X earnings	$9,354,219	—[a]	—
Adjusted earnings	6,541,102	—	—
Adjusted returns	2,576,880	$1,517,151	$1,059,729
Percent of Title X earnings	27.5	16.2	11.3
Percent of adjusted earnings	39.4	23.2	16.2
Percent of returns	100.0	58.9	41.1
Savings per employee	$1,309	$771	$538
Federal share	1,824,382	1,135,045	689,337
State share	752,498	382,106	370,392
Net adjusted wage/salary cost to government	6,717,339	—	—

[a] Data not available.
Source: Compiled by the authors.

TABLE D.4

Adjusted Tax Revenues from Title X Labor Expenditures: Employee Sample

Type of Tax	Revenue from Tax	Percent of Total Tax Revenue	Federal Share	State Share
Personal income	$325,873	21.5	$290,612	$ 35,261
FICA—employee	380,822	25.1	380,822	—
FICA—employer	380,822	25.1	280,822	—
Sales	125,494	8.3	—[a]	125,494
Excise, on tobacco	74,736	4.9	42,596	32,140
Escise, on gasoline	61,765	4.0	14,199	47,566
Unemployment insurance	167,639	11.1	25,994	141,645
Total tax revenue	1,517,151	100.0	1,135,045	382,106

[a] Data not available.
Source: Compiled by the authors.

TABLE D.5

Adjusted Reductions in Transfer Payments from Title X Labor Expenditures: Employee Sample

Type of Transfer Payment	Savings to Government	Percent of Total Transfer Savings	Federal Share	State Share
Unemployment compensation	$522,444	49.3	$315,233	$207,211
Social Security	35,236	3.3	35,236	—
AFDC	101,331	9.6	87,011	14,320
General Relief	91,692	8.6	—[a]	91,692
SSI	12,724	1.2	12,488	236
Food stamps	156,015	14.7	156,015	—
Medicaid	125,975	11.9	69,042	56,933
Public housing	14,312	1.4	14,312	—
Total reduction in transfer payments	1,059,729	100.0	689,337	370,392

[a] Data not available.

Source: Compiled by the authors.

APPENDIX E

OCCUPATIONAL-CLASSIFICATION STRUCTURE

The occupational-classification codes utilized on the ED–110X report forms are the two-digit occupational divisions of the *Dictionary of Occupational Titles*. Initial analysis of aggregate data from ED–110X reports, however, revealed that these codes were not very useful in describing Title X jobs. Either the codes themselves were inappropriate to the job structures, or they were being misused by projects in reporting the jobs of their employees.

For example, fully 61 percent of the employees analyzed came under only four of 84 available occupational codes. Moreover, these four codes were very general or catchall categories—other construction occupations (30.1 percent); excavating, grading, paving, and related occupations (14 percent); forestry occupations (10.4 percent); and miscellaneous personal-service occupations (6.5 percent). Such a concentration of employees in so very few general occupational categories provides very little useful information of analytic relevance. In contrast, many categories were rarely used. Fifty of the 84 codes were applied to less than two-tenths of 1 percent of the reported employees; collectively, these 50 categories accounted for less than 2.5 percent of employees.

The types of occupational analysis desired in this study required a more sensitive and appropriate coding structure. Moreover, it required that that structure be applied uniformly to the jobs of sample participants. Therefore, ED–110X occupation data were not used in the study. Rather, respondents were asked to describe the work they did in terms of job title and job responsibilities. This information was postcoded by Abt Associates, utilizing a revised two-digit code structure. This code structure, presented below, is adapted from the ED–110X codes, but also draws from the more precise three-digit categories defined in the *Dictionary of Occupational Titles*.

The occupational-code structure for the Title X employee survey serves several purposes. First, by more precisely specifying certain occupations, it greatly reduces the concentration of employees in a small number of general or miscellaneous occupational categories. Second, it permits a rough ability to detect levels of responsibility by providing distinct codes for managers, supervisors/foremen, and workers in different industry groups. Third, it provides codes for responses that are of interest but are not encompassed in standard occupational frameworks (for example, housewife, student, a self-employed person in an unspecified occupation).

The occupational-code structure developed for the Title X employee survey is presented below, along with the equivalent codes (where applicable) from the DOT and the ED–110X form.

OCCUPATIONAL-CODE STRUCTURE
FOR TITLE X EMPLOYEE SURVEY

		DOT Code	ED-110X Code
00	No answer		
01-09	Managers, administrators, and officials	18	18
	01 Agriculture, forestry, and fishing-industry managers and officials	180	nc[a]
	02 Construction-industry managers and officials	182	nc
	03 Manufacturing-industry managers and officials	183	nc
	04 Transportation-, communication-, and utilities-industry managers and officials	184	nc
	05 Wholesale- and retail-trade managers and officials	185	nc
	06 Finance, insurance, and real estate managers and officials	186	nc
	07 Service industry managers and officials	187	nc
	08 Public administration managers and officials	188	nc
	09 Miscellaneous managers and officials, not elsewhere classified	189	nc
10-19	Professional and technical work	$0,1$[b]	$0,1$[b]
	10 Museum, library, and archival sciences	10	10
	11 Law and jurisprudence	11	11
	12 Education (including teachers at all levels)	05, 09	05, 09
	13 Creative and performing arts (art, graphics, drama, music, writing, etc.)	13, 14, 97 part 15, part 96	13, 14, 97 part 15, part 96
	14 Recreational professions (e.g., coach, athlete)	part 15, part 96	part 15, part 96
	15 Architecture, engineering	01	01
	16 Accounting, auditing, budget and management analysis, personnel, purchasing	160-166	16
	17 Medicine and health (including RNs)	07	07
	18 Mathematics, physical sciences, life sciences	02, 04	02, 04
	19 Other professional and technical (including religion, unspecified military professional, etc.)	12, 19, nc	12, 19, nc

		DOT Code	ED-110X Code
20-25	Clerical and sales work		
	20 Stenography, typing, filing, and related	20	20
	21 Computing and account recording	21	21
	22 Material and production recording	22	22
	23 Information and message distribution	23	23
	24 Miscellaneous clerical	24	24
	25 Sales of all kinds (including insurance, real estate, retail, door-to-door, etc.)	25-29	25-29
26	Student	nc	nc
27	Housewife	nc	nc
28	Other (invalids)	nc	nc
29	Self-employed in otherwise uncodable work	nc	nc
30-38	Service occupations		
	30 Domestic	30	30
	31 Food and beverage preparation	31	31
	32 Lodging and related services	32	32
	33 Barbering, cosmetology, and related services	33	33
	34 Amusement and recreation	34	34
	35 Miscellaneous personal services	35	35
	36 Apparel and furnishings	36	36
	37 Protective services	37	37
	38 Building and related services (porters, janitors, etc.)	38	38
	39 Miscellaneous	35	35
40-48	Forestry, parks, recreation, farming, and fishing		
	40 Farmer, fisherman, hunter	40-43, 45-46	40-43, 45-46
	41 Farmworker	nc	nc
	42 Tree cutter, brush clearer, sawyer	nc	nc
	43 Lumberjack	nc	nc
	47 Environmental monitor or technician	nc	nc
	48 Other forestry/parks/recreation occupation	nc	nc
50-59	Government and social-service occupations		
	50 Licensed Practical Nurse (LPN)	nc	nc
	51 Social worker, counselor	nc	nc
	59 Other government/social-service	nc	nc
60-69	Operatives and technicians		
	60 Operatives—processing plants	50-59	50-59
	61 Manufacturing-assembly or bench work	70-79	70-79

		DOT Code	ED-110X Code
62	Nonmanufacturing skilled operative or technician	60-61, 64-69	60-61, 64-69
63	Mechanic or repair person	62, 63, part 82	62, 63, part 82
64	Draftsperson	017	nc
65	Heavy-equipment operator (crane, bulldozer, tractor, etc.)	nc	nc
66	Truck driver or bus driver	part 90	part 90
67	Computer programmer	nc	nc
69	Other operative or technician	599, 699, 799	nc
70-79	Supervisors and foremen		
70	Agriculture, forestry, and fishing industry	nc	nc
71	Mining industry	nc	nc
72	Construction industry	nc	nc
73	Manufacturing industry	nc	nc
74	Transportation, communication, and utilities industry	nc	nc
75	Wholesale and retail trades	nc	nc
76	Finance, insurance, and real estate	nc	nc
77	Service industry	nc	nc
78	Public administration	nc	nc
79	Miscellaneous	nc	nc
80-89	Construction and structural work		
80	Welders, riveters, and other metalworkers	80, 81	80, 81
81	Excavating, grading, etc.	850-851	part 85
82	Cement worker, concrete laying, paving, or finishing	852, 853, 844	part 84, part 85
83	Painting and plastering	840-843, 845, 846	part 84
84	Carpenter or other construction woodworker	860	part 86
85	Brickmason, stone mason, tile setter	861	part 86
86	Plumber	862	part 86
87	Electrician	83	83
88	Roofer	866	part 86
89	Miscellaneous (e.g., floor layer, glazier)	89, part 86	89, part 86
90	Construction worker or laborer, otherwise unspecified	nc	nc

	DOT Code	ED-110X Code
91–99 Other work		
91 Building maintenance (exclusive of janitorial)	nc	nc
92 Miner	93	93
93 Cab driver	nc	nc
94 Miscellaneous laborer, manufacturing or nonmanufacturing	nc	nc
95 Odd jobs	nc	nc
96 None, nothing	nc	nc
97 Miscellaneous	nc	nc
98 No response	nc	nc
99 Don't know	nc	nc

---

[a]No counterpart.
[b]Does not include managerial positions that are encompassed by DOT and ED-110X codes.

BIBLIOGRAPHY

Abt Associates, Inc. *An Evaluation for the Massachusetts Local Initiatives Program.* Vols. 1-3. Cambridge: Abt, 1977.

————. *An Evaluation of the Special Impact Program.* Vols. 1-4. Cambridge: Abt, 1973.

Barocci, Thomas A. *The Canadian Job Creation Program and Its Applicability to the United States.* Joint Economic Committee, Paper #2, vol. 1. Washington, D.C.: Government Printing Office, 1976.

————. "Planning and Economic Development Under CETA." *Adherent* 2, no. 2 (1976).

————. "The Recession is a Regressive Tax." Mimeographed, Cambridge, Mass.: MIT, 1977.

————, and William Spring. "Jobs and the Management of the Economy." Paper presented at the Boston University Regional Institute on Employment, Training and Labor Market Policy, Boston, 1975.

Blinder, Alan, and Robert Solow. "The Analytical Foundations of Fiscal Policy." In *The Economics of Public Finance,* edited by Alan Blinder and Robert Solow et al., pp. 3-115. Washington, D.C.: Brookings Institution, 1974.

Boise Cascade Center for Community Development. *An Evaluation of EDA Public Works Projects.* Vol. 1. Mimeographed, U.S. Department of Commerce, Economic Development Administration.

Briscoe, Alden F. "Public Service Employment in the 1930's: The WPA." In *The Political Economy of Public Service Employment,* edited by Harold Sheppard et al. Lexington, Mass.: D. C. Heath, 1972.

Bureau of Labor Statistics. *Employment and Earnings.* Washington, D.C.: Department of Labor, issued monthly.

————. *Factbook for Estimating Manpower Need of Federal Programs.* BLS Bulletin 1832. Washington, D.C.: Department of Labor, 1975.

————. "Work Experience of the Population in 1975." *Special Labor Force Report 192.* Washington, D.C.: Department of Labor, 1976.

Burns, Arthur, and Edward Williams. *Federal Work, Security and Relief Programs.* Washington, D.C.: Government Printing Office, 1941.

Centaur Management Consultants, Inc. *Re-Evaluation of the Impacts of Fifty Public Works Projects and EDA, An Updated Evaluation of EDA Funded Industrial Parks, 1968-74.* Washington, D.C.: EDA, 1975.

Committee on Social Security. *Work Relief Experience in the U.S.* New York: Social Science Research Council, n.d.

Congressional Budget Office. *Temporary Measures to Stimulate Employment*. Washington, D.C.: Government Printing Office, 1975.

Craig, Lois. "Beyond Leaf-Raking, WPA's Lasting Legacy." *City*, October–November 1970, p. 23.

Crosslin, Robert L., and David W. Stevens. "The Asking Wage–Duration of Unemployment Relation Revisited." *Southern Economic Journal* 43, no. 3 (January 1977).

Economic Report of the President, 1955. Washington, D.C.: Government Printing Office, 1956.

Economic Report of the President, 1976. Washington, D.C.: Government Printing Office, 1977.

Economic Development Administration. *Developing Methodologies for Evaluating the Impact of the EDA Programs*. Washington, D.C.: Department of Commerce, 1972.

———. *The EDA Experience in the Evolution of Policy, A Brief History, 1965-73*. Washington, D.C.: Department of Commerce, 1974.

———. *Public Works Impact Program: An Evaluation*. Vols. 1 and 2. Washington, D.C.: Department of Commerce, 1970.

———. "Summary of Title X Proposals." Mimeographed. Washington, D.C.: Department of Commerce, March 7, 1976.

Evans, Michael K. *Macroeconomic Activity: Theory, Forecasting and Control*. New York: Harper and Row, 1969.

Faux, Geoffrey. *CDCs: New Hope for the Inner Cities*. New York: Twentieth Century Fund, 1971.

Galbraith, John K. *The Economic Effects of the Federal Public Works Expenditures, 1933-38*. Washington, D.C.: Government Printing Office, 1940.

Gorn, Harvey, et al. *Community Development Corporations*. Washington, D.C.: Urban Institute, 1976.

Gramlich, Edward. "The Distributional Effects of Higher Unemployment." *Brookings Papers on Economic Activity*. Vol. 2. Washington, D.C.: Brookings Institution, 1974.

Hall, Robert E. "Turnover in the Labor Force." *Brookings Papers on Economic Activity*. Vol. 3. Washington, D.C.: Brookings Institution, 1974.

Hansen, W. Lee. "The Cyclical Sensitivity of the Labor Supply." *American Economics Review* 51 (June 1961): 299-309.

Harrison, Bennett. *The Economic Development of Massachusetts*. Boston: Massachusetts Senate, Commerce and Labor Committee, 1974.

————, and Sandra Kanter. "The Political Economy of State Job Creation Business Incentives." In *The Declining Northeast*, edited by George Sternlieb. New Brunswick: Rutgers University Press, 1979.

Hoeber, Johannes U. "Some Characteristics of Accelerated Public Works Projects." *Redevelopment*, September 1964.

Isakoff, Jack. "The Public Works Administration." *Illinois Studies in the Social Sciences* 33, no. 3 (University of Illinois Press, 1978): 137.

Jusenius, Carol, and Richard Shortledge. *Dual Careers: A Longitudinal Study of Labor Market Experience of Women*. Manpower Research Monograph, no. 21, vol. 3, U.S. Department of Labor. Columbus: Ohio University Press, 1975.

Levitan, Sar, and Robert Taggart. *The Emergency Employment Act: The PEP Generation*. Salt Lake City, Utah: Olympus, 1973.

Levitan, Sar A. *Federal Aid to Depressed Areas: An Evaluation of the Area Redevelopment Administration*. Baltimore: Johns Hopkins Press, 1964.

————, and Joyce K. Zickler. *Too Little But Not Too Late: Federal Aid to Lagging Areas*. Lexington, Mass.: Lexington Books, 1976.

MacMahon, Arthur W., et al. *The Administration of Federal Work Relief*. Chicago: Public Administration Service, 1941.

Mangum, Garth L. "New Deal Job Creation Programs." In *Emergency Employment Act Background Information*. Subcommittee on Employment, Manpower and Poverty, Committee on Labor and the Public Welfare, Washington, D.C., 1967.

Marston, Stephen. "Employment Instability and High Unemployment Rates." *Brookings Papers on Economic Activity*. Vol. 1. Washington, D.C.: Brookings Institution, 1976.

Miernyk, William H. *Elements of Input-Output Analysis*. New York: Random House, 1965.

Milkman, Raymond, et al. *Alleviating Economic Distress: Evaluating a Federal Effort*. Lexington, Mass.: Lexington Books, 1972.

Oliphant, Thomas. "Will Carter's Promises Become Economic Progress for the Northeast?" *New England Magazine (Boston Globe)*, January 30, 1977.

Perry, George L. "Unemployment Flows in the U.S. Labor Market." *Brookings Papers on Economic Activity*. Vol. 2. Washington, D.C.: Brookings Institution, 1972.

Pressman, Jeffrey, and Aaron Wildavsky. *Implementation: How Great Expectations in Washington Are Dashed in Oakland*. Berkeley: University of California Press, 1973.

Smith, Ralph E. "A Simulation Model of the Demographic Composition of Employment, Unemployment, and Labor Force Participation." Urban Institute Working Paper. Washington, D.C.: June 1976.

Stein, Herbert. "Twentieth Anniversary of the Employment Act of 1946." In *Supplement to the Joint Economic Committee Symposium*, pp. 143–52. Washington, D.C.: Government Printing Office, 1967.

Studenski, Paul, and Herman Krooss. *Financial History of the United States*. New York: McGraw-Hill, 1963.

Sulvetta, Anthony, et al., eds. House Report No. 92-92, *Alleviating Unemployment Through Accelerated Public Works in the United States: An Historical Perspective*. Washington, D.C.: Economic Development Administration, 1976.

Sulvetta, Anthony, and Norman Thompson. *An Evaluation of the Public Works Impact Program*. Washington, D.C.: Department of Commerce, 1975.

Sum, Andrew, and Thomas P. Rush. "The Geographic Structures of Unemployment Rates." *Monthly Labor Review*, March 1975.

Teeters, Nancy H. "The 1972 Budget: Where It Stands and Whither It Might Go." *Brookings Papers on Economic Activity*. Vol. 1, p. 233. Washington, D.C.: Brookings Institution, 1971.

Tobin, William J. *Public Works and Unemployment: A History of Federally Funded Programs*. Washington, D.C.: Department of Commerce, 1975.

U.S. Community Improvements Appraisal. *A Report on the Programs of the WPA*. Washington, D.C.: Government Printing Office, 1939.

U.S. Department of Commerce. *Statistical Abstract of the United States, 1941*. Washington, D.C.: Government Printing Office, 1941.

———. *Statistical Abstract of the United States, 1976*. Washington, D.C.: Government Printing Office, 1976.

U.S. Department of Labor. *Employment and Training Report of the President, 1976*. Washington, D.C.: Government Printing Office, 1976.

U.S. Senate. *Hearings Before a Subcommittee of the Committee on Banking and Currency, U.S. Senate, 79th Congress, 1st Session on S. 380*. Washington, D.C.: Government Printing Office, 1945.

Vaughan, Roger. *Public Works as a Councercyclical Device: A Review of the Issues*. A Report to the EDA. Santa Monica: Rand Corp., 1976.

Vernez, Georges, et al. *Regional Cycles and Employment Effects of Public Works Investments*. Santa Monica: Rand Corp., 1977.

Watson, Donald. "The Reconstruction Finance Corporation." In *The Municipal Yearbook*. Chicago: International City Managers Association, 1937.

Westat, Inc. *Continuous Longitudinal Manpower Survey Report No. 4: Characteristics of Enrollees Who Entered CETA Programs During Calendar Year 1975*. Washington, D.C.: Department of Labor, November 1976.

Wiseman, Michael. *Achieving the Goals of the Employment Act of 1946–30th Anniversary Review, Paper No. 1, On Giving a Job: The Implementation and Allocation of Public Service Employment*. Joint Economic Committee. Washington, D.C.: Government Printing Office, 1975.

ABOUT THE AUTHORS

ROBERT JERRETT, III is a vice-president at Abt Associates Inc., in charge of employment-related research and development. He holds an A.B. from Brown University and a Ph.D. in history of American civilization from Harvard University. In his eight years at Abt, Jerrett has been engaged in a wide variety of employment-related research for the Department of Labor, the Economic Development Administration, and the Department of Housing and Urban Development. He is currently directing a nationwide microeconomic evaluation of the Local Public Works Program and an impact evaluation of the Youth Incentive Entitlement Pilot Program.

THOMAS A. BAROCCI is an associate professor (as of July 1, 1979) at the Alfred P. Sloan School of Management, Massachusetts Institute of Technology. Prior to MIT, he taught at Cornell University and worked as a staff economist for the U.S. secretary of labor and the governor of Massachusetts. He is the author of several articles relating to job-creation programs, employment and training policy, and collective bargaining.

Barocci received his B.A., M.A., and Ph.D. degrees from the University of Wisconsin, Madison, in 1968, 1969, and 1972, respectively. He is currently working with Jerrett and others on the national microeconomic evaluation of the Local Public Works Program.